THE GOLDEN HARVESTER

the vision of
EDWIN MUIR

AUP titles of related interest

THE HISTORY OF SCOTTISH LITERATURE
general editor Cairns Craig
Volume 1 Medieval and Renaissance *editor R D S Jack*
Volume 2 1660 to 1800 *editor Andrew Hook*
Volume 3 Nineteenth Century *editor Douglas Gifford*
Volume 4 Twentieth Century *editor Cairns Craig*

THE TRUTH OF IMAGINATION
essays and reviews by *Edwin Muir*
edited and introduced by P H Butter

TEN MODERN SCOTTISH NOVELS
Isobel Murray and Bob Tait

A BLASPHEMER AND REFORMER
a study of James Leslie Mitchell/Lewis Grassic Gibbon
William Malcolm

LITERATURE OF THE NORTH
edited by David Hewitt and Michael Spiller

POPULAR LITERATURE IN VICTORIAN SCOTLAND
Language, fiction and the press
William Donaldson

LANDSCAPE AND LIGHT
Essays by *Neil M Gunn*
edited by Alistair McCleery

A BIBLIOGRAPHY OF THE WORKS OF NEIL M GUNN
C J L Stokoe

GRAMPIAN HAIRST
an anthology of Northeast prose
edited by William Donaldson and Douglas Young

FROM THE CLYDE TO CALIFORNIA
Robert Louis Stevenson
edited and introduced by Andrew Noble

THE LAIRD OF DRAMMOCHDYLE
William Alexander
Introduction by William Donaldson

THE GOLDEN HARVESTER

the vision of

EDWIN MUIR

JAMES AITCHISON

ABERDEEN UNIVERSITY PRESS

First Published 1988
Aberdeen University Press
A member of the Pergamon Group

© James Aitchison 1988

The publisher acknowledges subsidy from the
Scottish Arts Council towards the publication
of this volume.

British Library Cataloguing in Publication Data

Aitchison, James
   The golden harvester: the vision of
   Edwin Muir.
   1. Poetry in English. Muir, Edwin, 1887–1959
   Critical studies
   I. Title
   821'.912

   ISBN 0 08 036400 4

Printed in Great Britain
The University Press
Aberdeen

Contents

STRANGE BLESSINGS

Acknowledgements

I am grateful to Professor I F Clarke, Dr Douglas Gifford and the late Keith Wright for their generous assistance with an early draft of this work.

COLLECTED POEMS
All references are to the second edition of Edwin Muir's *Collected Poems*, published in 1963.

CHRONOLOGY
In this study the chronology of Muir's publications is based on Elgin W Mcl-lown's *Bibliography Of The Writings Of Edwin Muir*. Biographical details are based on Peter Butter's *Edwin Muir: Man And Poet* and his *Selected Letters Of Edwin Muir*, on Willa Muir's *Belonging: A Memoir*, and on Muir's *An Autobiography*.

RADIO SCRIPTS
Reference is made to radio scripts, broadcast but otherwise unpublished, by Edwin Muir and others. Most of this material was broadcast on the old Scottish Home Service, and I am grateful to the BBC in Edinburgh for making these scripts available.

The Work And The Myth

INTRODUCTION

The entire work, from *We Moderns* published under the pseudonym of Edward Moore in 1918 to *The Estate of Poetry* written in the mid 1950s and published posthumously in 1962, shows a deepening and clarifying of vision. And Muir's last books—*The Labyrinth* of 1949 and *One Foot in Eden* of 1956, and the prose works, *An Autobiography* of 1954 and *The Estate of Poetry* of 1962—have a completeness of vision that includes moments of perfection.

What emerges most clearly from Muir's work is his continuing pre-occupation with certain themes: the origin of man, the fall, the conflict, the journey, and reconciliation. His exploration of the fall begins in the second chapter of *We Moderns*, finds its fullest expression in *One Foot in Eden*, and continues into his last poems. And from the start Muir was fully aware that he was dealing with the great myths of man's existence.

If readers of Muir's work do not feel themselves to be involved in these myths, do not accept that they are participants in the fall or the conflict or the search for reconciliation, then it is understandable that these readers may feel that Muir's poetry and prose is dominated by emblematic, archetypal elements. These readers may be more aware of the similarities and occasional repetitions than of the development as Muir returns again and again to his great themes. But for the reader who accepts the validity of myth—and this is not a matter of doctrine but of imagination, not so much a question of faith as one of vulnerability—for the reader who accepts, Muir's work becomes a re-discovery, a re-enactment of the life of everyman. In this fundamental sense Muir's work is dramatic: the collision and eventually the resolution of human and cosmic forces.

Over the course of Muir's work as a whole the treatment of myth is not a regular, progressive development, but there is a clear movement from the fall and the conflict to acceptance and reconciliation. The development is clear, but it has to be admitted that there are times in Muir's career when the development is arrested.

This is most obvious in the three novels: *The Marionette* of 1927, *The Three Brothers* of 1931, and *Poor Tom* of 1932. The novels are fascinating failures, and they fail because unlike his poems and criticism they are products of an intelligence rather than an imagination. Another feature of the novels, and an unusual one, is that each is more autobiographical than the one before, with longer and longer passages transposed from the life, so that with each novel Muir moves further from the art and spirit of fiction.

The Marionette combines a version of the Faust legend with a study in autism; *The Three Brothers*, set in sixteenth-century Scotland, is concerned with conflict—political, religious, and personal—and all of it recognisably Muir's own; in *Poor Tom* the Mansons of the novel are undisguisedly the Muirs. *Poor Tom* was to have been the first of a trilogy, the second volume of which Muir said, in a letter to his sister, would be 'noisily comic—if I can bring it off'. But *Poor Tom* was his last attempt at a novel, and one is led to the belief that *Poor Tom*, and to a lesser extent *The Marionette* and *The Three Brothers*, served a psychological rather than a literary purpose, allowing Muir to express through the medium of fiction those experiences that were otherwise inadmissible; that is, the novels may have been a form of abreaction process, a release and acceptance of emotion that had previously been intolerable.

Even so they remain novels, and Muir as novelist shows less confidence and authority than he does as a critic of the novel. In *The Structure of the Novel* of 1928 and elsewhere he is an excellent commentator on individual novels and on the whole mode of fiction. He captures the essential qualities of the society that the novelist creates and also the society in which the novel was created, so that at one and the same time he conveys the spirit of the art, of the artist, and of the age in which the novel was written, relating that age to the one from which he observes. The striking example of this is *Scott and Scotland* of 1936 and several pieces in *Essays on Literature and Society* of 1949.

Muir's first volume of criticism, *Latitudes* of 1924, is wilfully clever, with opinions presented in a legislative tone and a highly polished style, a polish that is surely intended to dazzle the reader rather than illuminate the subject matter. But with *Transition* in 1926 Muir begins to use a language that is polished not as a mirror but as a lens. And he begins to offer criticism that is remarkably free from opinions, or even judgements, a criticism in which he is as much concerned with people and society, with human values and civilisation, as with works of art.

His best criticism is in *The Structure of the Novel*, *Scott and Scotland*, *Essays on Literature and Society*, *The Estate of Poetry*, and in several essays, some of them still uncollected: 'Time and the Modern Novel', 'Bolshevism and Calvinism', 'Toys and Abstractions', 'Yesterday's Mirror', 'The Decline of the Imagination'. In these works Muir writes with the authority of insight, and the reader is persuaded of the truth of the account Muir gives of the literature, of its authors, of the age, and of the various forces—psychological, moral, political, religious—that helped to shape the writer and the society. There is a similar range and depth of concern in *Scottish Journey* of 1935, *An Autobiography*, and to a lesser extent in the biography, *John Knox* of 1929.

The notable exception to all this is *The Present Age* of 1939. The book is surprisingly bad, coming as it does after the excellent *Scott and Scotland* and just before the first autobiography, *The Story and the Fable* of 1940, which Muir began to write in 1938 as soon as *The Present Age* had gone to press. *The Present Age* is Muir's weakest volume of criticism and, apart from *We*

Moderns, the only book that shows none of his compassionate vision or generosity of spirit. In it he limits himself exclusively to literary values; elsewhere he treats literature not as an end in itself but as the expression of a mind, of an imagination, and as a measure of a civilisation. What makes Muir a great critic is the extent to which he goes beyond literary values. Knowing that a work of art is the expression of an individual imagination, Muir considers the nature of that imagination, and once he is committed to this line of enquiry he is led beyond individual values to the collective experience, the collective imagination of mankind.

It is impossible to give a precise summary of what Muir means by 'imagination' but the attempt must be made. Clearly, Muir's concept includes collective as well as individual experience, collective in the sense of the common, the shared fate of mankind. The imagination contains and is enriched by the past as well as the present, ancestral voices as well as contemporary, unconscious forces as well as conscious; the imagination is animated by the interaction of consciousness and the unconscious, the interaction of waking reality and dream. Muir attaches great importance to dreams because he knows that the dream as an expression of unconscious forces can be to the individual as myths are to the race. He knows that through acknowledging the dream there can come a wholeness, a harmony between the unconscious and consciousness, between myth and actuality, between archetypes and individuals. In reading what Muir has to say about imagination, one has the sense of an individual identity emerging from—being individuated from—a collective identity, the sense of an articulate consciousness emerging from an undifferentiated and semi-conscious folk mentality; emerging from it but never severing the connection.

There is a similarity between this and Jung's theories of archetypes and the collective unconscious, and it is possible that there is a line of influence from Jung to Muir through Maurice Nicoll, the Jungian psychiatrist who treated Muir in 1919, but it would of course be foolish to see this as a causal connection. The *Autobiography* and the letters make it clear that Muir arrived at his own attitudes and concepts from his reading of the evidence of his own life, and the evidence led him to see his life as a re-enactment of the evolution of the race. The state of childhood, for example, is comparatively unconscious and, especially when recollected in adulthood, comparatively timeless; emerging from this state into consciousness is like a fall, and Muir fell further than most, from the paradise of unconscious childhood in Orkney to industrial Glasgow at the turn of the century. The beginning of consciousness brings with it a sense of time and mutability, and through this a sense of the lost timelessness that made a paradise of childhood; it also brings a sense of separation, of having lost one's tribe, one's people, so that the individual with a certain kind of intelligence and imagination—the individual with a highly differentiated consciousness—feels himself to be one of the dispossessed. Inevitably, the individual reacts against this loss and tries to resolve the dilemma; Muir's attempt leads to his lifelong quest for reconciliation.

For Muir, then, criticism is not so much a matter of judgement on others as an act of imaginative participation and communion. He is a great critic, and he is above all a critic of the imagination whose observations on others are informed by his awareness of the development of his own imagination.

Muir's prose had a minor revival in the late 1970s and early 1980s with the re-publication in Scotland of *Scottish Journey, Scott and Scotland, Poor Tom*, and some previously uncollected essays. His poetry has been almost continuously available since the publication of *Collected Poems 1921–1951*, and the complete *Collected Poems* of 1963 was republished in a new edition in 1984.

Muir's poetry has had some sympathetic critics, including Peter Butter, John Holloway, Helen Gardner, and Kathleen Raine, but the discussion has been sparse and intermittent. Two issues on which even Muir's sympathetic critics have been hesitant are those of his technical skill and his level of achievement. On the question of technique, Muir is a more accomplished practitioner than his critics have allowed. He was never concerned with technical innovation; never concerned with structural, metrical, or linguistic experiment; never concerned to be ahead of or even up to date with changing fashions. He knew that he was out of fashion, and that it was important for him to be out. In an age when writers were expressing the fragmented, discontinuous, chaotic nature of existence, Muir was concerned to express the order and wholeness that he saw beyond the chaos. Admittedly, there are times when this search for an ideal order beyond the reach of time leads to a more orderly poem, a more firmly organised statement, than the theme requires. Similarly, there are moments when his attentiveness to ancestral voices leads to archaism in the poems. But in the great bulk of his work there is an indivisible unity of theme and expression, form and content; technique is employed in the service of his vision so that technique and vision are inseparable. His technique is such that the technical components, the mechanics, are almost imperceptible. This, the illusion of simplicity, is one of the measures of the mastery of a craft, but it is a measure that might be misunderstood, especially by a critic who is not a practitioner of the craft or by the practitioner whose craft lies in ornamentation and innovation.

This illusion of simplicity may have led readers to undervalue Muir's poetry in a more serious way. Like simplicity, fluency and spontaneity are seldom innate natural gifts but rather qualities that have to be developed; these qualities are levels of achievement that can never be taken for granted but have to be worked for, or waited for, in poem after poem, as if each poem were the first. Muir is at his most fluent and spontaneous in his lyrics: in the love poems, 'The Annunciation', 'The Confirmation', 'The Commemoration'; in his songs of joy, 'A Birthday', 'All We', 'In Love for Long'; in the celebrations, 'The Animals' and 'The Days'; in the reflective lyrics, 'The Late Wasp', 'The Late Swallow', and the song, 'This that I give'; and in the late lyrics, 'The Brothers', 'Sunset', and 'I have been taught'. In these poems Muir combines awe and delight, gravity and joy, the incarnate and the numinous, the sombre and the felicitous to make a harmony that is unique in English poetry.

There remains an even more serious mis-reading of Muir's poetry, prompted by the assumption that a great poem should be a difficult poem, perhaps an obscure poem, and generally a long poem. But the great poems of Muir's maturity are fashioned in such a way that they seem to unfold effortlessly; changes of theme or emphasis within the poem are carefully modulated or clearly indicated; there is an almost total absence of disjunctive devices. Instead, there is a strong sense of structural cohesion and thematic integrity. The reader, relieved of the burden of decoding, may not feel the full immensity of the poems and yet no poet of the present century has tackled bigger themes than Muir does in 'The Labyrinth', 'The Journey Back', 'Adam's Dream', 'One Foot in Eden', 'The Horses', 'Into Thirty Centuries Born', and from an earlier period, 'Ballad of the Soul' and *Variations on a Time Theme*. There, Muir's subjects are the creation of the world and the evolution of man, the fall of man and the mystery of time, the relationship of men and gods, the destruction of civilisation.

Few poets have dared to venture so far towards the limits of experience; fewer still have returned with messages of such wisdom and reconciliation.

THE RISE AND FALL OF THE SUPERMAN

Muir's first attempt to explore the myth of the fall appears in 'Original Sin', the second chapter of *We Moderns*, where it soon becomes clear that the attitude Muir adopts to myth and archetype is the attitude he has borrowed from Nietzsche. Muir writes:

> To glorify Humanity at its source it set there a Superman. The fall from innocence—that was the fall from the Superman into Man. And how, then, is Man to be redeemed? By the return of the Superman! Let that be our reading of the myth![1]

And on the same page in the same Nietzschean rhetoric he adds:

> In the early world myth was used to dignify Man by idealizing his origin. Henceforward it must be used to dignify him by idealizing his goal. *That* is the task of the poets and artists.

In 1919, the year after the publication *We Moderns*, Muir commented on the influence of Nietzsche in a letter to H L Mencken, who wrote the preface to the American edition of *We Moderns*, published in 1920. Muir wrote to Mencken:

> From the very moment when I first became acquainted with Nietzsche (when I was about 22) I have been more attracted to him than to any other writer. He has *spoken* to me as no one else has. I suppose everyone who has understood Nietzsche in any degree at all must have felt that. The kind of life I had lived before I met him also pre-disposed me, I have no doubt, to listen. I was born up in the Orkney islands in the north of Scotland, where my father was a small crofter. We all came to Glasgow when I was 14; my brothers, who were older than me, went into warehouses and I was sent into an office. Within four years, my father and mother and two brothers were dead, and I was left to fend for myself. Very bad health supervened for a while, and it was when I was emerging from it that Nietzsche came my way. He discovered a number of things for me.[2]

Much later, when Muir came to write *An Autobiography*, he saw that his belief in Nietzsche was a 'willed belief', but when he first began to adopt Nietzsche or to be possessed by him—as early as 1909 or 1910 according to Muir's letter to Mencken—the philosophy was a means of survival without which Muir might have lost his sanity or even his life. His experience in Glasgow and Greenock (Fairport in the *Autobiography*) drove him to such extremes of despair that he admits in the *Autobiography*:

> All the hopes that I brought from Glasgow withered one by one. At last one night, as I was walking along the Clyde with a friend, I said casually, hardly knowing what I was saying, merely speaking my thoughts, 'If I don't get out of this place I expect I'll jump in there some night.'[3]

Nietzsche's archetype of the Superman, and to some extent his myth of Eternal Recurrence, was a faith that gave Muir's life a significance during the years of squalor.

In the fourth chapter of *We Moderns*, 'Art and Literature', Muir returns to the question of myth and archetype:

> The only modern poet who has dared to be a poet through and through, that is, a liar in the noble and tragic sense, is the author of the Superman. In Nietzsche, again, after centuries of divine toying, the poet has appeared in his great *role* of a creator of gods, a figure beside whom the 'poet' seems like nothing more than the page boy of the Muses.[4]

This concept of the poet as 'a creator of gods' suggests that Muir's dependence on the myth of the Superman was so acute that it became a form of hysteria, an abandoning of his own identity for the preferred identity of Nietzsche and the Superman. Later in the same chapter, in the section entitled 'Myth', Muir lists the archetypal figures that fascinate him: Faust, Mephistopheles, Brand, Peer Gynt, and Zarathustra. Muir comments: '. . . there were no greater figures in the literature of the last century—were all myths, and all forecasts of the future.'[5] The prophetic element that these figures have in common seems to blind Muir to the fact that they, or rather their authors, were prophesying totally different futures, and in the grip of his fascination for Neitzsche Muir seems blind to the fact that Zarathustra is a psychotic figure who tries to resolve his conflict and frustration through the totalitarian fantasies of the Superman and the will to power.[6]

We Moderns reflects Muir's concept of myth up to the year 1918, but in the following year his attitude changed radically. Perhaps the publication in book form of the 'We Modern' series of essays he had been writing for *New Age* magazine was a form of exorcism for Muir. The *Autobiography* implies this when Muir writes:

> The perpetration of the book left me naked; the wings, having performed their act, fell from me; I felt the lack of them greatly, but was the better for it.[7]

The fundamental change in Muir's attitude to myth, and to life, began during his psychoanalysis in the autumn and winter of 1919. (The reader's attitude to psychoanalysis is comparatively unimportant; what is important is that Muir's psychoanalysis was a crucial period in his life.) The process of psycho-analysis does not of course 'explain' the change in Muir's concept of myth; it was the circumstance in which the change took place, and it was the process that gave Muir access to a completely different kind of myth, one that emerged from the collective unconscious. The new mythology arose spontaneously in dreams and waking visions, and Muir's account of them is one of the most exciting and satisfying sections of *An Autobiography*.[8] Since Muir's own account is readily available, it is foolish to attempt to paraphrase it. What is not available in Muir's account is a comment on the identity and the methods of the analyst, Maurice Nicoll.

The first edition of Nicoll's book, *Dream Psychology*, was published in 1917, so that it is reasonable to assume that the attitudes he expresses in that work were those he brought to bear on Muir's case in 1919. The second edition of *Dream Psychology* appeared in 1920, and it is possible that some of the conclusions Nicoll arrives at, conclusions based on case studies, might have been influenced by his analysis of Muir. The second edition repeats the preface to the first, in which Nicoll writes: 'I desire to place on record here the debt that I owe personally to Dr Jung'; later in *Dream Psychology* Nicoll distinguishes between the 'reductive associations' in the interpretation of dreams practised by Freud and the 'constructive associations' made by Jung.[9] Much of Jung's work is concerned with myth, archetypes, and religion, and it is probable that Nicoll's Jungian approach influenced Muir's concept of myth.

Muir admits that the publication of *We Moderns* in 1918 left him naked and without wings; his analysis by Nicoll in the following year helped him to meet the difficulties of this period in his life, not so much by covering up the nakedness and providing a new set of wings as by helping him to see something of the courage, the dignity, and the beauty of naked and wingless man. Muir and Nicoll sometimes differed in their interpretations of Muir's dreams,[10] but the analyst may have been more sympathetic than Muir thought, because Nicoll's fundamental approach to dream material was this:

> I believe that dream symbolism is a primary form of expression, a primary form of (primitive) thinking still surviving in us, that is creative and of value to life, and that it is not produced by distortion as a secondary product.[11]

Dream symbolism, Nicoll argues, is not only a valid form of expression but a valuable and creative form. And at this point in his Introduction Nicoll concludes:

> Finally, I believe that we find in the unconscious material—in the dream—a typical doctrine or tendency, which is not unrelated to the central teaching of many religions. I believe that doctrine or tendency to be relative to the necessity of the development of the individuality—the rebirth of the self from collective values to individual ones.[12]

Nicoll suggests that the dream material, as well as being a primary and undistorted form of expression that is creative and of value to life, also contains a numinous element, and that the process of individuation is 'not unrelated to' the religious concept of the rebirth of the individual. Nicoll, like Jung, stresses the therapeutic rather than the pathological qualities of the dream material;[13] like Jung he relates the symbol to the individual[14] rather than impose the kind of categorical interpretation that Freud makes in *The Interpretation Of Dreams*; and like Jung, Nicoll acknowledges a numinous or religious element in the dream material.

It may be mere co-incidence that Muir's attitude to dreams and the unconscious mind has these features in common with the attitudes of Jung and Nicoll, but a remark of Muir's in the *Autobiography* suggests that the similarities are not entirely accidental. Recalling the period of his analysis, Muir writes:

> My whole world of ideas invisibly changed; the Superman, after attending me so faithfully, took himself off without a word after his appearance on the cross, and I could not see even a perfectly analysed human being as a Superman.[15]

The change in Muir's 'whole world of ideas' included a change in his concept of myth and archetype. The archetype of the Superman is replaced by that of everyman:

> I saw that my lot was the human lot, that when I faced my own unvarnished likeness I was one among all men and women, all of whom had the same desires and thoughts, the same failures and frustrations, the same unacknowledged hatred of themselves and others, the same hidden shames and griefs, and that if they confronted these things they could win a certain liberation from them.[16]

The change from the Superman to everyman was part of a greater change in Muir's concept of myth; it was during his analysis that he came to see that myth is not a product of the will, of the conscious mind, but rather of the unconscious mind. He came to see that dreams, the expressions of the unconscious, could be the substance of myth, that there is no division between the dream and the myth, and that dreams are to the individual as myths are to the race. This link between dream and myth may have been suggested to Muir by Nicoll; it was certainly a connection that Jung made.[17] But even if Nicoll did not make the suggestion, Muir would have been led to make the link between dream and myth when he experienced that astonishing vision, the waking dream that was a cosmogonic myth.[18] The dream became the subject of a poem, 'Ballad Of Eternal Life', published in *New Age* in 1922 and then in *First Poems* in 1925; in a revised form it appears in *Collected Poems* as 'Ballad Of The Soul'.[19]

The vision that is the basis of 'Ballad Of The Soul' is of fundamental importance in any study of Muir's work. The vision marked a turning point in his analysis, and in his life. It is this vision that reveals most vividly Muir's changed attitude to dream and myth, and reveals too his discovery of the numinous element in life, a sense of the divine that is not exclusively Christian, or even exclusively religious in a formal or doctrinal sense. The vision as it is expressed in 'Ballad Of The Soul' brings together the myths of the fall, the conflict, the journey, and the reconciliation so that, in its densely symbolic and sometimes obscure way, the poem is a great prefiguration of Muir's later work.

'Ballad Of The Soul' evokes an ambivalent response even from the most sympathetic of Muir's critics. Kathleen Raine, in her highly favourable review of the *Collected Poems* in April 1960 said of 'Ballad Of The Soul' and 'Ballad Of The Flood' that they

> . . . are halting and obscure; the archetypal images come so thick and fast that they fail by reason of their too great purity, their insufficiently incarnated quality.[20]

Peter Butter in *Edwin Muir: Man And Poet* writes of the poem in these terms:

> The trouble was that he was trying merely to reproduce the dream, not working creatively on it. The visions he describes are of great interest from a psychological point of view, but the poem does not help the reader to see nor to feel them more vividly than the prose account does.[21]

And Elizabeth Huberman in *The Poetry Of Edwin Muir: The Field Of Good And Ill* offers a similar comment, suggesting that the poem is obscure because the vision on which it is based 'was confused to begin with'.[22]

What these comments have in common is that they note the difficulty and then shy away from it. Muir is dealing with symbols that are ultimately irreducible and with unconscious material that cannot be paraphrased in fully conscious terms, but one can borrow from the techniques of the psychologist and consider the poem further. When one turns to Maurice Nicoll, the analyst with whom Muir discussed the dream, one finds that Nicoll is aware of this kind of dream sequence:

> But this coherence is not relative to intelligibility, but is rather a coherence in the sequence of events, which are related to one another by a kind of naturalness.[23]

And when one turns to Nicoll's mentor, Jung, one finds that he has examined this kind of dream sequence in a literary context. In the essay, 'Psychology And Literature', Jung writes:

> The vision is not something derived or secondary, and it is not a symptom of something else. It is true symbolic expression—that is, the expression of something existent in its own right, but imperfectly known.[24]

Muir's own comment on the Scottish ballads is revealing. His essay, 'A Note On The Scottish Ballads', appeared in the American magazine *Freeman* in

January 1923, only months after the first version of 'Ballad Of The Soul' had appeared in *New Age*, and one feels that some of his observations refer just as directly to his own ballads as to the Scottish ballads generally. He writes:

> There is nothing in the ballads but passion, terror, instinct, action: the states in which soul and body alike live most intensely; and this accounts for the impression of full and moving life which, stark and bare as they are, they leave with us.[25]

And later in the essay:

> This world in which there is no reflection, no regard for the unity of action, nothing but pure passion seen through pure vision, is, if anything is, the world of art.

The poem, like the vision on which it is based, reflects a critical stage in Muir's individuation process, that is, the process by which he gained a new awareness of selfhood and a degree of psychological wholeness. The vision marks a sudden development in his long analysis, a period of intense interaction between the conscious and the unconscious, and it is this compression of conflicting experience that gives the poem its extraordinary wealth of symbolism and its astonishingly rapid sequence of events. Jung's comment on the individuation process is helpful:

> Then, under the influence of therapy . . . the identity breaks down and is accompanied by an intensification (sometimes technically induced) of fantasy, with the result that archaic or mythological features become increasingly apparent. Further transformations run true to the hero myth. The theme of 'mighty feats' is generally absent, but on the other hand the mythical dangers play all the greater part. At this stage there is usually another identification, this time with the hero, whose role is attractive for a variety of reasons. The identification is often extremely stubborn and dangerous to the psychic equilibrium. If it can be broken down and if consciousness can be reduced to human proportions, the figure of the hero can gradually be differentiated into a symbol of the self.[26]

It is exactly this pattern of experience that Muir expresses in 'Ballad Of The Soul'. In the opening lines of the poem Muir has a heightened awareness of his own breathing:

> I did not know whence came my breath
> Nor where had hid my clay.

In the *Autobiography* he recalls that during the vision his wife was correcting students' scripts in the same room, and that there was a continuous 'curiously loud' rustling of papers in the background. This, along with the sound of his breathing, is like the sound of the lapping water of a rising tide or the premonitory breath of a ministering wind. The awareness of the act of breathing intensifies into autoscopic detachment:

> Until my soul stood by my side
> As on my bed I lay.

This sense of detachment, a recurring experience in Muir's life, can be interpreted as the separation of the conscious and the unconscious without contradicting Muir's religious and traditional terms of the flesh and the spirit—'my clay' and 'my soul'. From this point onwards the 'I' of the poem is the dreamer's soul. In the second stanza, as the dreamer is poised on the brink of 'a dark blue shore' beneath 'a dark blue sky', he marvels at a mysterious light that has no visible source and suggests the dawn of creation. The dreamer is suddenly plunged into the waters:

> The waters rose, down sank the land,
> The sea closed in like lead.

The dreamer is plunged into the confusion of his unconscious, the symbolic waters that dissolve all logical concepts. (Of this phenomenon Jung writes: 'The psychological equivalent of the chaotic water of the beginning is the unconscious'.[27])

When he surfaces from the depths—but not back into consciousness—the dreamer finds himself in a featureless sea, 'the vast and moveless mere'. It is a world of unknowing, the world of the undifferentiated creaturehood of the 'headless things' against which he has to fight before he can come ashore. And when he finally gains the land, he is alone, the first man among the other animals:

> The low-browed voiceless animals
> Were my companions.

These closing stanzas of the first section of the poem seem to echo the story of man's evolution, but the echo is so compressed in symbolic terms that evolution and the creation—the story and the fable—are as one. The dreamer has to struggle free from the formless sea creatures, define himself against the amoeboids just as later, on land, he must define himself against the animals. And these two concerns, man's origins and his relationship to the animal world, are recurring themes in Muir's work.

The mysterious, strangely beautiful account of creation and evolution in the first section of the poem gives way to the absurdity and violence of the second section. The dreamer finds himself alone in 'a waste of jagged rock' where 'what seemed a palace lay/Like ruins of the sky'. This is like the broken landscape of the lost way that Muir explores in many of his early poems. Here, the ledge is covered with wooden scaffolding, and the dreamer climbs down so rapidly that he 'Dived deep and knew my fall'; then 'like spouted light' he climbs up again until he is trapped beneath a roof. Jung's interpretation of this kind of symbolic action is helpful here: 'Ascent and descent, above and below, up and down, represent an emotional realisation of opposites, and this realisation gradually leads, or should lead, to their equilibrium'.[28] And Muir himself gives a clue to the symbolism in the *Autobiography* when he speaks of his new self-knowledge gained from the unconscious 'making great breaches and gashes' in his conscious resistance to that knowledge.[29] In the closing stanzas of the second section the dreamer makes a desperate attempt to find the equilibrium of opposites that Jung speaks of, or to discover a sense of direction that will release him from his entombment. In a state of blind aggression he batters his head against the roof:

> And the dumb stone shuddered and cried,
>   Turned back and made a way.
> The sky leaped up, the stars showered out,
>   In peace the planets lay.

The dreamer is released into a recognisable world, and the imagery of sky and stars and planets gives a sense of infinite space and harmony.

But in the third section of the poem there is the intensification of the mythological dangers Jung refers to, and a closer identification with the role of the hero. The confrontation of the dreamer's conscious and unconscious generates a symbolism of cosmic upheaval in which newly created planets rush together and collide with tremendous destructive force:

> They met, they broke in fiery smoke,
>   A red ball in the sky,
> A ball of fire, it raged and turned
>   To ashes suddenly.

It is a vision of an inchoate universe, a chaos of matter and energy symbolised by the black spinning sun that throws out its final flames like writhing serpents; it is primeval turmoil in which the mind seems to burst apart to release its monstrous fears, in which planets burst asunder to spawn grotesque mythological creatures:

> But now its rage in furious spawn
>   A hundred legs gave birth;
> Like a great spider down the air
>   It clambered to the earth.

As the spider comes closer the dreamer has to fight for his life: 'The sword in lightnings wild/Rove and rent', but paradoxically, with the non-rational logic and inevitability of dream, the adversary 'softly, softly smiled' and then submits 'Obedient as a child'. Although the conflict, one that combines elements of the epic and the absurd, is over, the dreamer strikes again and again until the creature is split apart and:

> The white-robed white-winged spirit up
>   In wavering circles flew.

The closing stanza of this section gives the sense of release and the stillness of exhaustion after the final battle:

> Hastily sank the empty mail
>   Deep in the secret ground.
> Nothing was there but trampled grass,
>   The tarn, the watching mound.

By the end of the third section the turmoil has ceased. The dreamer has survived his three conflicts—the struggle with the shapeless sea creatures, the fight to burst free from the place of entombment, the battle with the monstrous spider—and from this ordeal of conflict and voyaging he has emerged into a universe of peace. Aggression is replaced by ecstasy at the beginning of the fourth section:

> Then as I looked above I saw
>   The sweet sky rain with wings.
> I was so happy I longed to be
>   With one of these fair things.

The sky that had flashed with colliding planets and had been darkened by the great spider is now filled with winged spirits; and in the prose account of the vision Muir recalls that the spirits led the way to the throne of God. Winged and weightless, the dreamer finds himself floating upwards with another figure:

> Two linked their hands till one they seemed,
>   Rose up in wavering rings.

In the prose version of the vision the two are Muir and his wife; as they rise upwards, each sheds the wing nearer the other person so that they fly up on the two outer wings:

> Two plumes fell down the glittering air,
>   They mounted on two wings.

The closing image of the poem is that of the syzygy, the male–female deity that symbolises reconciliation and perfect harmony.

Muir writes that when Maurice Nicoll read his notes of the dream, Nicoll agreed that it was a vision of the creation; but when Muir said that he felt the dream suggested immortality, Nicoll rejected this and instead pointed out the sexual symbolism. The symbolism of swimming and diving in the first two sections could be given the Freudian interpretation of 'phantasies of intra-uterine life';[30] the sword and the blazing serpents could have phallic connotations; the giant spider might symbolise the devouring mother; the syzygy might symbolise a sexual union and nothing else. But Freudian interpretations can become a form of dialectic, a procrustean device that reduces all experience and all phenomena to rigid categories, the limitations of which frequently reflect the limitations of the interpreter. If 'Ballad Of The Soul' is a dream of procreation, then it is the procreation of the race rather than of an individual, an archetypal event rather than a clinical one. But if this is so, then procreation is creation, and the idea of personal sexuality becomes inappropriate. The Freudian interpretation depersonalises the dreamer by reducing him to a clinical case study, it de-mythologises the dream by reducing it to a set of sexual impulses, and it is grounded on pathological rather than therapeutic concepts. The anagogical approach that Muir so clearly preferred and which is also the Jungian approach, preserves the individuality of the dreamer and at the same time allows an identification between the individual and the archetype, between a man and mankind. In psychological terms the poem is an account of a critical stage in an individuation process; at the same time it is a mythopoeic—and in its closing stages a mystical—account of man's encounter with archetypal man in the dawn of creation, and of archetypal man's journey through the millenia of evolution. 'Ballad Of The Soul' is a vision of immemorial events, a vision of the creation of man, of his journey through time, of his conflict, and ultimately his purification.

The case for this poem has been argued at some length partly because it is a better poem than critics have allowed and also because it is a much more important poem than has been allowed; inseparable from the question of the psychological vision that is the basis of the poem, there is also the question of Muir's wider vision of life. It is here, at this crucial turning point, that Muir ranges to the limits of his vision. Vast areas of experience are left uncharted in 'Ballad Of The Soul', but in this poem more than any other of Muir's the reader has the impression of the poet reaching to the limits of his imagination. In this sense it is a great prefiguration of his later work; it marks the boundaries, while the later work explores within these boundaries, gradually clarifying the obscurity and penetrating the mystery. Willa Muir saw the importance of the poem, and in a radio broadcast in 1964 she said:

> That particular one was the inspiration for so many things and a lot of his beliefs. He really did think he had had a view of the creation. It was a very wonderful vision.[31]

In concept and structure too 'Ballad Of The Soul' foreshadows Muir's later work. The poem expresses the enormity and intensity of the warring opposites in the mind of man, and it acknowledges that the conflict of the individual is the conflict of everyman. The battle is expressed in mythological terms and with a grotesque, spectacular violence on a cosmic scale. And yet the civil war within the self can be a creative conflict; the symbolism and the action of the poem show a development from the amorphous to the numinous, from chaos to order, from universal violence to universal peace. It is as if by giving expression to the violence, by acknowledging it, the poet begins to exorcise it until, in the final section, the conflict is resolved in the image of the divine syzygy, the symbol of reconciliation. And the search for reconciliation becomes the great theme of Muir's late work.

During the period of his psychoanalysis Muir had access to his personal unconscious and to the collective unconscious through his dreams and waking visions; he entered an area of experience that changed his vision of life, and having once gained access to this area he returned to it from time to time for the next forty years. After his psychoanalysis of 1919, Muir found that the Nietzschean myths were no longer valid, and as these myths faded, so the Superman disappeared.

VERSIONS OF EVERYMAN

In his letter to Mencken, Muir writes as if Nietzsche were his constant companion, a real and reassuring presence during his years in Glasgow and Greenock. And Nietzsche's Superman clearly played a double role in Muir's life at that time: in an absurd and yet necessary way the Superman was Muir's intellectual and spiritual guide, and it was also part of Muir's assumed identity, what Muir himself calls a 'willed belief'. After his analysis Muir saw the absurdity, and in that rare moment of irony in the *Autobiography* he writes: 'I could not see even a perfectly analysed human being as a Superman.' When the Superman withdrew Muir was able to face his 'own unvarnished likeness' and see that he was 'one among all men and women'. He was everyman, sharing the same human lot as millions of his contemporaries but equally sharing in the identity of the archetypal everyman of 'Ballad Of The Soul'.

Questions of man's identity, and particularly this sense of the archetypal everyman within each individual man, are central to Muir's developing vision of life. Muir was haunted, enchanted, by the mystery of finding one's self in everyday life and yet finding archetypal versions of that self, undeniably one's own, in dream and myth. Muir touches on the mystery at an early stage in the *Autobiography*:

> It is clear that no autobiography can begin with a man's birth, that we extend far beyond any boundary line which we can set for ourselves in the past or the future, and that the life of every man is an endlessly repeated performance of the life of man. It is clear for the same reason that no autobiography can confine itself to conscious life, and that sleep, in which we pass a third of our existence, is a mode of experience, and our dreams a part of reality.[1]

Muir of course is not alone amongst twentieth-century writers in acknowledging the power of myth. A new awareness of myth and the associated archetypes and symbolism became an accepted part of the intellectual equipment of writers following the publication of work by Freud and Jung; and Frazer's *The Golden Bough*, first published in 1922 and reprinted five times in the 1920s, achieved wide popularity. But Muir's awareness of the power of myth, as the previous chapter has shown, was an independent and involuntary discovery.

Among Muir's Scottish contemporaries mythological themes, especially Celtic and Norse, appear in the work of Naomi Mitchison, Lewis Grassic Gibbon, Neil Gunn, and Muir's fellow-Orcadian, Eric Linklater. But Muir's attitude to myth differs from theirs. Apart from the difference in literary form—poetry rather than fiction—there is the fact that myth is not only the subject of Muir's work; it *is* the work. He not only re-created the myths; he lived them. And his work includes not only established myth—Biblical, Greek, Celtic, Norse—but also the new mythology that arose from his dreams. Muir's work is more truly mythopoeic than that of most of his contemporaries.

In his life and his art the myth that emerges from Muir's dreams is inseparable from the myth of his childhood. The child's world, like the world of the dreamer in sleep, is an unconscious or partly conscious one; but even in this partly conscious state the mind can recognise the importance of the symbolic events and characters, and when the child gains adult consciousness or when the dreamer awakes, then the symbolism recollected from the other world can take on a mysterious, fabulous, or even a numinous quality.

Muir's early childhood, especially the first seven years, was a period of almost total emotional security. It was spent on a small farm on the island of Wyre in Orkney where the way of life followed an archetypal pattern based on ancestral custom and ritual, on the ancestral tasks of farming and fishing, sowing and harvesting, and where the pace of life was governed by sunrise and sunset and the cycle of the seasons. The way of life was unchanging, as if it were beyond the reach of time. Muir writes of Orkney and his earliest years in terms of profound gratitude, and he recalls that part of his life as a mythical experience:

> The Orkney I was born into was a place where there was no great distinction between the ordinary and the fabulous; the lives of living men turned into legend. A man I knew once sailed out in a boat to look for a mermaid, and claimed afterwards that he had talked with her. Fantastic feats of strength were commonly reported. Fairies, or 'fairicks', as they were called, were encountered dancing on the sands on moonlight nights.[2]

Childhood is in a sense an adult experience. The sensation of childhood belongs to the child but an understanding, however imperfect, of childhood comes later. As recollected by the adult, then, the state of childhood may be subject to distortion. At the simplest level the adult may forget some things and invent others; at another level, since childhood is a partly unconscious state, there is an almost irresistible tendency for the adult to interpret in adult terms or sometimes childishly to idealise. Muir is aware of this possibility of self-deception when he recalls his parents:

> I never thought that they were like other men and women; to me they were fixed allegorical figures in a timeless landscape. Their allegorical changelessness made them more, not less, solid, as if they were condensed into something more real than humanity; as if the image 'mother' meant more than 'woman', and the image 'father' more than 'man'.[3]

Muir's recollections of his childhood become an integral part of his wider vision of life, and when he began to write poetry in the 1920s he felt that the source of these first poems lay in his childhood:

> I must have been influenced by something, since we all are, but when I try to find out what it was that influenced me, I can only think of the years of childhood which I spent on my father's farm in the little island of Wyre in Orkney, and the beauty I apprehended then, before I knew there was beauty. These years had come alive, after being forgotten for so long, and when I wrote about horses they were my father's plough-horses as I saw them when I was four or five; and a poem on Achilles pursuing Hector round the walls of Troy was really a resuscitation of the afternoon when I ran away, in real terror, from another boy as I returned from school. The bare landscape of the little island became, without my knowing it, a universal landscape over which Abraham and Moses and Achilles and Tristram and all sorts of pilgrims passed; and Troy was associated with the Castle, a mere green mound, near my father's house.[4]

His childhood had a mythological quality through which the ordinary was inseparable from the fabulous; his childhood, both psychologically and geographically, became 'a universal landscape' inhabited by legendary figures. His actual parents on the actual island became part of the fable. For Muir, as perhaps for most of us, the act of recollecting is an act of the imagination, so that his mother and father are both real and imaginary. Muir himself was aware of this process of the imagination, and on the same page of the *Autobiography* he writes:

> In any case we need a symbolic stage on which the drama of human life can play itself out for us, and I doubt whether we have the liberty to choose it. The little island was not too big for a child to see in it an image of life; land and sea and sky, good and evil, happiness and grief, life and death discovered themselves to me there; and the landscape was so simple that it made these things simple too.

This 'symbolic stage', this 'universal landscape' is a timeless region. In Muir's vision the landscape of childhood and the landscape of dreams exist in the same world, and the world of the child, like the world of the dreamer, is beyond the reach of time. The symbols and archetypes that emerge from this partly conscious world have, as Muir writes of his parents, an 'allegorical changelessness', and he speaks of the timeless world of childhood in these terms:

> That world was a perfectly solid world, for the days did not undermine it but merely rounded it, or rather repeated it, as if there were only one day endlessly rising and setting. Our first childhood is the only time in our lives when we exist within immortality, and perhaps all our ideas of immortality are influenced by it. I do not mean that the belief in immortality is a mere rationalization of childish impressions; I have quite other reasons for holding it. But we think and feel and believe immortally in our first few years, simply because time does not exist for us. We pay no attention to time until he tugs us by the sleeve or claps his policeman's hand on our shoulders; it is in our nature to ignore him, but he will not be ignored.[5]

Time tugs us by the sleeve when we outgrow the timeless paradise of uncon-scious childhood and begin to find ourselves in the fallen world of con-sciousness and separation and time. This dilemma, between time and time-lessness, between mutability and immortality, becomes one of the great preoccupations in Muir's work. He is able partly to resolve the dilemma through his rediscovery of the childlike vision and through his adult accept-ance of the elements of innocence and immortality that are still discernible in the adult world.

The sense of striving for reconciliation in the 1934 collection, *Variations On A Time Theme*, gives way to a calmly assured vision of reconciliation in his late work, notably the 1956 collection, *One Foot In Eden*, and it is clear that Muir's mature vision of life was influenced by the emergence of another archetype of innocence and immortality, the Christ-image. The circumstances in which the archetype emerged are similar to those of the waking dream that prompted the poem, 'Ballad Of The Soul'.

In *An Autobiography* Muir prints an entry from his diary of the spring of 1939:

> Last night, going to bed alone, I suddenly found myself (I was taking off my waistcoat) reciting the Lord's Prayer in a loud, emphatic voice—a thing I had not done for many years—with deep urgency and profound disturbed emotion. While I went on I grew more composed; as if it had been empty and craving and were being replenished, my soul grew still; every word had a strange fullness of meaning which astonished and delighted me. It was late; I had sat up reading; I was sleepy; but as I stood in the middle of the floor half-undressed, saying the prayer over and over, meaning after meaning sprang from it, overcoming me again with joyful surprise; and I realized that this simple petition was always universal and always inexhaustible, and day by day sanctified human life.[6]

The image that irrupted so suddenly into consciousness had, one feels, been taking shape for some time in his unconscious mind. In a letter to the poet George Barker written in the spring of 1937 Muir discusses a point Barker had made about poetry and religion, and Muir concludes:

> The religious Christ, theoretically at any rate, can be taken away, by historical research, science, etc.; or if not taken away can at any rate be modified. But it is hard to see what can be done with the imaginative Christ, since he is quite inside the mind.[7]

The image of Christ, 'quite inside the mind' was taking shape until it emerged that night two years later. The *Autobiography* offers only one paragraph, quoted above, from the diary entry for that night, but Peter Butter in *Edwin Muir: Man And Poet* quotes another extract that shows how Muir's concept of everyman had developed since the vision of 1919:

> I never realized before so clearly the primary importance of 'we' and 'us' in prayer: it is collective, for all societies, for all mankind as a great society. . . . And this collective form of prayer was the form enjoined by Jesus . . .

The difference here between 'I' and 'we' tremendous: there is no end to the conclusions that follow from it. In 'we' it is man, or mankind, or the community, or all the communities, that is speaking: it is human life, and therefore society is the formal embodiment of human life. And to pray as 'we' is not only to embrace in the prayer all human life, all the aspiration of mankind for the perfect kingdom when God's will shall be done on earth; it is for the individual soul a pledge for all other souls, an act of responsibility, and an action of union which strengthens him from within and at the same time lends him infinite strength from without.[8]

This vision of unity is similar to the identification Muir made at the time of his psychoanalysis in 1919 when he saw that his lot was the human lot and that he was one among all men and women, but in the 1939 diary entry the identification is more than that of the individual with others or of a man with everyman; it is also the identification of the individual soul with all other souls through Christ. The psycholanalysis of 1919 liberated Muir from his assumed identity with the Superman and gave him a renewed sense of himself as a member of a community of mankind; the diary entry some twenty years later suggests that the process of individuation was a continuous one and led to this greater sense of identity, this further insight into the dimensions of the human condition in which he sees the self as everyman, not only in psychological terms but in Christian terms.

Almost a year later, in February 1940, Muir replied to a letter from the poet William Soutar in these terms:

> The difficulty that strikes me about life is not that it is uninteresting (as so many uninteresting people call it) but that it is interesting in too many different ways, that is, confusing; so that it takes a genius, and a very great genius at that, to pierce through its countless meanings to the one that illumines them all.[9]

And in the same paragraph he adds:

> I believe in God, in the immortality of the soul, and that Christ is the greatest figure who ever appeared in the history of mankind. I believe in the Fall too, and the need for salvation.

The conclusions seems irresistible: for Muir, Christ has become the genius who can pierce through life's countless meanings to the one that illumines them all.

By 1949 Muir is writing about religion in a less assertive and more convincing way. In December of that year, when he was Director of the British Council in Rome, he wrote to the writer Joseph Chiari and spoke of his sense of the presence of gods in the city:

> It has brought very palpably to my mind the theme of Incarnation and I feel that probably I shall write a few poems about that high and difficult theme sometime: I hope so. Edinburgh I love, but in Edinburgh you never come upon anything that brings the thought of Incarnation to your mind, and here you do so often, and quite unexpectedly. I'm rather afraid of writing on such a theme

and though it occupies my mind whenever my mind is free from daily affairs, I feel nothing is ready yet to be written down.[10]

The long process of individuation has led to the Incarnation, a constant preoccupation with the sense of the living presence of the incarnate god.

The similarities between Muir's developing concept of archetype—self, everyman, and Christ—and Jung's are so striking that it is helpful again to quote Jung. *In Psychology And Religion: East And West* he writes:

> The goal of psychological, as of biological development is self-realisation, or individuation. But since man knows himself only as an ego, and the self, as a totality, is indescribable and indistinguishable from the God-image, self-realis-ation—to put it in its religious or metaphysical terms—amounts of God's incarnation. That is already expressed in the fact that Christ is the son of God. And because individuation is an heroic and often tragic task, the most difficult of all, it involves suffering, a passion of the ego: the ordinary, empirical man we once were is burdened with the fate of losing himself in a greater dimension and being robbed of his fancied freedom of will. He suffers, so to speak, from the violence done to him by the self. The analogous passion of Christ signifies God's suffering on account of the injustice of the world and the darkness of man. The human and the divine suffering set up a relationship of complementarity with compensating effects. Through the Christ-symbol, man can get to know the real meaning of his suffering: he is on the way towards realising his wholeness. As a result of the integration of conscious and unconscious, his ego enters the 'divine' realm, where it participates in 'God's suffering'. The cause of the suffering is in both cases the same, namely 'incarnation', which on the human level appears as 'individuation'. The divine hero born of man is already threatened with murder; he has nowhere to lay his head, and his death is a gruesome tragedy. The self is no mere concept or logical postulate; it is a psychic reality, only part of it conscious, while for the rest it embraces the life of the unconscious and is therefore inconceivable except in the form of symbols. The drama of the arche-typal life of Christ describes in symbolic images the events in the conscious life—as well as in the life that transcends consciousness—of a man who has been transformed by his own higher destiny.[11]

Jung's argument is that the development of the self, a life-long process rather than a once-and-for-all event, is similar to the life of Christ; that an awareness of the unconscious as well as the conscious dimensions of the self can bring an awareness of the Christ-image; and that the Christ-image gives meaning to the life of man. But Jung is also suggesting that the Christ-image can be an immanent symbol, an archetype of the unconscious, so that identification of the immanent image with the historical Christ could bring a sense of having found one's self, a sense of completeness and —in a poet—a unity and clarity of vision. And in comparing the incarnation of the god with the individuation of man Jung expresses an essential element of Muir's experience, especially during his time in Rome: the experience of the divine god participating in human life and of man participating in immortality.

In this chapter Muir's letters, diary and *Autobiography* have been quoted at some length because it is here, much more explicitly than in the poems or the criticism, that he reveals the extent to which his awareness of the self and his archetype of everyman became associated with the archetypal life of Christ, and because the preoccupations he discloses in the letters are those that appear, in a transmuted form, in the poems. The letters and the *Autobiography* show the development of Muir's concept of archetype and myth; the reader who knows of this development may gain a fuller understanding of the poems. The question of the reader's religious belief is, of course, largely irrelevant. What is important is that the Incarnation became a living myth for Edwin Muir, and that the great poems—not all of them religious—are the achievement of Edwin Muir, not of a religion. Similarly, a reader may remain sceptical about Jung's philosophy as a pattern of belief and yet still see that Jung's commentaries are a reasoned attempt to interpret, or at least to describe, the working of the mind; and to the extent that these commentaries complement what Muir's says about the imagination they may bring a better understanding of Muir's work.

It is clear that in the last twenty years of his life Muir accepted Christ as a dominant archetype and a symbol of reconciliation. Throughout his life Muir searched for a way of making a pattern of the various truths he found in myth, a way of unifying his vision of life, and the sense of unity is strongest in his last twenty years when the Christ-image encompassed all other versions of everyman and confirmed Muir's belief in immortality and in the divinity that shapes man's origin and end.

The Fall

CHILDHOOD AND PARADISE

This unifying vision was lost for a time in 1948. Muir had gone to Czecho-slovakia in 1945 as Director of the British Council in Prague, and for two and a half years he watched the people gradually recover from the terror of the Nazi occupation until, just when their recovery seemed assured, a new tyranny was imposed with the Communist seizure of power early in 1948. When Muir came back to Britain in July that year he was exhausted and in despair. He recalls the period in the *Autobiography*:

> As soon as I arrived I had a breakdown, and fell plumb into a dead pocket of life which I had never guessed at before. It was hard to live there, simply because it was unimaginably uninteresting. I awoke each morning feeling that I had lost or mislaid something which I was accustomed to but could not name; I slowly realized that it was the little spring of hope, or of interest, with which the day once began. It had stopped playing, and it did not return for several weeks.[1]

And twenty years later when Willa Muir recalled that bleak time in her book, *Belonging: A Memoir*, she wrote of it in terms of the fall:

> It was the Fall of Man and the consequent inherited guilt of the whole human race that kept haunting his imagination, and, I suspected, at times had paralysed him like his own Enchanted Knight.[2]

On the same page, as if the memory of that period brought back other memories of other falls, she adds:

> Ever since the beginning of our marriage, I had been aware of his preoccupation with the Fall and with Original Sin, and had thought that it burdened him unduly.

Muir's long preoccupation with the fall begins in his first book, *We Moderns*, published in 1918 but consisting of essays from the magazine, *New Age*, for which Muir had been writing since 1913. Encouraged by A R Orage, editor of *New Age*, Muir contributed essays on the arts, literature, religion and philosophy as well as reviews, satirical verse and epigrams. *We Moderns*, published under the pseudonym Edward Moore, contains material ranging in length from the fragmentary single sentence to statements of several thousand words; the prose style is carefully polished to produce a knowingly assertive tone, broken by occasional outbursts of exclamatory rhetoric. Muir soon came to disapprove of his first book, saying that in it he 'generalized in excited ignorance',[3] but *We Moderns* remains a fascinating document. It shows a young man responding to the world of ideas with great energy and curiosity, launching exploratory forays into the arts and religion and philosophy, and pronouncing his conclusions with an air of witty gravity. After a preliminary attack on a subject Muir will withdraw for a few paragraphs and then approach his theme from a different angle, sometimes surprising the subject by the sheer irregularity of his assault. But the importance of *We Moderns* today is that it shows the young Edwin Muir grappling for the first time with some of the themes that were to remain with him for the rest of his life: the antitheses of the Superman and everyman, past and present, time and eternity. And in the chapter entitled 'Original Sin' Muir makes his first attempt to come to terms with what what was to become a central theme—the myth of the fall of man.

When he was writing for *New Age* Muir had rejected Christianity in favour of the Nietzschean Superman and eternal recurrence. In the *Autobiography* he writes:

> I did not believe in the immortality of the soul at that time; I was deep in the study of Nietzsche, and had cast off with a great sense of liberation all belief in any other life than the life we live here and now, as an imputation on the purity of immediate experience, which I had intellectually convinced myself was guiltless and beyond good and evil.[4]

There are sections of *We Moderns* where this intellectual conviction is obviously contrived and when the witty, superior manner seems to be a self-conscious, defensive mask. But as Muir is drawn further into the subject of the fall there are times when the mask slips and the brashly assertive language gives way to the language of genuine intellectual enquiry. 'Original Sin' offers insights into the myth of the fall that are assimilated into the poet's growing vision of the myth.

In a section entitled 'The Fall Of Man' Muir writes:

> In very early times Man must have had a deep sense of the tragicality of existence: life was then so full of pain; death, as a rule, so sudden and unforeseen, and the world generally so beset with terrors. The few who were fortunate enough to escape violent death had yet to toil incessantly to retain a footing on this unkind star ... And it was to explain this human misfortune, and not sin at all, that the whole fable of Adam and Eve was invented.[5]

Muir flatly denies there was any element of sin and stresses instead the purely natural pains and terrors of existence on 'this unkind star', so that when he uses the word 'explain' at this point the reader suspects that Muir may be trying to explain the whole thing away. But despite his sceptical introduction to the subject, Muir has chanced on a line of enquiry that begins to lead him to the centre of the myth.

Having 'explained' what he calls 'the whole fable of Adam and Eve' in terms of physical necessity, Muir goes on to deal with sin. 'The doctrine of Original Sin,' he writes, ' was simply an interpretation which was afterwards read into the story.'[6] Doctrinally, Muir is right; the doctrine of original sin is retrospective legislation, but Muir reaches this conclusion through a stream of intuitive assertions and denials. He continues:

> How would the fable arise? Well, a primitive poet one day in a fit of melancholy made the whole thing up. Out of his misery his desires created for him an imaginary state, its opposite, the Garden of Eden.[7]

Muir offers a simple compensation theory: the Garden of Eden was invented by man—or by Muir's primitive poet—to counterpoise the intolerable reality of life on 'this unkind star'. His theory of the primitive poet making the whole thing up is frivolous, and perhaps an example of his Superman philosophy at that time. But as Muir goes on in his dismissive way he moves, perhaps unintentionally, towards the centre of the myth of the fall. He writes:

> But this state being created, the problem arose: how did Man fall from it? And the Tree was brought in. But to the naive, untheological poet, this tree had nothing to do with metaphysics or sin, the child of metaphysics. It was simply a magical tree, and if Man ate of the fruit of it, something terrible would happen to him.[8]

In saying that it was 'simply a magical tree' that threatened terrible consequences if man ate its fruit, Muir seems unaware that these questions—magic and primitive man, tree totemism, guilt, and indeed the myth of the fall— were already being discussed by Frazer and Freud. This seems puzzling, since Muir writes in the *Autobiography* of his time with *New Age*:

> For some years *New Age* had been publishing articles on psychoanalysis, in which Freud's and Jung's theories were discussed from every angle, philosophical, religious, and literary, as well as scientific.[9]

Freud's *Totem and Taboo*, which uses Frazer's anthropological material as a starting point for a conjectural reconstruction of the psychology of primitive man, had been published in 1913. Freud argues that in magic, and particularly in eating the totem animal or in eating fruit of the totem tree, lies the beginning of religion and morality.[10] And Frazer in *The Golden Bough* and to some extent in *Folk-Lore In The Old Testament* argues that the scientific knowledge of primitive man was magic.[11]

Frazer, Freud, and many theological commentators[12] have shown that Eden and the fall is a complex myth; it contains elements of tree and vegetation cults, of totemism and associated taboos, of a new knowledge of sexuality, a new awareness of man's separate existence, and with this a new awareness of insecurity. Clearly, the myth tells of a great crisis in the human condition, perhaps of the beginning of man's consciousness. In *We Moderns* Muir operates in an intuitive, impetuous and sometimes contradictory way, and yet he chances on the train of thought that leads him to the ideas magic and totemism, and later to the ideas of consciousness, conscience and guilt—the themes that lie at the centre of the myth.

Muir makes the assertion: 'The Fall of Man was a *mystery* to the poet, which he did not rationalize or theologize.'[13] But Muir, unlike his primitive poet, cannot resist rationalising and theologising, and as he does so his initial hostility gradually gives way to curiosity, and even fascination as his enquiry proceeds. He argues that the primitive man who ate the fruit of the tree felt no guilt and regarded the fall as a misfortune rather than a punishment for a crime; the idea that this was a criminal act, says Muir, 'came much later, when the conscience had become deeper, more subtle and more neurotic; when individualism had been introduced into morality.'[14] And a few pages later in a fragment entitled 'Before The Fall' he returns to the question of conscience:

> Innocence is the morality of the instincts. Original Sin—that was war upon the instincts, morality become abstract, separate, self-centred, accusing and tyrannical. The self-consciousness of morality, this disruption in the nature of Man, was the Fall.[15]

The statement is to some extent a show of his agnosticism, but at the same time it leads him even closer to the main elements of the myth, and on the next page he writes:

> The knowledge of Good and Evil was not an instantaneous 'illumination'; it was the result of long experiment and analysis: the apple took perhaps hundreds of years to eat! Before that, in the happy days of innocence, Good and Evil were not, for instinct and morality were one and not twain.[16]

Muir identifies innocence with instinct, and he argues that the concept of original sin, a 'war upon the instincts', disrupts the nature of man: the innocence of the instincts is adulterated by the 'separate, self-centred' morality. Developing this line of thought, Muir imagines a period in primitive history, 'the happy days of innocence', when questions of good and evil could not be asked since there was no morality apart from instinct; it was only afterwards, during the centuries of apple-eating, that these questions could be asked.

The agnostic Muir, believing himself to be beyond good and evil at that time, does not admit the possibility that it is just 'this disruption in the nature of Man', the development of consciousness and conscience, that makes man fully human; his interpretation seems closer to those of the anthropologist and the psychologist of the period. In *The Golden Bough* Frazer comments on the failure of primitive man to make distinctions between good and evil, holiness and pollution;[17] and in *Totem and Taboo* Freud argues that conscience emerged 'on a basis of emotional ambivalence'.[18] And amongst the theological commentators N P Williams in *The Ideas Of The Fall And Of Original Sin* makes the point that there can be no sense of sin without a moral struggle between conscience and desire,[19] which is similar to Muir's idea of the conflict between the new self-centred morality and the old instinctive innocence; and there is a further similarity in that Williams points out that the moral struggle pre-supposes a development in self-consciousness.[20] Muir has begun to adopt a position that is not inconsistent with that of the theologians.

His argument is that primitive man was instinctive man, lacking any awareness of himself as a separate being and lacking, therefore, conscience and morality. Without this there could be no guilt, no original sin. Such an existence implies an almost total absence of self-consciousness in primitive man; it implies that primitive man was—and, since the primitive still exists in modern man, is—unconscious man. On questions of consciousness and the unconscious, and on the importance of the myth of the fall, Jung is again persuasive. In *The Structure And Dynamics Of The Psyche* he writes:

> Every problem, therefore, brings the possibility of a widening of consciousness, but also the necessity of saying goodbye to childlike unconsciousness and trust in nature. This necessity is a psychic fact of such importance that it constitutes one of the most essential symbolic teachings of the Christian religion. It is the sacrifice of the merely natural man, of the unconscious, ingenuous being whose tragic career began with the eating of the apple in Paradise. The biblical fall of man represents the dawn of consciousness as a curse. And as a matter of fact it is in this light that we first look upon every problem that forces us to greater consciousness and separates us even further from the paradise of unconscious childhood.[21]

This, the concept of 'the paradise of unconscious childhood', is where Muir's train of thought has led him.

Throughout *We Moderns* and notably in the chapter, 'Original Sin', Muir adopts attitudes that he was soon to outgrow. There is the Nietzschean rhetoric of 'And how, then, is Man to be redeemed? By the return of the Superman!', and the dismissive wit of 'The belief in Original Sin—that was itself Man's original sin'.[22] But behind the intellectual posturing there is a genuine spirit of enquiry that leads Muir towards a deeper understanding of the myth of the fall. It is a train of thought that leads him to write of 'the happy days of innocence' before the fall, the days that preceded the eating of the apple and the gaining of knowledge of good and evil, the days of primitive instinctive man, without sin because he had no conscience, and without conscience because he had no consciousness of self.

The manner in which Muir discusses the myth of the fall in *We Moderns* is wilful and sometimes frivolous, a juggling with ideas rather than the expression of a genuinely held vision; and as has been shown, some of these ideas were soon to disappear along with the Superman. Even so, the underlying pattern of ideas in Muir's first book prefigures the attitudes that emerge in the poems; but between the publication of *We Moderns* in 1918 and *First Poems* in 1925 Muir had rediscovered his childhood and the self that had been lost.

The fact that Muir's childhood was spent on farms in Orkney and his adolescence and early manhood were spent in Glasgow has led some readers to equate Orkney with Eden, and industrial Glasgow—or the capitalist system—with the fall. This seems a plausible interpretation, and one that seems to be confirmed by the *Autobiography*, but the second chapter of the *Autobiography*, 'Garth', makes it clear that innocence ended long before Muir left Orkney. The fall from the paradise of unconscious childhood is the fall of everyman; the effect of Muir's years in Glasgow and Greenock was to extend and intensify his experience of the fall.

Only once does Muir himself make a connection between the move from Orkney and the fall. In the novel, *Poor Tom*, published in 1932, the Manson family, like the Muirs in reality, have come to Glasgow from an island in the far north. Muir writes of Mrs Manson:

> In her heart she blamed Glasgow for all the misfortunes that had happened since they had come south, though she did not say this for fear of being laughed at. ... It was simply the portion of the corruption of Glasgow alloted to them, their private share of the corruption that was visible in the troubled, dirty atmosphere, the filth and confusion of the street, the cynical frankness, hitherto unknown to her, with which people here talked of their privatest affairs, their fathers and mothers, sisters and brothers.[23]

The idea, placed in the thoughts of Mrs Manson rather than those of the central character, Mansie, is not repeated, and even here there is no mention of a fall.

On the question of the importance of Orkney, Neil M Gunn, whose work shares some of Muir's preoccupations and whose childhood was acted out in circumstances similar to Muir's, said in a radio broadcast:

> I would be against putting too much stress on the Orkney experience because there would seem to be an easy way out for unusual visionary experiences. I think experiences of Edwin's kind have been had by people brought up in surroundings quite different from Edwin's, and if I want to stress that, it's because I want to stress that Edwin wasn't having some kind of experience which, let me say, could be explained away by the single tree and the single house and so on.[24]

The visionary experiences, argues Gunn, arise not simply from Orkney but in the mind of the boy growing up in Orkney; or rather, the experiences are rediscovered and recreated with a new significance in the adult mind. The geography was an important part of the experience for Muir, but the essential experience was childhood itself; the mystery lies in that state rather than a physical location. And Gunn's point, that unusual visionary experiences can be had by people brought up in surroundings quite different from Muir's, is one that many readers will confirm—so many, indeed, that the experience may not be unusual. C S Lewis, writing of the childhood of the race and of individual childhood in the chapter entitled 'The Fall Of Man' in *The Problem Of Pain*, says:

> From our own childhood we remember that before our elders thought us capable of 'understanding' anything, we already had spiritual experiences as pure and as

momentous as any we have undergone since, though not, of course, as rich in factual content.[25]

It is these visionary, spiritual experiences—intimations of innocence and of the paradise of unconscious childhood—that Muir rediscovers in the poems, 'Childhood', from *First Poems* of 1925, 'The Myth' from *The Voyage* of 1946, 'The Young Princes' from *One Foot in Eden* of 1956, and 'The Brothers' in the posthumously published *Collected Poems*.

'Childhood'[26] is Muir's first attempt to express in poetry the timeless pre-lapsarian state of childhood. It is a minor poem in ballad form with a slightly plodding rhythm and traces of archaic diction, but even so it creates and sustains the state of mind that hovers between the vacancy of idle daydream and a sense of timeless communion. (And one notes that when Muir began to write poems in the early 1920s he disregarded contemporary modernist modes, choosing instead the ballad as his form and his Orkney childhood as his subject.)

The child in the poem—Muir's recollection of his childhood self on the island of Wyre—lies in the sun and looks across at the other islands:

> In thought he saw the still light on the sand,
> The shallow water clear in tranquil air.

And as he gazes he sees a ship appear, passing so slowly that 'time seemed finished ere the ship passed by', until the trance of innocence and timelessness is gently broken in the closing line:

> And from the house his mother called his name.

'The Myth'[27] is a more confident statement of the theme. It opens:

> My childhood all a myth
> Enacted in a distant isle

Once again Muir sees childhood as a timeless state; time 'did not move the whole day long', but here he introduces the tension between timelessness and time, innocence and experience:

> That immobility might save
> Continually the dying song,
> The flower, the falling wave.

The effect is of the suspension of time and the passing of time, so that the song dies and yet continues, the flower blooms even as it withers, and the falling wave never quite completes its fall. In the last four lines of the first stanza Muir suggests a mysterious, protective haunting:

> And at each corner of the wood
> In which I played the ancient play,
> Guarding the traditional day
> The faithful watchers stood.

Muir's sense of the innocence of his early childhood is so strong that he recalls the innocence as being physically present—'the faithful watchers'— like the archetypes of myth; it may even be that Muir is using the word, 'watchers', with its religious meaning, 'angels'. And as the poem continues through the 'tragi-comedy' of youth in the second stanza to late middle-age when 'designs grow halt and lame' in the third and final stanza, so the innocence persists. Muir weakens the impact of the poem by using the word, 'reverie', in the second and third stanzas when it seems certain he means the myth of the title, but the poem ends unequivocally: 'The risen watchers stand'. The watchers are still present (and the tense of the verb has changed from 'stood' to 'stand', from past to present) like guardian spirits of the original innocence.

In 'The Young Princes'[28] the mythical element of 'The Myth' is developed into a picture of a golden age. introducing 'The Young Princes' in a radio broadcast in 1954, Muir made a rare public explanatory comment in which he stated explicitly his concept of the innocence of childhood and, less explicitly, his feeling that the original innocence remains part of our adult identity:

> 'The Young Princes' is about childhood and the fact that we all come into the world unspoiled, as if we were stepping into an Eden, but that sooner or later doubt falls across our lives, so that we pass out of innocence into experience. The young princes in the poem are children; and the last two lines suggest that we only know what we are by remembering our first state.[29]

The impression of stepping into an Eden is given immediately in the opening lines:

> There was a time: we were young princes then
> In artless state, with brows as bright and clear
> As morning light on a new morning land.

Muir says the 'artless state' is childhood, but the nature of this 'new morning land' is such that it suggests the childhood of the race as well as of the individual, the archetypal infancy of man in the dawn of creation. The princes give and take 'with innocent hands' and like 'absentminded kings' in an infinitely courteous and generous and gentle world. This is man's estate through the morning of his childhood until 'the irreversible noonday came', bringing with it 'Doubt that kills courtesy and gratitude'. The princes fall

from their paradise into the adult, conscious world, but the fall is not quite
absolute because the poem ends:

> And yet sometimes
> We still, as through a dream that comes and goes,
> Know what we are, remembering what we were.

Beyond the distortions of the adult world the original innocence remains as
part of our full identity. The visionary quality of 'The Young Princes' is such
that, although Muir paints too idyllic a picture of the golden age, the poem
is closer to prophecy than to recollection.

Muir returns to the theme in his late poem, 'The Brothers',[30] in which the
figures are Muir's own brothers, Willie and Johnny, who appeared in a dream
Muir had late in 1956 or early in 1957, some fifty years after their deaths.[31]
Through the dream the boys are released from time and death into eternal
play:

> For still they raced about the green
> And were like two revolving suns;
> A brightness poured from head to head,
> So strong I could not see their eyes
> Or look into their paradise.

Muir wonders how he had failed to see this loveliness fifty years ago, but
when he tries to put the question the dream ends. Awake, the poet recalls the
antagonisms of the brothers when they lived:

> A darkness covered every head,
> Frowns twisted the original face

But Muir's point is that the frowns twisted the *original* face, and in the next
two lines he writes:

> And through the mask we could not see
> The beauty and the buried grace.

The beauty and the grace, he says, are not simply aspects of the dream but
qualities that had been present in the boys' lives. The 'paradise' of the earlier
line, then, can be read as an allusion to the immortality of the spirit and also
to the original innocence, the paradise of unconscious childhood that Muir
rediscovers through the unconsciousness of his dream.

In the final stanza Muir acknowledges the reality of man's fallen condition;
he has seen

> ... indifferent justice done
> By everyone on everyone

But in the closing lines he reaffirms the other reality, and in doing so he allows himself the word, 'vision', a more positive and appropriate term than the 'reverie' of 'The Myth' or the 'dream that comes and goes' of 'The Young Princes'. 'The Brothers' ends:

> And in a vision I have seen
> My brothers playing on the green.

There is some similarity between the exploratory attitudes the young Muir juggled with in *We Moderns* and the themes that emerge from the poems considered in this chapter. The essential difference is that the early prose expresses ideas whereas the poems express a faith and a personal vision. The manner too changes in the intervening years: bold assertion is replaced by quiet affirmation, cleverness by wisdom, and polished rhetoric by a testimony that may on occasion be faltering or even confused but is always truthful.

THE BROKEN CITADEL

In his poems on the loss of childhood innocence Muir treats the fall as a corruption of the imagination and the spirit. In his poems of the broken citadel he sees the fall as a violent physical event—the destruction of a castle, a city, a civilisation.

One of the key poems in this treatment of the fall is 'The Castle'[1] from the volume, *The Voyage* of 1946. The opening stanza establishes an atmosphere of leisurely security:

> All through that summer at ease we lay,
> And daily from the turret wall
> We watched the mowers in the hay
> And the enemy half a mile away.
> They seemed no threat to us at all.

The castle is under siege but the defenders know that the place is impregnable and that their allies are approaching, so that the presence of the enemy beyond the fields that are still being safely harvested serves to intensify the sweetness of the way of life that continues undisturbed behind the walls. When Muir has established the sense of security the poem changes course:

> There was a little private gate,
> A little wicked wicket gate.
> The wizened warder let them through.

And then the enemy is inside and the castle taken:

> The famous citadel overthrown,
> And all its secret galleries bare.

The fall expressed in 'The Castle', with the act of betrayal and the sense that the sheer physical bulk of the walls is so reassuring that it becomes paradoxically a weakness, echoes an incident in the opening chapter of Muir's novel, *The Three Brothers* of 1931. (And there are slight similarities between poem and novel and the incident in the ballad, 'Edom o' Gordon'.[2]) In the novel young David Blackadder overhears his father saying that Cardinal Beaton has been murdered in St Andrews Castle, and the boy is disturbed not by the murder of the cardinal but that the castle has been breached. He begins to question his father:

'But how could he slip in when the door was barred? And then he would have
to go through the second door and it's barred as well, and then the next door,
and then another door still.'[3]

The many doors, a defence mechanism in the mind of the frightened boy as
well as an architectural feature of the castle, correspond with the 'maze of
tunnelled stone' and the 'secret galleries' of the castle in the poem. In the
novel David's father explains how the killers got in:

'Ay, but just listen a wee. If you go round the corner of the castle what should
you come to but another gate, a wee thing that you would hardly notice, a wee,
wicked-looking, wee gate.'[4]

The 'wicked-looking, wee gate' is of course the 'little wicked wicket gate' of
the poem. The account in the novel ends with David's awed and unwilling
acceptance of the fall of the castle:

'Then a castle isna safe after all, father? And a man can be killed in the middle
of a castle?'[5]

The capture of the castle and the murder of Beaton in *The Three Brothers*
give a physical and historical reality to the fall, but more importantly they
implant a sense of insecurity in David's mind that puts an end to the innocence
of childhood. The castle of the poem, by contrast, is set in any place at any
time and its fall is a universal event. But having established this Muir goes
further:

> How can this shameful tale be told?
> I will maintain until my death
> We could do nothing, being sold;
> Our only enemy was gold,
> And we had no arms to fight it with.

It is a defeat that has been brought about by the defenders themselves, not
just by the guard who took the bribe to open the gate. There are ambiguities
in the closing stanza of the poem, but one feels that Muir's intention is that
the narrator of the poem should be seen to be protesting too much: 'I will
maintain . . . We could do nothing'. The enemy was more than the besieging
army and more than the greed of a guard; the enemy was the state of mind
that made defeat possible, the oblivious certainty of those inside the castle
that the place could not be taken and that the old dispensation was assured.
Their sense of comfort was so unquestioning that their strength became their
weakness and the old way of life was lost; it is a conclusion Muir reaches in
other poems on this theme.

In 'The Castle' the fall is presented in a way that transforms the physical
reality into a near-abstraction and modifies the horror of the event into
the ambiguous self-justification of the narrator, leaving the reader with the
impression of a universal and yet anonymous fall that has been brought

about, at least partly, by the defenders themselves. In 'Troy' and 'A Trojan Slave',[6] companion poems in *Journeys And Places* of 1937, the broken citadel is more precisely located and the theme is expressed more forcefully. What is merely implied in 'The Castle', that the defenders of the besieged citadel contributed to their own defeat, is stated explicitly in 'A Trojan Slave'; the Trojans are aware of the potential threat from within and yet despite, or perhaps because of, this suspicion Troy falls to the Greeks.

The poem opens with a recollection of Troy and of Paris and Hector growing up from boyhood to early manhood, and then the reminiscence is cut short:

> That was before the fall,
> When high still stood Troy's many-tunnelled wall.
> Now I am shackled to a Grecian dolt.

The monologue is that of a man who has been a slave in Troy for thirty years and has survived the fall of the city only to become a slave in a Greek galley. He is constantly reminded of Troy, but all the memories lead to the image of the city in flames: 'Troy's towers burn like a winter wood'. And the memory of the fire brings the other recollection:

> But in my heart a deeper spite has grown,
> This, that they would not arm us, and preferred
> Troy's ruin lest a slave should snatch a sword
> And fight even at their side.

The narrator says the slaves and the common people of Troy would have fought for the city; instead, they had no choice but to watch the slaughter:

> And so we watched with dogs outside the ring
> Heroes fall cheap as meat, king slaughtering king
> Like fatted cattle.

But it was not only vanity and the aristocratic code that prevented the Trojans from asking the slaves for help; they were afraid that if the slaves were armed and let loose they might turn on their masters rather than the enemy:

> And while they feared the Greeks they feared us most,
> And ancient Troy was lost and we were lost.

At the centre of the poem is the irony that the defenders were so alert to what they imagined to be the threat from within that they refused to arm the slaves and so lost an opportunity to save the city. Despite the irony and bitterness of 'A Trojan Slave' the poem ends on a note of acceptance:

> Yet through that rage shines Troy's untroubled hill,
> And many a tumbled wall and vanished tree
> Remains, as if in spite, a happy memory.

By contrast, the companion poem, 'Troy', tells of a fall of unrelieved futility. The central figure in the poem has lost everything; the destruction of Troy has driven the man insane, and he lives in the sewers beneath the ruined city, imagining when he fights the rats for scraps of food that he is still beating back the advancing Greeks: ' "Achilles, Ajax, turn and fight!/Stop cowards!" ' And in the middle lines of the poem Muir intensifies the degradation by expressing the man's entire existence in terms of the rats:

> The light was rat-grey,
> The hills and dells, the common drain, his Simois,
> Rat-grey. Mysterious shadows fell
> Affrighting him whenever a cloud offended
> The sun up in the other world. The rat-hordes,
> Moving, were grey dust shifting in grey dust.

The crazed old man sees and thinks and lives like a rat, and Muir comments: 'Proud history has such sack-ends'. Even so this last survivor, fighting out his hallucinatory battles in the sewers of the city, might have died with a kind of lunatic dignity had he been left among the rats but here the poem changes course, rising back into the sunlight, into 'the other world' and into another level of wretchedness. Some wandering thieves find the old man and drag him from the rat-grey dust of the sewers. Above ground he faces the fact of fallen Troy for the first time and loses the delusions that had helped to keep him alive:

> And there he saw Troy like a burial ground . . .
> . . . No sail from edge to edge, the Greeks clean gone.
> They stretched him on a rock and wrenched his limbs,
> Asking: 'Where is the treasure?' till he died.

In the closing lines of the poem the man loses his shabby dignity, and his death by torture is futile. The crazed old Trojan, sharply defined in this firmly constructed poem, is both an individual and an archetypal figure; he is the last of the Trojans after the fall of Troy and he is any man stumbling blindly in the ruins of any fallen city.

It is a situation Muir explores several times but seldom, until his nuclear poems of the 1950s, in such savagely unrelieved terms. 'The Town Betrayed',[7] also from *Journeys and Places*, and 'The Good Town'[8] from *The Labyrinth* of 1949 lack the completeness and inevitability of 'Troy' but they capture the demoralisation of a people and the destruction of their way of life after a fall, and with their mid-twentieth-century settings these poems place the fall in the modern world.

The first stanza of 'The Town Betrayed' speaks of the shock and degradation of the people in the aftermath of war:

> Our homes are eaten out by time,
>   Our lawns strewn with our listless sons,
> Our harlot daughters lean and watch
>   The ships crammed down with shells and guns.

It is an existence without hope or purpose, and in the fifth stanza Muir confirms this impression when he gives a glimpse of the forces that now control the fallen town:

> Yet here there is no word, no sign
>   But quiet murder in the street.
> Our leaf-light lives are spared or taken
>   By men obsessed and neat.

It is the world of informers, secret police, casual and arbitrary arrest and execution, a world in which order has been replaced by 'dark disorder'. But Muir's vision of this fallen state is not sustained; the opening stanza with its image of a broken family and a broken people is followed by the stylised, emblematic imagery of 'glittering swords', 'dubious field' and 'dubious trumpet'; the grim impersonality of the modern police state is followed by allusions to 'our ancestral ghosts'—Agamemnon, Achilles, Siegfried and Lancelot. Muir is trying to set the particular experience of the town in a timeless and universal context, and perhaps trying to introduce an element of hope by suggesting the undying presence of ancestral heroes, but the unfortunate effect is that the language and the vision of the poem seem inconsistent, almost contradictory. 'The Town Betrayed' could have been a chillingly effective, strikingly modern poem; instead, it is an interesting failure.

A longer and more successful exploration of the fallen town and of the conditions of the people after their defeat is 'The Good Town'. In a radio broadcast in 1952 Muir commented on the origin of the poem:

> A little before writing "The Labyrinth"—as I was walking one day in a park near our house in Prague—I had an idea for two poems about towns, one to be called "The Good Town", and the other "The Bad Town"; and I intended the towns to stand as symbols of two ways of life. But as things were then shaping in Prague, I saw that the only way to treat the theme was to describe a good town turning into a bad one. Yet the poem is not really about Prague or any other place, but about something that was happening in Europe. Stories of what was happening in other countries to whole families, whole communities, became absorbed into the poem, which I tried to make into a symbolical picture of a vast change.[9]

This poem, like 'The Town Betrayed', is set in a place that has been taken by the enemy, but the opening section of 'The Good Town', as Muir indicated in his radio broadcast, recalls the conditions before the fall:

> Look at it well. This was a good town once,
> Known everywhere, with streets of friendly neighbours,
> Street friend to street and house to house.

And the narrator goes on to recall an ideal order, an idyllic state of almost prelapsarian perfection. Muir's narrator overstates his case for the city as it was before the fall, perhaps to make a more striking comparison with the new conditions, but the idyll of the first twenty-one lines is too much for the poet and critic, Edwin Morgan, who wrote of 'The Good Town':

> The poem 'The Good Town', for instance, leaves a melodramatic impression because one knows very well what the poet is talking about but one simply doesn't accept the 'universalising' black-and-white opposition between the Danny Kaye 'streets of friendly neighbours' where lock and key were 'quaint antiquities fit for museums' while ivy trailed 'across the prison door' and their later metamorphosis . . .[10]

One concedes that there is something unjustified in the opening lines of the poem; the details are catalogued rather than fully expressed, but it is possible that the friendly neighbours and the unused prison may have been facts, as the later description of the shattered city is fact. What Muir attempts in the opening sequence is the presentation of a lost way of life that is so far removed from the present as to seem like a different order of reality, an innocent and unfallen world:

> There is a virtue in tranquility
> That makes all fitting, childhood and youth and age,
> Each in its place.

When the narrator turns from the past to the present in a juxtaposition that is deliberately harsh, this order and continuity is lost:

> Look well. These mounds of rubble,
> And shattered piers, half-windows, broken arches
> And groping arms were once inwoven in walls
> Covered with saints and angels, bore the roof,
> Shot up the towering spire.

The church, the building that symbolised the old way of life with its faith and order, has been destroyed. The physical details of the ruined church and the wider destruction throughout the city are almost certainly prompted by Muir's impressions of Cologne in 1945 when he drove across Europe to Prague.[11] There has been some rebuilding in the city of the poem but what has been done is shapeless, part of the disorder of the fall:

> These gaping bridges
> Once spanned the quiet river which you see
> Beyond that patch of raw and angry earth
> Where the new concrete houses sit and stare.

The old order, and with it man's sense of place in the scheme of life, is lost; spiritually as well as physically the people are displaced persons, and the narrator says his friends have disappeared in 'parties, armies, camps, conspiracies'. Of those who remain he says:

We avoid each other. If you see a man
Who smiles good-day or waves a lordly greeting
Be sure he's a policeman or a spy.

Muir himself had witnessed such things in Prague before and after the Communist coup of 1948, and he writes of these conditions in the *Autobiography*:

We were living in the midst of these changes without any clear notion of what was happening, but aware of a constant invisible pressure, which seemed more dangerous than the isolated acts of intimidation or terror which came to our ears. The pressure produced, as by an exactly calculated process, a deepening of the apprehension which already anticipated the future; people were not so much afraid of what was happening as of what would happen yet. At first the apprehension seemed the worst effect of the new State; then the moral anguish of those who had to choose Communism against their conscience to keep their families alive seemed worse still: until at last one saw that the impersonality of the system which imposed these miseries was the worst of all.[12]

The narrator says the fall of the good town has been brought about by 'these two wars which trampled on us twice'—which could be either the two world wars of the twentieth century or the two tyrannies, Nazi and Communist, in the city of Prague—and the wars, says the narrator, have caused the land to look awry, the roads to run crooked, the light to fall wrong, and the fields to lie like a randomly dealt pack of cheating cards. And then he questions the source of the disorder: 'Could it have come from us?'

The answer to the question in the closing section of the poem is in Muir's own voice as well as that of his persona. The city fell because within the people themselves the fine balance between good and evil was lost, and the critical moment of imbalance was 'So finely reckoned' as to be imperceptible. Regaining goodness, or restoring the balance, is so enormous a task that Muir uses the imagery not of the city but of the cosmos to express the difficulty:

No: when evil comes
All things turn adverse, and we must begin
At the beginning, heave the groaning world
Back in its place again, and clamp it there.

The conclusion Muir arrives at—'Our peace betrayed us; we betrayed our peace'—is the one he reaches in 'The Castle' and 'The Trojan Slave', and the poem ends with the stark understatement: 'These thoughts we have, walking among our ruins'.

Clearly, beneath the twentieth century detail of 'The Good Town' Muir is exploring the endless struggle between good and evil, a struggle that has its expression in the political arena but has its origin in the mind of man; and the fallen state of the city in the aftermath of defeat is an aspect of the human condition in which man has fallen from his original innocence. The poems of the broken citadel explore the physical and political, as well as the spiritual and psychological, consequences of the fall. Muir accepts that the citadel will be breached, that we cannot build an impregnable wall around our peace of mind, and that there is no security in the fallen world. It is a bleak, almost despairing vision of existence, and in his nuclear poems of the 1950s Muir looks even deeper into the abyss to consider the fact that man can bring about a fall that might finally destroy the world.

THE HOLOCAUST

When Muir came to write the extension of his autobiography in the early 1950s he realised that the world had changed in a fundamental way. The first volume of autobiography, *The Story And The Fable*, had been published in 1940 and when he was bringing it up to date Muir grew increasingly aware of the nature and extent of the change. He writes:

> I finished the first part of this book thirteen years ago. Since then there has been a great war and a succession of revolutions; the world has been divided into two hostile camps; and our concern has ceased to be the community or country we live in, and has become the single disunited world: a vast abstraction, and at the same time a dilemma which, as it seems, we must all solve together or on which we must all be impaled together.[1]

As early as 1953 Muir sees that the Second World War and the series of lesser wars and coups that followed it—in Czechoslovakia, China, Korea, the Middle East—have at one and the same time made the world a smaller and yet a more deeply divided and dangerous place. The war ended the threat of Nazism only to reveal the new threat of the hostile division between East and West. But the conflict of ideologies is not the only change in those intervening thirteen years, and Muir adds:

> This world was set going when we began to make nature serve us, hoping that we should eventually reach a stage where we would not have to adapt ourselves at all: machinery would save the trouble. We did not foresee that the machinery would grow into a great impersonal power, that we should have to serve it instead of co-operating with nature as our fathers did, and that as it grew more perfect we should become more powerless and be forced at last into a position not chosen by us, or chosen in blindness before we knew where our desires were leading.[2]

The stimulus of war intensified the other process—man's development of machines and his insatiable desire to impose his control on nature. As Muir sees it, the process accelerates until man's concern becomes an obsession and he becomes the slave of the machine. Muir does not mention atomic energy or the atomic bomb, but this must have been part of his thinking at the time. The first British test of an atomic bomb took place on the Monte Bello Islands off the west coast of Australia in October 1952; in November 1952 the Americans tested their first thermonuclear bomb on the Eniwetok atoll in the Marshall Islands in the Pacific, and in the following year the Americans tested

47

an even bigger bomb on the Bikini atoll in the Marshall Islands. These tests were widely reported in the news media at the time.

In the *Autobiography* Muir writes not of the bombs but of the new sense of insecurity with which man faced the future:

> The generation to which I belong has survived an age, and the part of our life which is still immobilized there is like a sentence broken off before it could be completed; the future in which it would have written its last word was snatched away and a raw new present abruptly substituted; and that present is reluctant now to formulate its own sentence, for the fear that what it has to say will in turn be cut short by yet another raw present.[3]

Muir's vision of continuity is one of the ways in which he finds meaning in life, but here he says the continuity is broken and that he cannot relate the past to the present or the present to the future. In this sense Muir's world had changed almost beyond recognition. The war of course caused many of the changes, but the 'raw new present' and the fear that this might be 'cut short by yet another raw present' was prompted not only by war but by the conflicts that followed it. For Muir the most disturbing event was the Prague coup of 1948, and as the Gottwald regime was consolidating its position in Czechoslovakia the Soviet Union was applying the year-long Berlin Blockade, an episode that intensified the hostility between East and West. And throughout this period the United States, followed by Britain and the Soviet Union, were testing the new bombs. These were the events that led Muir to speak of a raw new present and to admit the fear that it might suddenly be cut short. It is this fear that underlies several of his last poems, in the most disturbing of which he faces the possibility of the final fall of man in a nuclear holocaust.

One of Muir's earliest poems on the theme is 'The Horses'[4] from *One Foot In Eden* of 1956. The poem is the monologue of a member of a remote community that has survived the war; the speaker recalls the immediate aftermath of the holocaust, and then he remembers the event that occurred almost a year afterwards. Along with this apparent simplicity of structure the poem has that achieved simplicity of diction and imagery that characterises much of Muir's best work, but beneath these simplicities there is an intricate organisation of material and a complex pattern of associations:

> Barely a twelvemonth after
> The seven days war that put the world to sleep,
> Late in the evening the strange horses came.

The understatement of the opening lines delays the shock until, beneath the quiet tone, one realises that the narrator is speaking about the destruction of civilisation; but he is speaking too about survival and about the mysterious arrival of the horses a year after the war. The speaker is drawn back to the days immediately after the war, and the images of death re-assert themselves in his mind:

On the second day
The radios failed; we turned the knobs; no answer.
On the third day a warship passed us, heading north,
Dead bodies piled on the deck. On the sixth day
A plane plunged over us into the sea. Thereafter
Nothing.

The radio is useless, and its silence, as well as being an ironic comment on the failure of the machine and man's failure to communicate, also symbolises the absolute and universal silence in the days that followed the war. The warship and the plane, symbols of man's power of life or death, are also useless, the ship a floating hearse and the plane swallowed up by the sea. Even the abandoned rusting tractors seem to be sinking back into the earth 'like other loam'. Radio, warship, aircraft—the instruments of man's ingenuity have become the instruments of his fall.

The lines seem to echo in twentieth century imagery the warning in *Genesis*: 'But of the tree of the knowledge of good and evil, thou shalt not eat of it: for in the day that thou eatest thereof thou shalt surely die'. And the six lines that recall the course of the war form a black parody on the Creation myth: in six days man *destroys* the world, and on the seventh day there is silence. In the year that follows the war the survivors come to reject the lost civilisation, 'That old bad world' as their spokesman call it, but they remain aware of the enormity of the loss and there are moments of spontaneous bewildered mourning:

Sometimes we think of the nations lying asleep,
Curled blindly in impenetrable sorrow,
And then the thought confounds us with its strangeness.

They mourn the dead and reject the civilisation that caused the deaths, preferring instead a primitive existence in which they know they 'have gone back/Far past our fathers' land'.

It is here, with the broken line, that the poem changes course. The coming of the horses breaks the universal silence of the fall:

We heard a distant tapping on the road,
A deepening drumming; it stopped, went on again
And at the corner changed to hollow thunder.

And the horses break the year-long isolation of the survivors, bringing back the forgotten culture, 'that long-lost archaic companionship'. The horses establish again something the community can barely remember but which they know to be good, the immemorial relationship between man and the horse, and the survivors rediscover 'that free servitude still can pierce our hearts'. But more than this, the return of the horses is the return of an element of innocence:

> Among them were some half-a-dozen colts
> Dropped in some wilderness of the broken world,
> Yet new as if they had come from their own Eden.

Innocence, and with it a spark of a transfiguring grace, is rekindled in the survivors, for with the line: 'Yet new as if they had come from their own Eden', Muir brings an unfallen element into the fallen world and offers a new beginning to man who had all but destroyed his world.

'The Horses' is not of course an argument that man must go back to a peasant economy based on the horse. The horses in the poem—'good plough-horses' Muir wrote of them in a letter[5]—clearly suggest a simple agrarian way of life but their greater function in the poem is to symbolise the possibility of harmony between man and the natural world. Instead of enslaving ourselves to the machine so as to conquer the forces of nature, we must rediscover the 'free servitude' that will allow us, as Muir says in the *Autobiography*, to go on 'co-operating with nature as our father did'.

'The Horses' is one of Muir's great poems. Its wholeness of vision—reaching back to Eden and the beginning of time in the first fall, reaching further back with that echo of the Creation, and then soaring forward again through time into the narrator's present, which is our indeterminate future—the completeness of vision is such that the poem becomes an act of mythopoesis, recreating in twentieth century terms the myth of the fall and the redemption of man. In his later explorations of the theme of nuclear war the fear of extinction becomes dominant. As existence in the raw present of the 1950s became increasingly uncertain so the poems became more grimly prophetic.

The harshness of these poems was to some extent pre-figured in Muir's radio broadcast, 'The Decline Of The Imagination' in 1951.[6] In this essay he argues that as the power of the imagination has declined so the dominance of science has increased and: 'As we do not know what to do with this power, it becomes a dangerous possession, an explosive possibility'. The phrase, 'an explosive possibility', is clearly an allusion to the destructive power of the new weapons as well as to science in general. Muir pursues the theme, expressing his sense of a divided world in uncharacteristically forceful terms:

> The world has changed radically as a place for human beings to live in, and has become the blundering, sometimes frightening, embodiment of an increasingly perfect intellectual process: the visible creation of science; or perhaps more truly a distortion of science, and the misbegotten offspring of a union between science in its purity and the ordinary ignorant unregenerate insatiable natural man.

The fear and pessimism of this passage—and at the same time its chilling clarity—is the spirit that underlies the later poems of the nuclear holocaust.

Every age is an age of anxiety, but the anxiety of the 1950s was prompted by the new and terrifying prospect of the destruction of the human race. Muir was one of the first writers to respond to the new situation, and the 'anti-vision' of 'After 1984'[7] and 'The Refugees Born For A Land Unknown'[8] expresses his deepest fears.

The title, 'after 1984' seems to suggest that after the publication of Orwell's novel the human situation had to be viewed differently, although Muir was of course independently aware of the new political realities. The poem is not explicitly about nuclear war but instead asks how the new situation, the post-1984 conditions, came about. Probing behind the anxiety, Muir wonders how man has come to be the slave of the machine, how he has brought about his own imprisonment:

> Because no one could see or touch
> Our fetters locked so far within,
> And not a key in the world to fit.

As a poem develops, the image of imprisonment recurs until it becomes a metaphor for the human condition: 'Shut from ourselves even in our mind'. In the search for escape the poem generates an air of sombre urgency, raising again the spiritual and psychological questions of the final section of 'The Good Town' as Muir speculates on the origin of this fall:

> Was it chaos that set us straight,
> The elements that rebelled, not we?

And with a growing sense of inevitability, as if the train of thought were being drawn irresistibly down into the 'twisting chaos within', the questions lead to the final question:

> In the Nought
> Did we beget it in our thought?

The question implies the answer, the answer that Muir continually reaches from various directions and in varying forms in his poems on the theme of the fall: the 'Nought', the blindness and imprisonment of the human condition in 'After 1984', is of man's own making.

Muir returns to the problem in 'The Refugees Born For A Land Unknown'. The poem is little more than a fragment and the deliberately juxtaposed and sharply defined images lead to a bleak conclusion. Again, the poem is the monologue of a survivor who sees his past life as: 'waste water drawn down through a hole'. And then in total contrast Muir introduces an image of order and tranquility:

> And in an English garden all afternoon
> I watch the bees among the lavender.

The garden is almost certainly that of Priory Cottage in Swaffham Prior where Muir spent the last years of his life, but here he writes as if he were somehow excluded from the scene, as if the present reality of the garden were already in the past, the hills 'unreal' and seen through 'alien eyes'. After the garden imagery, the closing image of the poem is again of imprisonment and the tone is fatalistic:

> Footsteps on the stairs, two heavy, two light,
> The door opens. Since then I remember nothing,
> But this room in a place where no doors open.
> I think the world died many years ago.

The final line reinforces one of the main impressions of 'After 1984', 'The Horses', and the poems of the broken citadel—that Muir writes from a convincingly post-lapsarian viewpoint because of the intensity with which he has imagined the fall.

This is the viewpoint in 'After A Hypothetical War'.[9] The opening lines take the reader beyond the immediate horror of the war into the nuclear wasteland:

> No rule nor ruler: only water and clay,
> And the purblind peasant squatting, elbows out
> To nudge his neighbour from his inch of ground
> Clutched fast through flood and drought but never loved.

Man has been reduced to a half-blind imbecile and his world transformed to a wilderness of mud. The linked images of spiritual and physical decay of the opening lines are developed throughout the poem—'The soil on its perpetual death-bed', and 'murderer choking murderer in the dark'—until the two are fused in an image of total deformity:

> Soil and air breed crookedly here, and men
> Are dumb and twisted as the envious scrub
> That spreads in silent malice on the fields.

And in the closing lines of the poem the image is repeated and extended so that the deformed, sub-human survivors of the nuclear war seem to be sinking in a sea of mud; it is as if they are about to be swallowed up by their poisoned world:

> The mud has sucked half in
> People and cattle until they eat and breathe
> Nothing but mud.

At the centre of the poem, giving it a grotesque authority, is one of Muir's more direct references to nuclear war:

> Even the dust-cart meteors on their rounds
> Stop here to void their refuse, leaving this
> Chaotic breed of misbegotten things,
> Embryos of what could never wish to be.

In his poems as in his prose Muir seems reluctant to name the apparatus of nuclear war, and even here it is not explicitly stated. He may have felt that simply to name the thing might evoke a quick and possibly spurious reaction of horror in his readers; at the same time one notes that Muir's war poems are not simply about war but also about that element in the human condition that makes war inevitable. But in the middle lines of the poem, despite the inadequacy of the image of the 'dust-cart meteors' voiding their refuse—an inadequacy which is partly that of language and poetry when dealing with the enormity of the facts—the detail is inescapable. Muir is of course referring to the radioactive fallout caused by a nuclear explosion, the poisonous material that would be carried through the atmosphere to descend later almost anywhere on earth in the form of dust or in droplets of rain. He is referring too to the radiation sickness that would affect animals and humans contaminated by the fallout. (Nuclear weapons are now infinitely more powerful than they were in the 1950s, and one consequence of nuclear war now being discussed is that dust and ash would obscure the sun to bring about the darkness of a 'nuclear winter'.)

Information on radiation sickness is now easily available but at the time Muir was writing 'After A Hypothetical War' the facts were little known or discussed. The poem first appeared under the title, 'The Bad Lands', in the *Listener* in January 1956 and it was probably written in 1955; one of the first non-specialist books on the subject of radiation sickness, *Atomic Radiation And Life* by Peter Alexander,[10] was published in 1957. Alexander considers various forms of radiation sickness, including irradiation of the eye which would cause the blindness of Muir's 'purblind peasant',[11] and in the following chapter, 'The Sins Of The Fathers', Alexander explains that the irradiation of one generation can have disastrous consequences for future generations, causing grotesque mutations. He writes:

> These malformations can be very great, so as to give horrible and distressing monsters, which are, however, quite capable of living for a time. The incidence is particularly high in the early stages of active development of the embryo . . .

Alexander continues:

> once the mutation has been established it becomes permanent, and genetic damage is cumulative and irreversible.[12]

Muir clearly knew some of these facts, and the poem shows that he has assimilated the knowledge into his vision of the human condition after the nuclear fall.

Muir's vision of a final fall is only part of his total vision, and nuclear war is seen as a possibility rather than an inevitability. Even so, the lasting impression of the poems on the theme of the holocaust is the completeness of the imagined participation in the event. Muir images the unimaginable and then reports from beyond the inferno, beyond despair. This is the effect of his longest poem on the theme, 'The Last War,[13] which first appeared in the *New Statesman* in June 1958 just a few months before his death.

'The Last War' is a set of five variations, and although there is no continuous narrative or even continuous development of theme the poem achieves a unity through the imagery of death and the hauntingly elegiac tone that comes from the acceptance of death. The separate sections of the poem were originally different poems which Muir came to see as a set of variations.[14] Each variation is prompted by an awareness of approaching death, and in the first section it is clearly the death of mankind in a nuclear war: 'the enemy / Hidden in boundless air'. And once again Muir is possessed by the enormity of the possibility: such a war would bring an end to the timeless continuity of the human race, would bring an end to time itself:

> The thought Again
> That made a promise to mortality—
> Gave pathos and distance, reason and rhyme—
> Will walk a little before us to the grave
> While we are still in time for a little time.

In the second variation he imagines the earth as a silent, empty planet where the cycle of night and day punctuates nothing: 'night and day / Vacantly visiting the vacant earth', and where the sun 'Shines on oes where thought of birth / Will never be'. This sense of finality then prompts another image of the universal fall, an image of coldly lyrical beauty:

> Or shall we picture bird and tree
> Silently falling, and think of all the words
> By which we forged earth, night and day
> And ruled with such a strange ease our work and play?
> Now only the lexicon of a dream.
> And we see our bodies buried in falling birds.

After the 'strange ease' of section II there is an abrupt change of tone in section III, as if the poet has caught himself thinking too fondly of death and now sees the end as a great sickness and terror:

> Perhaps nothing at all will be but pain,
> A choking and floundering, or gigantic stupor
> Of a world-wide deserted hospital ward.

But the moment of terror is brief and almost stylised, lacking the desolation of 'The Horses' or the grotesque detail of 'After A Hypothetical War', and this variation closes with an awareness of the daily guilt in our lives, the accumulation of little falls:

> Or shall we remember shameful things concealed,
> Mean coldnesses and wounds too eagerly given?

The question prompts a characteristic response and change of direction in Muir's train of thought. In section IV he considers the nature of the coldness and the wounding, trying again to trace them to their source, and he expresses his sense of the fallen world in terms of a stunted tree and a twisted smile on a human face:

> A tree thin sick and pale by a north wall,
> A smile splintering a face—

As this section develops the tree and the face come to symbolise nature and man; but the tree shrivels and dies, and the face is distorted from within until Muir imagines 'a common face/Aped from the crowd-face', a mask of impersonality and indifference. If the human face is to re-appear and the tree to be made whole then man must look again at himself and the natural world:

> I thought, our help is in all that is full-grown
> In nature, and all that is with hands well-made

If man can only rediscover this natural completeness and the deep satisfaction of tasks then: 'There is the harmony / By which we know our own and the world's health'.

The conclusion, although too simply arrived at in this case, is the one Muir reaches in the *Autobiography*: that we must go on 'co-operating with nature as our fathers did'; it is the attitude of 'free servitude' finally adopted by the survivors in 'The Horses', the answer that would end the tyranny of the raw present and allow man to complete the unfinished sentence and so relate past, present and future in a continuity of being.

Muir's attitude to nature raises a crucial issue in the interpretation of his work, an issue of which Muir himself was aware. In 'The Natural Estate', the first lecture in *The Estate Of Poetry*, he speaks of man's sense of himself in the past and in the present, and he argues:

> I am not advocating a return to the past that has gone forever, or romanticizing the coarseness of peasant life, or its poverty and hardship. All I want to suggest is that the vast dissemination of secondary objects isolates us from the natural world in a way which is new to mankind, and that this cannot help affecting our sensibilities and our imagination.[15]

Clearly, in his poems on the nuclear holocaust when Muir refers to nature he means not simply the countryside but the world of natural forces. In section IV of 'The Last War' he is referring to a condition of completeness and fulfilment that might help to free us from the world of secondary objects and the impersonal power of the machine. It is to express this ideal of wholeness and to suggest a way of breaking through the impersonality in order to gain a form of communion with one's self and with one's fellow men that Muir introduces the 'harvest yield'—his recurring symbol of the fruition that comes from man working in harmony with the natural world—in 'The Last War'.

But even as he says this Muir realises that it is too late, and the fourth section ends on a fatalistic note:

> Because we could not wait
> To untwist the twisted smile and make it straight
> Or render restitution to the tree . . .
> . . . Did not have time to call on pity
> For all that is sick, and heal and remake our city.

The short final section of the poem moves into another area of meaning; reflection intensifies into mysticism in a vision of first and last things, of life and death, of man's origin and end:

> About the well of life where we are made
> Spirits of earth and heaven together lie.

It is a vision of ultimate harmony in which the spirits of earth and heaven lie together in a 'dream of pure commingled being'; and then in two lines of almost surrealist imagery the unity extends to include not only heaven and earth but the underworld:

> Their bodies lie in shadow or buried in earth,
> Their heads shine in the light of the underworld.

The closing lines of this section, which has echoes of the early poem 'Ballad Of The Soul', add ambiguity to the mystery:

> Loaded with fear and crowned with every hope
> The born stream past them to the longed for place.

Is the longed for place of this world or of the mystical world of the watchers about the well of life? The slender evidence of the last line, in which the born stream past them whose heads shine in the light of the underworld, suggests that the longed for place is this world. If this is so then an element of ambiguity remains since the born are entering a world that might be ended by the final war. It is as if the judgement day has been brought forward to the moment of birth rather than death; the born are 'Loaded with fear' lest the judgement be the finality of a ruined planet, and yet at the same time they are 'crowned with every hope'. No clear interpretation emerges in this final section; one is left with the ambiguous but deeply satisfying vision that makes a unity of hope and fear, of life and death, of heaven and earth.

Muir's final poem on the theme of war, 'The Day Before The Last Day,'[16] contains some of the elements of his earlier poems of the holocaust and touches on some of his life-long preoccupations—man and the natural world, community and impersonality, death, resurrection and immortality. 'The Day Before The Last Day' was written very shortly before Muir's death and is clearly a draft rather than a final version;[17] the sombre elegiac first section, which may have been intended as a sonnet, does not connect with the longer second section, and the attempt to link the two—'Let us essay a hypothetical picture'—is probably Muir's note to himself rather than a line in the poem. (One imagines the poet, by this time very weak and ill, being prompted to some extent by the knowledge of his own imminent death.)

The opening sonnet-like sequence is an attempt to see the totality of the destruction after a nuclear fall. The human race could destroy itself in a day or a week:

> For so we murder all
> That ever has been, all species and forms,
> Man and woman and child, beast and bird,
> Tree, flower and herb, and that by which they were known,
> Sight and hearing and touch, feeling and thought,
> And memory of our friends among the dead.

All life on the planet would be extinguished so that no thing and no one would be left even to witness the fact of the extinction; death would continue to generate its own negative force, spreading from the present to cancel the future and even the past. Man's destructive ingenuity would not only eliminate all 'memory of our friends among the dead' but would reach back through the millenia to undo time and the Creation:

> We would not know even the silence
> Where all was now as if it had never been.

Muir faces the possibility of the destruction of his world and then he looks beyond the immediate destruction to the infinite nothingness.

This section of the poem is followed by the three-line linking device, including the line: 'Mechanical parody of the Judgement Day', and the longer section of the poem is Muir's vision of that judgement day. At first the imagery of death has a certain beauty, an opalescent splendour, and one feels that the 'dark ancestral dreams' referred to here are Muir's own dreams as he approaches death, a mythological vision that emerges from the unconscious mind rather than a vision of the nuclear holocaust.

> And those who were drowned a year or a thousand years
> Come out with staring eyes, foam on their faces,
> And quaint sea-creatures fixed like jewelled worms
> Upon their salt-white crowns, sea-tangle breasts,
> That they, the once dead, might know the second death.

The sea imagery suggests that this is the language of dream, and the 'quaint sea-creatures' surface from the unconscious into consciousness like figures in a surreal resurrection. But they rise from the dead only to experience 'the second death', and in the closing lines the beauty is replaced by a universal hopelessness:

> And women faint with child-birth lay their babes
> Beside them on the earth and turn away
> And lovers two by two estranged for ever
> Lie each in place without a parting look.

Muir goes on to present a picture of the day of judgement similar to the one had had written almost thirty years earlier in the closing chapter of his novel, *The Three Brothers*.[18] (Professor Peter Butter states that Muir had been re-reading the novel shortly before he wrote the poem.[19]) But the nature of the judgement in the two versions, the novel and the late poem, is different. In the novel some of the congregation are transfigured, and the central character, David Blackadder, feels his soul fill with joy and says the vision has brought him great comfort; in the poem there is no transfiguration, no joy, no comfort. The people are utterly impassive until the final moment when they cry out:

> ' "Choose! Choose again, you who have chosen this!
> Too late! Too late!"
> And then: "Where and by whom shall we be remembered?" ' '

There is no possibility of salvation; the judgement is inescapable and universal. And in saying 'you who have chosen this', Muir makes it clear, as he does in the poems of the broken citadel, that the fall in 'The Day Before The Last Day' is man's judgement on himself.

In his poems on the nuclear fall Muir is responding to the greatest problem mankind has ever had to face. He was not the first writer to respond to the problem; Edith Sitwell's *Three Poems Of The Atomic Bomb*[20]—'Dirge For The New Sunrise', 'The Shadow Of Cain', and 'The Canticle Of The Rose'—was published in 1947. Edith Sitwell's poems are ornate literary collages, attractive examples of the 'apocalyptic' poetry of the time. Muir's treatment of the theme, although uneven in quality, has a unity and completeness of vision that is profoundly pessimistic; and the completeness and pessimism, one feels, come from the depth of his imaginative involvement in the possibility of the holocaust. He imagined the grotesque mutation that would be caused by the radioactive fallout after the holocaust and he saw the possible survivors as a 'Chaotic breed of misbegotten things'. He looked further into the void and imagined the finality that nuclear war might bring—'For so we murder all/That ever has been'—with all forms of life extinguished on a silent and sterile planet.

With these realisations Muir is forced to abandon—at least in his poems on the holocaust—his belief that the fall is a recurring crisis, an inescapable part of the human condition. He sees that a nuclear war could cause the final fall, and in these poems he concludes that such a fall would be brought about by man himself. One is led, therefore, to look to Muir's work for the origins of this part of the human condition that might bring about the destruction of humanity, and in Muir's poems on the subject of the primal fall one finds a strange and compelling re-creation of the Eden myth.

THE LOST GARDEN

In his writings on the themes of the broken citadel and the holocaust Muir expresses the idea of the fall in historical as well as spiritual terms, and with a physical detail that is sometimes grotesquely realistic. The historical setting changes from legendary Troy to sixteenth-century St Andrews and twentieth-century Cologne and Prague, but the essential pattern of the poems is similar: castles and cities and civilisations fall, and peoples are suppressed or exterminated. What intensifies the pessimism of these poems is their air of inevitability and the fact that Muir invariably identifies with the victims; in the nuclear poems of the 1950s the victims, of course, are all mankind. But when one takes a wider view and considers Muir's total treatment of the myth of the fall then one sees that it is a vision of hope rather than despair. The recurring fall could lead to a final fall and the extermination of mankind, but Muir's more characteristic conclusion is that the fall is not so much an end as a beginning.

The fall is the beginning of conflict, certainly, but a conflict that is eventually resolved. It is the beginning of man's awareness of time and of his journey through time but the end of the journey is reconciliation and acceptance. These ideas emerge from the poems in which Muir expresses the fall in terms of the Eden myth. Unlike the poems of the broken citadel or the holocaust, the Eden poems cannot be so precisely grouped around identifiable concerns; instead, they explore a number of conditions that Muir sees as consequences of the fall: man's feelings of loss and despair, his sense of incompleteness and separation, his awareness of time and death. But in the course of this exploration Muir begins to discover a new attitude of acceptance.

As his search continues over the years a pattern begins to emerge until it becomes clear that Muir's concept of Eden includes the elements of innocence and timelessness embodied in the archetypal figures of Adam and Eve in the garden of the Genesis myth; it includes too the lost world of innocence discussed in the earlier chapter, 'Childhood And Paradise'. The search is an attempt to discover what has been lost in the fall and so make possible a vision of wholeness that would allow man to see himself as part of a unified pattern of existence. It is an attempt to discover a state of reconciliation that will allow man to find the right relationship within the self, with his fellow men, and with his God, and it is an attempt to reconcile the temporal and the timeless. Muir achieves this vision of reconciliation in some of his later poems in which man's fallen state is re-invested with the timelessness and innocence of the unfallen. But the vision is not a permanent one; it has to be sought for or waited for and then achieved as if for the first time in each of the great poems in which it is expressed, because the fall is a recurring experience for Muir, a condition from which he can never finally be free. These concepts—the co-existence of the fallen and the unfallen in man, and the recurring fall—appear in Muir's essay, ' "Royal Man": Notes on the tragedies of George Chapman'. Discussing Chapman's heroes, Muir writes:

> We accept this hero and his drama as real, perhaps because with one part of him man still lives in the world before the Fall, and with another in the world after it, since the Fall—assuming that it stands for anything in human experience— is not a historical event but something which is always happening.[1]

The earliest attempt at the theme is in *First Poems* of 1925[2] in the poems 'The Lost Land',[3] 'Remembrance',[4] and 'Maya'.[5] In these early pieces the themes are not sustained and are sometimes partly obscured by poetic diction and a tendency to assume an attitude rather than develop the subject. *First Poems* was followed a year later by *Chorus Of The Newly Dead*.[6] This collection, which was never reprinted and does not appear in any of the collected editions, consists of a series of monologues by stylised figures, and in the Harlot's monologue Muir writes one of his first clear images of the fall:

> Where 'mid the powder and the scent,
> As down a dark and dusty well,
> Through all the toppling tenement,
> Laughing I fell, and fell, and fell!

The Harlot's fall into prostitution is paralleled by her physical fall as she plunges to her death, and the two elements are clearly an attempt to express an archetypal fall.

Muir's first sustained treatment of the theme appears in *Variations On A Time Theme*.[7] This sequence of ten poems, first published in 1934, shows a great advance on Muir's first two collections. Technically, Muir abandons the ballad stanza for the decasyllabic line which he uses with some fluency and a growing control of shifting rhythms and rhymes. There is a genuinely exploratory quality about these poems; instead of assuming romantic postures and tragic masks as he does in his first two collections Muir ventures into a series of metaphysical speculations about the human condition. Some of the subjects are similar to those he toyed with in *We Moderns* but now he writes with a new urgency and sincerity.

It is in *Variations On A Time Theme* that Muir finds what is to become his characteristic collective voice and his characteristic form, the 'collective monologue'. The voice is plural, 'we' rather than 'I', in order to suggest the shared fate of a tribe or an entire people rather than the experience of an individual, but for the purposes of criticism it seems appropriate to treat the 'we' of these poems as a single, archetypal narrator.

In the first of the variations the narrator regains consciousness after a period of oblivion: 'After the fever this long convalescence'. He looks round at the shattered landscape with its images of decay and corruption:

> How did we come here to this broken wood?
> Splintered stumps, flapping bark, ringwormed holes,
> Soft milk-white water prisoned in jagged holes
> Like gaps where tusks have been.

The diction of these lines—'broken', 'Splintered', 'flapping', 'ringwormed'—expresses man's sense of disorientation and degradation in a fallen world. In fact, the broken landscape of the poem is almost certainly the countryside around Glasgow that Muir knew as a young man. In the same year as the publication of *Variations On A Time Theme*, 1934, Muir was travelling about Scotland collecting material for *Scottish Journey*. On the outskirts of Glasgow he saw the broken landscape again, and in *Scottish Journey* he writes:

> After that came a country road called the Hundred Acre Dyke, dotted with a few ringwormed trees, and affording a bleak prospect of smoking pits and blackened fields . . . But the first stretch was, like the immediate surroundings of almost all industrial towns, a debased landscape in which every growing thing seemed to be poisoned and stunted, a landscape which involuntarily roused evil thoughts and seemed made to be the scene of murders and rapes.[8]

And in the same description Muir refers to a 'meanly wicked-looking wood', 'black slag paths', 'filthy pools', and 'tattered trees which rose from that scabbed landscape'. In *Scottish Journey* Muir was revisiting the area during the depression of the 1930s; in *An Autobiography* he recalls his first visits to the area some twenty years earlier during the long period of his emotional depression when he had lived and worked in Glasgow like a displaced person.[9] The descriptions in *Scottish Journey* and *An Autobiography* are strikingly similar, and the passage in the *Autobiography* ends:

> These roads became so associated in my mind with misery that after leaving the south side of Glasgow I could never bear to revisit them.

When Muir lived in Glasgow the landscape of the fall was all around him, and in Section I of *Variations On A Time Theme* he uses this terrain and the feelings associated with it to reflect the misery of the narrator. A wretched period in the poet's life is transformed into art, and the narrator's fallen condition is convincingly realised in the poem as the poet relives his personal experience of the fall.

The sense of confusion in the landscape is paralleled by the tortuous self-questioning of the narrator:

> Did we come here
> Through darkness or inexplicable light,
> The road all clear behind us and before us,
> An answer and a riddle?

They are the questions of a traveller lost in an alien country. As the questions continue they begin to sound like the reaction of someone emerging from a state of shock or amnesia, or from unconsciousness into the conscious world. He recalls fragments of the lost world:

> We have seen Heaven opening,
> And fields and souls in radiance. We have walked
> In radiance and darkness.

In his new fallen and conscious state man looks back to the lost past and sees it as a paradise; the present, 'this twilight', is strange and frightening. But towards the end of Section I the narrator begins to come to terms with his new existence, and his questions become purposeful:

> Can we build a house here, make friends with the mangled stumps
> And splintered stones, not looking too closely
> At one another?

The people do not look too closely because of their sense of guilt, and in this not looking lies the beginning of man's separation from his fellow man. The questions continue:

> Can we sing our songs here,
> Pray, lift a shrine to some god? Can we till these nameless fields?

The narrator, and the poet, is asking if man can make a civilisation in this fallen world, if art and faith are possible, if man can work in harmony with nature—'till these nameless fields'—and find fulfilment. The questions Muir asks in this, his earliest sustained treatment of the myth of the fall, are the ones he continues to ask throughout his life. The questions are unanswered in this poem, but the nature of the questioning in the closing lines shows man beginning to engage with the mystery of his fallen condition.

A new element of doubt is introduced in Section III of the *Variations*. The poem opens with a sequence of six lines that range across time from the Eden myth to the fall and to a prophetic final fall:

> A child in Adam's field I dreamed away
> My one eternity and hourless day,
> Ere from my wrist Time's bird had learned to fly,
> Or I had robbed the Tree of which I die,
> Whose boughs rain still, whose fruit wave-green shall fall
> Until the last great autumn reddens all.

The effect of the first two lines is to confirm the concept of the paradise of unconscious childhood of the individual and the race, and to suggest the timelessness of the prelapsarian existence. Time and mortality are consequences of the fall, and Muir links these ideas in the second couplet; the third

couplet suggests an apocalyptic vision of a universal death. These lines are a
miniature version of Muir's Eden myth, a prefiguration of the great vision
that develops throughout his work.

The quality of the poetry is not sustained in Section III, but the closing
lines introduce a feature that becomes a major theme in Muir's poems:

> Set free, or outlawed, now I walk the sand
> And search this rubble for the promised land.

Man does not know if he has been liberated or outlawed in the fallen world,
and it is partly this doubt—the lifelong paradox of independence and rejection—that prompts the search for the promised land.

It is essentially the same search in the opening lines of Section V of the
sequence, but by linking it to a particular image of time Muir changes the
nature of the journey:

> Slow-motion flight over a bottomless road,
> Or clinical fantasy begotten by
> The knife of demon Time the vivisector
> Incising nightmares.

In Section III the search is for the promised land, but now the search is a
retreat, the nightmare of 'Slow-motion flight' from the memory of the fall.
And in Section III the predatory nature of time is partly concealed in the
beauty of the poetry—'Time's bird' has not yet learned to fly and to kill—
but now time is 'the vivisector/Incising nightmares'. There is a new awareness
of time as the bringer of mortality, and the sense that temporal existence is
a state of spiritual desolation after the timelessness before the fall. The
narrator remembers:

> Once there were ancient cities here, and shrines
> That branched from Adam's world.

But now there is permanent exile in a land of dead stones:

> Now these dead stones
> Among dead stones, where the late nomads pitch
> Their nightly tents, leaving a little refuse,
> The comfortless smell of casual habitation,
> Human or bestial—indistinguishable.

(The condition Muir describes here—fallen man as a nomad in an arid
desert—is similar to that described by theologians commenting on the doctrine of the fall. In *Christ And Original Sin* Peter de Rosa writes:

> Sin brings shame and remorse. It means that man is a wanderer, an exile, on the
> earth. Its consequence is that man, the sinner, feels compelled to flee away from
> the one who made him and loves him because God is all-holy and he is not.[10]

De Rosa uses the language of dogma—'sinner', 'God', 'all-holy'—but he and Muir are describing essentially the same circumstances: a sense of rejection followed by flight and exile as consequences of the fall.) The sense of exile in Section V of the *Variations* is again intensified by the harshness of the landscape; the dead stones and the 'debris not yet overgrown' create the same effect as the broken wood of Section I and the scabbed landscape of *Scottish Journey* and *An Autobiography*. They are different regions of the same fallen world.

Afraid of the fallen world he now inhabits and haunted by the memory of the paradise that is lost, man is in a state of exile and alienation. Here again Muir's vision corresponds with the theological interpretation, but with a major difference. The theologians[11] are agreed that the division between man and God is caused by man's sin of pride, but in *Variations On A Time Theme* and in his later poems on the myth Muir says almost nothing about God and nothing about pride. What he stresses is the exile from paradise and the simultaneous alienation from a raw and hostile present. A further difference between Muir's treatment of the myth and the version of it offered by the theologians is Muir's preoccupation with time and his awareness of the tensions between the timelessness of the lost world and the circumscription of the present, an awareness that finds its strongest expression in the *Variations* and the succeeding volume, *Journeys And Places* of 1937.

The fundamental difference between the doctrinal versions of the myth of the fall and Muir's version is that the theologians approach the myth through a vast body of dogma whereas Muir confronts the living myth. The starting point of *Variations On A Time Theme* is the beginning of consciousness, and what follows is pure discovery; the poem is not so much a presentation of his established vision of the myth as an attempt—through his dreams, his imagination and his craft—to create his vision. Muir's poems of the lost garden are not professions of faith, or even a search for faith in the doctrinal sense, but an attempt to understand the consequences of the fall.

One of the objects of the search is to discover something of the nature of the vanished paradise. This is the theme of 'Isaiah', a poem that appears in *The Narrow Place* of 1943 but is not included in any of the collected editions;[12] and it is the theme of the poems, 'The Covenant',[13] and 'The Window'[14] in *The Voyage* of 1946. These three poems have several features in common, similarities of diction, imagery and structure that suggest they are attempts at the same subject. Each seems to recapture something of the paradise before the fall, and 'Isaiah' opens with the lines:

> Isaiah from the ledge could see
> Angel and man and animal
> At their everlasting play.

This vision, possibly based on chapter 11 of Isaiah, is one in which the divine, the human and the sub-human exist in a timeless harmony. But in the next stanza the harmony is broken, and Muir expresses the ideas of disintegration and rejection in a violent, sharply defined image:

> He saw the crack in the palace wall
> Open and shut like a mouth jerking,
> Spitting out teeth of stone.

The image suggests that paradise is suddenly breached and its inhabitants cast out through the gap, an impression confirmed in the closing lines of the poem:

> But the triple shadows crossing
> Framed an image in their fall,
> A shape against the breaking wall.

The pattern is repeated in 'The Covenant', which opens with the vision of all forms of being—'god and animal', 'fabulous creatures', 'woman and man'— existing in sublime harmony. Even as he creates the vision Muir realises that it was 'lost long ago in fields beyond the Fall'. The harmony is lost and yet the elements of which it consists 'Keep faith in sleep-walled night and there are found/On our long journey back where we began.' The 'palace wall' in 'Isaiah' has become the 'sleep-walled night', the world of dreams and the unconscious in which the covenant can still be found; the lines suggest that through his dreams man can participate in the lost harmony and that 'sleep-walled night' can be a stage on 'our long journey back' to a prelapsarian state, to the paradise of unconscious childhood. But here again the vision is not sustained, and 'the weariless wave/Roofs with its sliding horror all that realm.'

The 'weariless wave', one suggests, is time and mortality which Muir treats as a single violent force that endlessly breaches the timeless vision. In 'The Window' the antithetical pattern emerges again. The poem opens with a vision of the paradise:

> Within the great wall's perfect round
> Bird, beast and child serenely grew
> In endless change on changeless ground
> That in a single pattern bound
> The old perfection and the new.

Here Muir is suggesting more than he does in the two previous poems; the 'endless change on changeless ground' gives the impression of time contained within timelessness, and the 'single pattern' that bound the 'old perfection and the new' is one that includes the lost past and the fallen present. There is a momentary harmony and then, echoing the structure of 'Isaiah' and 'The Covenant', the imagery changes to that of violent disintegration and fall. Forests fall, ships sink, the tower falls, the last citadel is taken in a sequence of stylised falls at the end of which Muir introduces an intimately human note that gives an immediacy to the fall:

> Then turning towards you I beheld
> The wrinkle writhe across your brow,
> And felt time's cap clapped on my head.

Yet again the search for the sustainable vision that will unite the timeless and the temporal is abruptly ended by Muir's awareness of time and mortality, the inescapable condition of the fallen world. The poem ends with the now familiar image of the broken wall and the finality of the dead garden: 'The great wall breached, the garden dead'.

In each of these three short poems Muir succeeds in creating images of the lost garden, but in each poem it is clear that the opening image is merely the beginning of a search for a wider vision that will encompass the eternal and the temporal, Eden and the fallen world, and so reconcile man to his existence in the fallen world. In each case the timeless vision fails, and the failure is so clearly the central moment of these poems—so clearly the result of the poet's conscious craftsmanship—that the failure is the meaning of the poems. They are not so much attempts to reconcile the fallen and unfallen conditions as admissions of the impossibility of achieving a vision of reconciliation, or of achieving it at that stage in his career. But when Muir at the height of his powers returns to the Eden myth the result is a great visionary poem that penetrates the mystery of the fall.

'Adam's Dream',[15] from the volume *One Foot In Eden* of 1956, is an account of Adam's first dream after his expulsion from Eden and while he lay asleep in Eve's arms. The dream is almost certainly Muir's own, and if one accepts that dreams are dramas during which personal identities can give way to archetypal identities, then for the duration of the dream Muir is Adam, as if newly fallen from 'his agelong daydream in the Garden' into the world of time and mortality that he must now try to understand. This attempt at understanding, unlike the attempts that are overshadowed by the awareness of alienation and separation in the earlier poems, begins by stating the physical and spiritual intimacy of Adam and Eve. (A biographical interpretation—that Muir's experience of marriage informs this part of the poem— seems entirely appropriate.) Outside Eden, Adam and Eve find they are bound to each other more closely than before; in their shared experience of the fall they have been plunged so deeply into terror that they have gone beyond terror's reach:

> Fallen in Eve's fallen arms, his terror drowned
> In her engulfing terror, in the abyss
> Whence there's no further fall, and comfort is—

And then the dream begins. Adam overlooks an interminable plain which is gradually covered by an ever-increasing number of running figures; the creatures resemble men and women but they are so far away across the plain that they seem to have no features, no identities:

> He could not see their faces. On they ran,
> And fell, and rose again, and ran, and fell,
> And rising were the same yet not the same,
> Identical or interchangeable,
> Different in indifference.

There is an urgency in all that the creatures seem compelled to do by the absurd logic of the dream. Adam, whose dream it is but who is remote from the characters in it, can see no purpose in the ceaseless activity but only a growing confusion of colliding bodies 'Weaving no pattern'. Some of the figures 'ran straight against the frontier of the plain/Till the horizon drove them back', and at this point Adam's detachment breaks down; disturbed by the figures' urgent, hopeless efforts to break free he cries out: ' "What are you doing there?" ' And then he realises: ' "This is time." '

The dream is a vision of time, apparently limitless and yet finite and imprisoning, and a vision of the succeeding generations trapped by time in the fallen world. Here again 'Adam's Dream' differs significantly from other poems on the Eden myth; the reference to time evokes not fear or revulsion in Adam's mind but curiosity. He wants to know more about the creatures trapped in the illusory freedom of the endless plain of time; he wants to see their faces, and as he wishes this he draws closer to them and sees that all their frantic activity 'made up a story'. But he wants to know more than 'this mere moving pattern' and he draws closer still:

> At that he was among them, and saw each face
> Was like his face, so that he would have hailed them
> As sons of God but that something restrained him.

He identifies with them, accepting that these creatures of time are like himself, and here again Adam's reaction—which is also the poet's—differs from that of earlier poems. The realisation that he is one of them does not bring with it the former sense of loss; instead 'he would have hailed them/As sons of God'. And then for a moment it seems that the pattern of the previous poems will be repeated as Adam's surge of sympathy is interrupted by the memory of the fall:

> And he remembered all, Eden, the Fall,
> The Promise, and his place.

But even here, remembering the fall and God's promise that outside Eden Adam would experience sorrow and thorns and thistles and sweat and finally death,[16] even here he accepts and the closing lines of the poem are an unequivocal acceptance of the fallen world:

> and took their hands
> That were his hands, his and his children's hands,
> Cried out and was at peace, and turned again
> In love and grief in Eve's encircling arms.

'Adam's Dream' with its disturbing vision of the featureless creatures trapped on the plain of time, might have been a poem of despair but at the central moment in the poem the vision changes and Muir achieves the reconciliation, the attitude of acceptance he has been seeking for so long. And this is made possible for Muir through the dream, at once a personal and ancestral dream, that gives him access to a mythological world and to an archetypal identity. The mythological drama of Adam's dream resolves the great dilemma that could not be resolved, or even fully expressed, in the conscious world. The poem is a deeply satisfying interpretation of the myth of the fall and at the same time a recreation of the myth.

The Conflict

THE KILLING BEAST

It is only after the fall that man becomes a separate being. Before the fall he had been unthinkingly part of the pattern of creation, a pattern in which he felt his affinity with—even his descendancy from—trees or animals or birds. Afterwards there came consciousness and self-consciousness. Man could step outside the pattern and see that he was separate from the rest of creation, that as an individual he was separate from other individuals and, as he grew conscious of his consciousness, that he was sometimes separate from his own self.

Implicit in Muir's vision of life is the belief that in this fallen condition of separation lies the beginning of conflict. Muir sees humanity split into hostile nations and ideologies; he sees opportunities for new and humane social orders lost to political tyrannies; he sees an older, ancestral order being overwhelmed by impersonal forces and mechanical processes; he sees that man has usurped the power to create and destroy that belonged to the first creator; and he concludes that an underlying factor in all these ills is the separation and conflict within the self.

'Ballad Of The Soul', as an earlier chapter has shown, is both a mythological account of millenia of conflict, much of which takes place on a cosmic scale, and at the same time a symbolic expression of the divisions and violent contradictions within the self. In contrast to this, 'Ballad Of Hector In Hades',[1] another poem of the 1920s, is one of Muir's most lucid and explicit statements of the conflict expressed in terms of man's struggle with his fellow man. In 'Ballad Of Hector In Hades' the simplicity of the diction and form along with the familiarity of the myth allow the reader to make an immediate recognition and response, but the Homeric material is merely Muir's starting point for what becomes a personal version of the myth.

The poem, Hector's account if his fight with Achilles, has that quality of inevitability and detachment that is peculiarly Muir's:

> I wait. On all the empty plain
> A burnished stillness lies,
> Save for the chariot's tinkling hum,
> And a few distant cries.

The uneasy silence establishes the atmosphere for the combat and then, following Homer,[2] Muir's Hector suddenly avoids the challenge:

His helmet glitters near. The world
Slowly turns around,
With some new sleight compels my feet
From the fighting ground.

'Ballad Of Hector In Hades' becomes a poem of the chase, a hunt to the death in which the stylised, dream-like action heightens the sense of inevitability. As the hunt continues Muir counterpoints the central action with apparently insignificant detail:

The grasses puff a little dust
Where my footsteps fall,
I cast a shadow as I pass
The little wayside wall.

The seemingly irrelevant touches throw the main action into sharper relief until it takes on a nightmarish quality; as Homer says of the chase in *The Iliad*: 'It was like a chase in a nightmare, when no one, pursuer or pursued, can move a limb.' The grasses, the dust, the shadows, the wall—such trivial detail does in fact catch one's eye when one is in a state of fear; and then these parallel narratives—the chase and the incidental detail—converge in the second last stanza when the shadows on the grass merge:

Two shadows racing on the grass,
Silent and so near,
Until his shadow falls on mine.
And I am rid of fear.

As Achilles' shadow overlaps his, Hector knows that the chase is at an end, and this sense of the sealed fate echoes the primitive shadow magic recorded by Frazer in *The Golden Bough*: primitive man's belief that his shadow was 'a vital part of himself' and that he would be harmed or even killed if his shadow were obscured by an enemy.[3]

It is here that Muir departs from the Homeric myth. He omits the final confrontation when Hector, despite his fears and the fact that he knows the gods are conspiring against him, turns to face Achilles and takes the spear throught the throat. Muir omits the courage, the nobility, the heroism of the myth of champions in combat; instead, his closing stanza combines an air of detachment, almost fatalism, with a vividly heraldic image as Hector watches the last act of the drama become frozen in time:

The race is ended. Far away
I hang and do not care,
While round bright Troy Achilles whirls
A corpse with streaming hair.

Again, as with 'Ballad Of The Soul', the *Autobiography* provides an account of the experience that prompts the poem. It becomes clear that Muir is not using the myth of Hector and Achilles simply to retell their story but rather to recall an episode from his early childhood and, by giving expression to it, to gain some understanding of the emotions that have gathered, partly suppressed, since the time of the childhood incident. Muir uses the incident and its emotionally charged associations not only in this poem and the *Autobiography* but also in the novel *The Three Brothers*.[4] In the *Autobiography* Muir recalls a childhood fight in which he beat his opponent; some days later the other boy offered to renew the contest, and Muir writes:

> He was the boy I had fought over the knife, and this day he wanted to fight me again, but I was afraid. The road from the school to Helye lay on the crown of the island, and as I ran on, hollow with fear, there seemed to be nothing on either side of me but the sky. What I was so afraid of I did not know; it was not Freddie, but something else; yet I could no more have turned and faced him than I could have stopped the sun revolving. As I ran I was conscious only of a few huge things monstrously simplified and enlarged: Wyre, which I felt under my feet, the other islands lying round, the sun in the sky, and the sky itself, which was quite empty. For almost thirty years afterwards I was so ashamed of that moment of panic that I did not dare to speak of it to anyone, and drove it out of my mind. I was seven at the time, and in the middle of my guilty fears. On that summer afternoon they took the shape of Freddie Sinclair, and turned him into a terrifying figure of vengeance.[5]

In the *Autobiography* Muir says the feelings of fear and guilt and shame associated with the childhood incident were made admissible by writing the poem—'In any case the poem cleared my conscience'—but this leaves unanswered the question of what prompted the overwhelming fear that made him run. In the poem it is simply 'some new sleight' that drives Hector, and Muir's childhood fear was not of Freddie 'but something else'. The nature of this fear, not fear of one's opponent 'but something else', is important since it seems to suggest not cowardice or the instinct for survival so much as an almost instinctive pacifism, an avoidance of hurting as well as of being hurt, impulses that are central to the question of human conflict.

Recalling the childhood incident, Muir says he had already fought Freddie and knocked him down, and at that point he adds: 'He did not get up again, and that frightened me.'[6] The fear, one suggests, is the fear of death, and on the second occasion Muir could not bring himself to fight again lest the violence end in death, or at least in a disfigurement of mind as well as body. One notes too that in the novel *The Three Brothers*, in which Muir uses the same autobiographical material, the central character David Blackadder thinks of his childhood and realises why he could not fight:

> I mind fine when I was a bairn that I couldna bear to see anything hurt. That was why when I was at school I wouldna fight the other boys. It seemed to me an awful thing—ay, in a way unnatural—that folk's bodies or faces should ever be harmed, and worst of all that they should harm each other themselves. I canna explain it rightly. But when I saw one boy fighting another and trying to do

> something to disfigure him—it might only end in a bloody nose or a black eye—
> it gave me a pain in the stomach, it made me sick.[7]

In the *Autobiography* Muir says that at the time of the conflict with Freddie he, Muir, was in the middle of a period of guilty fear, a time when he became aware—however confused and immature that awareness was—of sin and separation and death. Muir as a child was unable to assimilate the new awareness and the fear that came with it. It was so powerful a sensation that it threatened to engulf his existing experience so that he had no choice but to run away from the challenge and the fear, and afterwards no choice but to deny the flight and the fear. This denial of experience, this editing of our childhood and periods of our adult life, is commonplace; the painful process of acknowledging and assimilating the experience is less common.

If the first fight brought the fear of death—his own or his friend's—then the seven-year-old Muir may have been on the threshold of the associated experience, the ancestral drama of brother killing brother in the field. Muir's conflict with his school friend led to his first awareness of the hatred that can kill, and in the 'universal landscape' and on the 'symbolic stage' of his Orkney childhood the incident took on a mythological quality in Muir's mind.

Muir's work offers other versions of this homicidal, almost fratricidal conflict. In a dream that is recorded in *An Autobiography* and used in *The Three Brothers* Muir finds himself in the uncharacteristic role of the aggressor rather than victim. In the *Autobiography* he writes:

> Also, I was persecuted by a dream which visited me every night. We were staying in a hotel which had once been a palace, and my dream might have been the resuscitation of an event which had once happened there, if such things do occur. In the dream I was a young man of twenty, dressed in what seemed to be a renaissance costume, a closely fitting suit of black. I was waiting in a dark archway for the approach of someone; it was late in the night; the moon was up, but I was hidden in the shadow of the arch. Presently I heard a man's footsteps growing louder; as he passed I leapt out, filled with rage from head to foot, a sort of possession, and plunged my dagger into his breast. The warm blood spouted out, covering my hand; this always wakened me.[8]

The dream came to Muir in Florence in 1923 when he and his wife were travelling in Italy with John and Dorothy Holms.[9] It may be, as Muir suggests, that the dream was a 'resuscitation' of an actual event; or it may have been an expression of his resentment—never expressed in waking terms—of the ever present Holms.[10] A precise interpretation of the nightmare is less important than the fact that even Muir, the gentlest of men, should have experienced this violent rage, if only in a dream.

Elements of nightmare appear in two of Muir's most disturbing poems on the theme of conflict, 'Then' and 'The Combat'. In contrast to the established mythology of 'Ballad Of Hector In Hades' or the realistic, representational terms of the Florence nightmare, 'Then' and 'The Combat' are expressed in symbolic terms, and the grotesque combatants endlessly engaged in absurd, violent action add a surrealist quality to the two poems.

'Then'[11] from *The Narrow Place* of 1943 is an ambiguous, almost obscure poem, but one feels that a more explicit expression would have distorted the inner experience—a vision of a succession of protomorphic creatures in bloody combat—that prompts the poem. The ambiguity arises not from an incomplete expression of the vision but from the inchoate nature of the conflict and the complexity of the symbolism. The opening lines of 'Then' clearly suggest that the conflict precedes life itself:

> There were no men or women then at all,
> But the flesh lying alone,
> And angry shadows fighting on a wall.

The struggling shadows seem to be cast by creatures inside the wall, and the groaning uttered by someone or something 'Buried in lime and stone'. This echoes the primitive magic of sacrificing a victim to a new building, a practice that Frazer states was widespread in Europe:

> . . . the old practice of immuring a living person in the walls, or crushing him under the foundation-stone of a new building, in order to give strength and durability to the structure . . .[12]

The closing lines of the first stanza, with their related images of sweat and blood and tortured wood, reinforce this impression of sacrifice:

> And sweated now and then like tortured wood
> Big drops that looked yet did not look like blood.

The second stanza extends the action and imagery of the first, the recurring conflict and sacrifice, the endless shedding of blood. In the third stanza the blood is 'poor blood, unowned, unwanted', as if the sacrifice were futile, but at that point a group of women mourners appear, giving meaning and humanity to the sacrifice:

> The wall was haunted
> By mute maternal presences whose sighing
> Fluttered the fighting shadows . . .

These 'mute maternal presences' remind one of the women who watched the crucifixion of Christ: 'And many women were there beholding afar off, which followed Jesus from Galilee, ministering unto him.'[13] This image of the watching women confirms the theme of sacrifice and suggests, perhaps, that they are witnessing a martyrdom, so that a Christian interpretation of 'Then' could be argued. But the ambiguities remain: the shadows in the wall are those of primitive man, reminders of the magical practice of immuring a sacrificial victim, and reminders too of the other primitive belief that a man's shadow was an extension of the man himself, with the same vulnerability when it is overshadowed, as Hector is doomed when his shadow is obscured by Achilles'.

The closing line of the poem: 'As if that fury of death itself were dying', suggests that the agony may be about to end, but the lasting impression, as in 'Ballad Of Hector In Hades' and 'The Combat', is not of an end to conflict but of a moment taken from an endless conflict and frozen in time.

'The Combat'[14] from *The Labyrinth* of 1949 also has its origin in a dream, and when one compares the poem with the prose account in *An Autobiography* one can see the development from the unconscious material to the conscious. Muir recalls an occasion in his childhood when at the age of five or six he first saw a heron;[15] the sighting, Muir feels, prompts the adult dream, and the account continues:

> In the dream I was walking with some people in the country, when I saw a shining grey bird in a field. I turned and said in an awed voice, 'It's a heron.' We went towards it, but as we came nearer it spread its tail like a peacock, so that we could see nothing else. As the tail grew I saw that it was not round, but square, an impenetrable grey hedge of feathers; and at once I knew that its body was not a bird's body now, but an animal's, and that behind that gleaming hedge it was walking away from us on four feet padded like a leopard's or a tiger's. Then, confronting it in the field, there appeared an ancient, dirty, earth-coloured animal with a head like that of an old sheep or a mangy dog. Its eyes were soft and brown; it was alone against the splendid-tailed beast; yet it stood its ground and prepared to fight the danger coming towards it, whether that was death or merely humiliation and pain. From their look I could see that the two animals knew each other, that they had fought a countless number of times and after this battle would fight again, that each meeting would be the first meeting, and that the dark, patient animal would always be defeated, and the bright, fierce animal would always win. I did not see the fight, but I knew it would be ruthless and shameful, with a meaning of some kind perhaps, but no comfort.[16]

The opening stanza of the poem creates a setting for the battle; with a few quick strokes Muir sketches in a location that is both a real topography and a landscape of nightmare:

> That combat on the shabby patch
> Of clods and trampled turf that lies
> Somewhere beneath the sodden skies
> For eye of toad or adder to catch.

Into this setting Muir introduces the killing beast, an animal that is distinctively Muir's creation and also everyman's, since mythological creatures like this have prowled man's mind for thousands of years:

> Body of leopard, eagle's head
> And whetted beak, and lion's mane,
> And frost-grey hedge of feathers spread
> Behind—he seemed of all things bred.

The griffon of Greek mythology, part eagle and part lion, is such a beast; something similar stirred in St John's unconscious in the Book of Revelation;[17] and there are monsters like this in Daniel's vision of the four beasts.[18] Eagle, leopard, lion—the creature seems irresistibly destructive when compared to the animal that confronts it:

> As for his enemy, there came in
> A soft round beast as brown as clay;
> All rent and patched his wretched skin;
> A battered bag he might have been,
> Some old used thing to throw away.

Clearly this second animal symbolises not goodness or innocence but something ordinary and vulgar and vulnerable. It is the eternal victim apparently defenceless against the eternal aggressor, and the result of the confrontation seems inevitable: 'The fury had him on his back.' But the brown animal breaks free:

> For ere the death-stroke he was gone,
> Writhed, whirled, huddled into his den,
> Safe somehow there.

After an interval of stillness in which the place seems to be 'Drowsing as in relief from pain', the combatants meet again and the battle is resumed. In the closing stanza of the poem the tense changes from past to present:

> And now, while the trees stand watching, still
> The unequal battle rages there.

The change of tense closes the distance between then and now, bridging the gulf between the mythological creatures of the dream and the forces of present reality so that the combat continues not only in the present but into the future. The closing lines create that characteristic effect of Muir's—an endlessly recurring action that is frozen in time:

> The killing beast that cannot kill
> Swells and swells in his fury till
> You'd almost think it was despair.

The combat continues, but the last line of the poem, like the last line of 'Then'—'As if that fury of death itself were dying'—brings a trace of hope into what seemed like hopelessness. But it is the hope, not of victory, but of an uncertain survival.

Writing in 1950 to the Scottish poet Douglas Young, Muir said: 'I think "The Combat" (from *The Labyrinth*) is one of my best poems',[19] but five years later when asked to comment on the poem Muir was reluctant to offer a firm interpretation:

> Helpless . . . little animal . . . might be a . . . or stand for something in humanity that can be killed—that, that cannot be killed, actually—that is always attacked,

that is in a very vulnerable position. It is very vulnerable . . . that after it has been . . . beaten or vanquished, it does return again. It's in a way, it's a . . . rather horrible [way?] but it's an expression of hope at the same time, at the end. Or it might be taken as humanity and all the enormous forces, particularly nowadays, ranged against humanity in every way.[20]

The combat, then, is between vulnerable man and all the glittering might of the forces ranged against humanity, the kind of combat that could lead to a nuclear holocaust. It is also the struggle between ordinary man and the crushing ideological forces of political tyrannies, forces that Muir saw at work in Czechoslovakia. It is the combat between the eternal victim and the eternal oppressor, between ordinary man quietly concerned with the ordinary business of surviving from one day into the next, and man as aggressor, predator, destroyer. At the end of the poem Muir brings the opposed forces to an uneasy equilibrium, with the balance tilted marginally towards survival.

THE THREATENING WORLD

Mankind survives the conflict, but the survival contains the element of defeat as well as victory, and the survivor is both victim and victor, the two in one. In a radio programme, 'The Inheritors', written by Muir in 1955 the narrator says:

> We are the descendants of the victors, but also of the defeated. The blood of both runs in our veins. We do not inherit only what we want to inherit.[1]

Victor and vanquished, the killing beast and the soft round beast, Achilles and Hector—Muir sees these irreconcilable opposites as part of the one inheritance in which episodes of physical violence are the historical expressions of a continuing mythological conflict.

Muir is aware of another area of conflict, as archetypal in its nature as that of 'The Combat' but expressed in a much less dramatic and more subtly persistent way. In 1921, just two years after his analysis by Maurice Nicoll, Muir published the essay, 'Against The Wise'—republished in *Latitudes* in 1924—in which he speaks of the contradictory dialogue between the conscious and the unconscious in the mind of man:

> The wise search for the flaw that has brought their work to nothing. But the flaw is not a flaw of reason; it is not wisdom but something else that is lacking. The *unconscious* wisdom of life judges not only our crimes; it condemns our most precious and holy things—virtue, self-sacrifice, beauty, truth—because they want to be final and are not.[2]

It is as if there are two co-existent patterns of belief in man's mind: the conscious vision of a world of moral values which is continually contradicted and undermined by the negative values—destructive, blasphemous, or simply absurd—of an alternative vision.

There is yet a third form of conflict expressed in Muir's work, a division that is both universal and intimately personal. In the novel, *Poor Tom*, the central character, Mansie Manson, recalls an incident from his childhood, an incident that also appears in the *Autobiography*. The account in the novel reads:

> At certain stages children seem to live in two separate worlds, both of which are real. In one world, the world which included his parents and all other grown people and himself, a place perfectly familiar to them but full of perplexities for

him, Mansie knew that what he did was, in spite of its simplicity, a sin of awful dimensions; but in the other world where he lived with his playmate there was no evil, or a purely fictitious evil which he could summon before his mind only by make-believe. So accompanying the clear knowledge that he was disobeying his father and mother, was the feeling that he was committing a fabulous sin, a sin which was not a sin to him, but to some shadowy figure—it might be God—in a world only visible to his elders.[3]

Muir is not explicit about the nature of Mansie's sin, and the point of Mansie's recollection is not to reconstruct an actual incident but rather to recall the time when as a child he became aware of the conflict between the adult's and the child's view of the world, and the way in which this conflict of views led to a division in the child's mind. In the *Autobiography* Muir associates the sense of sin with sex: '. . . the obsession which all young children have with sex, their brooding curiosity, natural in itself, but coloured with guilt by the thoughts of their elders.'[4]

Peter Butter takes this association further; in *Edwin Muir: Man And Poet* he offers the sympathetic and persuasive comment:

> . . . his obscure sense of guilt about sex may have been projected retrospectively on to his friendship with the little girl with whom he played throughout the long summer days in the roofless chapel. Their friendship had taken place in Eden and had been quite innocent, but the later consciousness of sex and of the feelings of guilt associated with it by adults may have cast a destructive light backwards upon it.[5]

If one accepts Butter's interpretation, then the childhood experience is a re-enactment of the fall: the new knowledge is accompanied by a sense of 'fabulous sin' and the prelapsarian innocence is lost in guilt. This impression is confirmed by the account in the *Autobiography* where Muir writes of a new sense of separation from his parents:

> The worst thing about my fears was that I could not tell my father and mother about them, since I did not understand them; and the knowledge that there were things in which their help, no matter how willing, could be of no use to me bewildered me most of all.[6]

Confused feelings of guilt made it impossible for the infant Muir to confide in his parents and he felt himself isolated from them; for the first time he was aware of himself as a separate being, and in his separation he saw, even as a child, that he was divided not only from his parents and their world but divided within himself. He writes of the experience as if it were an illness: 'And I had actually gone away into a world where every object was touched with fear'. It was certainly a time of acute distress for Muir but such experience—an abrupt enlargement of consciousness accompanied by a deeply disturbing sense of inner conflict—may be an inescapable part of childhood. The child's distress, one feels, lies not so much in a naturally occurring incident within childhood but in the collision of the two worlds, the child's and the adult's, the world of the unconscious and the world of consciousness.

And in Muir's case the conflict was intensified by an incident that he recalls with frightening clarity. The shock of adult values, and particularly adult censure, imposed on the unthinking child is compounded when an unthinking act in the adult world is seen by the child as an evil and horrifying event. Such an occasion is the killing of the pig.

This was an annual event on the Orkney farms, a recurring process as common as sowing and harvesting. But in the *Autobiography* the event is recorded in such sharply defined detail that it reads like a ritual sacrifice that is clumsily botched. Even after an interval of more than fifty years Muir recalls the slaughter of the pig on one occasion—perhaps the first occasion on which he witnessed the act in a conscious way—as an act of grotesque cruelty:

> When I reached the window the pig had a great gash in its throat, and blood was frothing from it into a basin which Sutherland was holding in his hands as he knelt on one knee on the ground. My father and the farmer were clinging to the pig to keep it still; but suddenly it broke loose, knocking Sutherland down; the basin toppled over; the blood poured over the ground, and Sutherland rose cursing, wiping his red hands on his trousers. It was a bright, windy day, and little flurries and ripples ran over the pool of blood. The pig seemed to be changed. It flew on, quite strange to me, as if seeking something, with an evil, purposive look, as if it were a partner in the crime, an associate of the pig-killer. As it ran it kept up a saw-like screaming which seemed to come from the slit in its throat. It stopped now and then to consider what it should do next; for it was not acting at random, but with a purpose which I could not fathom, and which therefore frightened me. Once it stopped to sniff at a docken in a corner of the yard, and then it looked like itself again and I was not afraid of it. But at once it made another stumbling charge, and what glared out of its eyes was mortal cruelty, the cruelty of the act itself, the killing. Then it began to make little top-heavy lurches; every moment it seemed about to fall forward on its snout. I ran into the house and hid my face, crying, in my mother's skirt.[7]

Muir uses the same event in the novel, *The Three Brothers*,[8] where the killing of the pig is presented in the same grotesquely detailed way, and the memory of the event visits David Blackadder, the central character in the novel, like a recurring nightmare. For both Blackadder and Muir the killing comes to symbolise the child's painful initiation into the necessary cruelties of the adult world. And for Muir the event is a first violent realisation of another form of conflict that is a secondary preoccupation in his work: man's predation on the animal world and the feelings of guilt associated with this.

The childhood idyll was at an end: Muir felt a deep division between himself and his parents as he was wrenched from the innocence of the child's world into an adult world of frightening cruelty, and at the same time he was abruptly made aware of the violence man exercised on the animal world. For a time there was no communion between Muir and his parents, and in his isolation he held the hurt inwards and felt the division grow within the self.

Although Muir experienced distress as a result of the conflict and division in his childhood, the suffering was probably not different in kind from that experienced by many children in the process of passing from unthinking innocence to a new state of consciousness. Muir's adolescence, however, was almost unimaginably painful. Those first years in Glasgow, when he watched both his parents and two older brothers die, are starkly recorded in the *Autobiography* and, thinly disguised as fiction, in the novel, *Poor Tom*. Forty years after the deaths Muir still regarded those Glasgow years as being 'so stupidly wretched, such a meaningless waste of inherited virtue, that I cannot write of them even now without grief and anger'.[9] For the man there remained the feeling of meaningless waste; for the boy to whom the deaths were an immediate reality there was a prolonged state of shock and anxiety from which Muir did not begin to emerge until after his analysis in 1919. There may also have been an associated sense of guilt, since he had survived while his parents and brothers had died. There was certainly a new sense of separation from, and fear of, the world.

This state of anxiety is explored in Muir's first novel, *The Marionette*, published in 1927. The novel is a persuasive study of the conflict between reality and fantasy in the mind of an autistic boy, Hans Scheffer. *The Marionette*, unlike *Poor Tom* or to a lesser extent *The Three Brothers*, is not autobiographical and yet the pattern of the novel—an almost total withdrawal from the real world followed by a gradual return to it—has a parallel in Muir's own life during his adolescence and early manhood.

Hans Scheffer in *The Marionette* lives in a toy world in which the marionettes are more real, more acceptable, to him than the people and objects of the actual physical world which seems to threaten him:

> But a lizard scuttling across the stones would make the place insecure. He saw nature as a terrifying heraldry. The cat, the lizard, and the wasp were embattled forces armed for war, carrying terror and death on their blazoned stripes, their stings, claws, and tongues. He could only run away from them to the vacancy of his room.[10]

The boy's mother is dead and in the early chapters of the novel he is largely ignored by his father; out of his insecurity comes the feeling of vulnerability. Here there is a similarity between the fiction and a state of mind that Muir records in the *Autobiography*:

> A jagged stone or thistle seemed to be bursting with malice, as if they had been put in the world to cut and gash; the dashing of breakers on rocks terrified me, for I was both the wave and the rock; it was as though I were both too close to things and immeasurably distant from them.[11]

For Muir as for Hans Sceffer the world is a 'terrifying heraldry' because it is too threateningly close, but at the same time it is 'immeasurably distant' because the threatened individuals have withdrawn so far in retreat from the world.

Hans Scheffer's anxiety is an extreme version of Muir's own. In both cases the individual's sense of himself, his central identity, has been attacked and almost overwhelmed by experience to the point where all experience is seen as dangerous to the self that has been hurt so deeply and so often by the world that the cat, the lizard, the wasp, the stone and the thistle are objects of terror. With this distorted vision of life the individual feels he is 'too close' to things that might tear him apart. He must withdraw until the dangers become 'immeasurably distant', but in this condition the individual cannot have an active relationship with the world because he lacks the right relationship within the self; he feels he must retreat from experience so as to preserve himself, but as he does so his vision of life grows more and more distorted as he withdraws further into the diminishing self.

In Muir's writings a recurring expression of this fear of the world is the feeling that stones or roofs or whole buildings are about to come crashing down on the individual. In *The Marionette*: 'Hans looked up at the houses towering above him; they seemed to be toppling at every moment; they would fall on him'.[12] Tom Manson in *Poor Tom*[13] and David Blackadder in *The Three Brothers*[14] have the same fear, and it appears again in the poem, 'The Refugees', in the volume *The Narrow Place* of 1943:

> Tenement roofs and towers
> Will fall upon the kind and the unkind
> Without election . . .[15]

The fear, of course, was Muir's own. In *Belonging: A Memoir* Willa Muir recalls that her husband in his first year in London still 'shivered with apprehension'; she explains:

> Sometimes he felt that buildings were going to crash on his head as he passed them, sometimes he cowered beneath the conviction that he barely existed, being an anonymous unit among a crowd of anonymous units . . . by day he was often hag-ridden by these obscure fears.[16]

The real and understandable fear was that the self might be crushed out of existence by the unbearable weight of painful experience. To save the self— as if to save his life—Muir tried to withdraw from life, retreating so far into the self that it too became threatened with extinction.[17]

Muir's most detailed expression of man's conflict with a hostile world, and of the inner conflict that follows this, appears in the three novels. Hans Scheffer in *The Marionette* eludes the conflict by retreating into a world of fantasy, but the price of his uneasy peace is that he forfeits part of his identity and becomes the prisoner of his fantasies. Mansie Manson, the central character in *Poor Tom*, remains in touch with reality and his suffering is the more acute because of this. He watches his brother, Tom—the poor Tom of the title—die a slow and painful death, and on the evening of the death Mansie leaves the house to be alone in the streets of Glasgow. As he walks up Union Street he feels the people around him become less than human; he sees them as 'two processions . . . each on a long raft', and then he experiences a vision of despair:

> Yet though their progress was so inexorable, it left time for a group of young men here and there to shout inviting or lewd words to the girls on the other raft as it floated past, words that evoked stony stares or tittering or raucous laughter. But at the same time these two rafts bearing all that human freightage floated just a little over the mud, were only a thin partition over a bottomless quagmire, and through the planks the mud oozed up and clung to the passengers' shoe-soles, though their heads were so high in the air. If the whole business were to collapse! Mansie pushed his way through the moving mass and stepped on to the roadway.[18]

'The whole business' is life itself, and at that moment its collapse is what Mansie both fears and wishes.

Of Muir's fictional characters it is David Blackadder in *The Three Brothers* who feels the conflict most acutely. Blackadder, like Mansie Manson and like Muir himself, watches an older brother die; close to death, the brother, Sandy, says:

> For when you've once seen the evil in folk, then you see it everywhere, you canna help seeing it, and you see it in some gey queer places, too—but I'll no' speak of that. And in the end you take pleasure in seeing it, and in seeing nothing else; the sight of goodness fills ye with a scunner, for you ken it's no' what it seems— it canna be; but the pleasure's a gey queer kind of pleasure too, you would be better without it. Folk are no better than beasts, Davie, when you see them in their right colours.[19]

Later in the novel Blackadder begins to see life in these 'right colours'. After the deaths of his mother, his brother, and Ellen Livingstone, the woman he loved, Blackadder is haunted by the imagery of putrefaction:

> He saw again the worm stretching its head out of his mother's open grave; he thought of Ellen, and it seemed to him that it was not there, in the dank churchyard among the banks of offal, that the worms were wreathing, but within his mind; and a taste of rottenness rose into his mouth.[20]

When the self is under this kind of attack—and the attack is no less terrifying for being 'illusory' or 'hysterical'—then it must try to shut out the world, but in withdrawing from the world the individual withdraws from other people so that communion becomes impossible. But people too may be part of the world's threat, and so the threatened individual may cultivate an indifference and practise an impersonality as part of his system of defence. This partly explains Muir's adoption of the Nietzschean Superman: in a state of extreme anxiety the individual may have no pity left over for others, and Muir writes that in his early manhood he 'eagerly embraced' Nietzsche's condemnation of pity as 'a treachery to man's highest hope'.[21]

Expressions of this willed pitilessness appear in the poems, long after Muir had abandoned the Superman. In Section IX of *Variations On A Time Theme*[22] Muir explores this 'Indifference' which he sees as a self within the self:

> Packed in my skin from head to toe
> Is one I know and do not know.
> He never speaks to me yet is at home
> More snug than embryo in the womb.

Muir's Indifference, the impersonal element that is a defence against suffering, observes life's triumphs and tragedies with the same impassive face, in contrast to what Muir calls 'my Soul, my Visitor', the element the poet thinks may be his true self:

> He comes but seldom and I cannot tell
> If he's myself or one that loves me well
> And comes in pity, for he pities all.

In the fourth stanza the two elements are juxtaposed to produce the dilemma:

> Pity would cancel what it feeds upon,
> And gladly cease, its office done.
> Yet could it end all passion, flaw, offence,
> Would come my homespun fiend Indifference
> And have me wholly.

Pity, the healing element, would eliminate all suffering, but Muir's fear is that man might then be incapable of any form of human feeling. If pity were to 'change the crown of thorns' the result would not be peace but the death of pity. Pity, and the suffering that prompts it, would then have to be rediscovered:

> And friends consent to meet
> To stage a slaughter and make up a story.

The poem's convoluted dilemma is a real one for Muir; for a time in his life he had cultivated the indifference of the Superman and had lost part of his humanity. Here he resolves the dilemma by saying that if he admits his vulnerability and the inevitability of suffering, then 'peace would burst into my heart'.

It is essentially the same dilemma, expressed in a less convoluted and paradoxical form, that is the theme of 'The Private Place' from *Journeys And Places* of 1937[23] and 'The Intercepter' from *The Labyrinth* of 1949.[24] In 'The Private Place' indifference is personified as 'This stranger' and 'This deaf usurper' and 'my ally and only enemy'. As an ally it allows the poet to shut out the horror of a hostile world, but as enemy it denies him a true relationship with the world. The intercepter of the later poem is an expression of the same negative force, paralysing the poet's will: 'And to my "Yes" says "no",' and reminding him that it, the impersonal element, is an aspect of the self: 'The Intercepter frowns at me/With my own frowning face'.

Although these poems cannot be claimed as examples of his best work, it is clear that he explores the dilemma of indifference and compassion with a craftsman's control of these states of mind; the original sensations have been assimilated and have become part of a pattern of mature experience that Muir is able to evaluate and reflect on without the process of reflection being distorted by emotion. The state of mind that prompts the poems is contained and to some extent re-shaped by them. In contrast, the central characters in the three novels—including the character of novelist as narrator—are sometimes possessed by the intensity of their emotions. The novels have an autobiographical immediacy and in places an undercurrent of hysteria that one associates with the prolonged crisis of Muir's adolescence and early manhood.

The process by which the enormity of immediate sensations and events becomes assimilated into an ordered pattern of experience is one of the commonplace mysteries of life. In Muir's case the process was helped by several factors: his marriage which he saw as 'the most fortunate event in my life',[25] his analysis by Maurice Nicoll, the healing power of dreams and unconscious images to which Muir remained attentive throughout his life, his sense of the living past and the continuity of mankind, and his highly personal form of Christianity. This healing process from raw sensation to experience is of course part of the process of the passing of time; ironically, in Muir's work time is also a major element in the conflict and the subject of some of his most perplexing poems.

AGAINST TIME

Muir's conflict with time is part of a wider conflict: unfallen, unconscious man lived in a timeless present; fallen, conscious man became aware of himself as a separate being existing in time and in its paradoxes. As Muir explores these paradoxes the nature of the conflict changes. The fight between warring opposites is a fight for physical survival, while the fight against the real and imagined fears of a threatening world is an attempt to maintain identity and sanity. Muir felt personally threatened by these two forms of conflict; in his nightmares and in his waking anxieties he was an unwilling actor in these violent, intimate dramas.

In contrast the conflict with time, although it is sometimes expressed in terms of physical combat and inevitably raises thoughts of death, begins as an intellectual struggle. In the poems that express this conflict Muir's voice is once again collective, that of the spokesman of a tribe, rather than personal, and the mode is metaphysical rather than physical or psychological as Muir explores the contradictions of time. He sees time as a progression and yet a recurring cycle; he sees it as absolute and infinite and yet also as an immediate and inescapably destructive process; he thinks of past and future yet he remains imprisoned in a continuous present. Acutely aware of his mortality, he imagines an immortal condition beyond time and he begins to see the conflict as a state of spiritual frustration, a search for faith.[1]

Muir admits to being 'obsessed with Time'. Towards the end of his first volume of autobiography, *The Story and The Fable*, published in 1940 he writes:

> I was born before the Industrial Revolution, and am now about two hundred years old. But I have skipped a hundred and fifty of them. I was really born in 1737, and till I was fourteen no time-accidents happened to me. Then in 1751 I set out from Orkney to Glasgow. When I arrived I found that it was not 1751, but 1901, and that a hundred and fifty years had been burned up in my two days' journey. But I myself was still in 1751, and remained there for a long time. All my life since I have been trying to overhaul that invisible leeway. No wonder I am obsessed with Time.[2]

Muir experienced a drastic sense of dislocation when he was wrenched from the ordered simplicities of Orkney life into the clamorous competition of Glasgow at the turn of the century, but the obsession he speaks of in *The Story and The Fable* is essentially modern Western man's preoccupation with time as history, as linear progression. When he resumes his autobiography thirteen years later Muir's attitude has changed. He is still pre-occupied with time but he is no longer concerned to make up the leeway; indeed, he seems to feel that in some respects mankind has travelled too far and too fast.

In the chapter, 'Interval', which links *The Story And The Fable* with *An Autobiography*, he writes:

> I cannot see even the life of Orkney as I saw it when I began this book, for remote as it seemed from history, it was already making for or being driven towards the present we know. The process which produced this universal effect seems, looking back, both blundering and inevitable: good and evil, our hopes and our fears, our dreams and our sober calculations, equally helped it on; as if nothing we could have done could have prevented us from reaching the exact point where we are now.[3]

It is as if a great mechanical force had brought man to his present state, as if time had passed like the unwinding of a reel of film, the images on which seemed pre-ordained and incontrovertible. For a moment Muir sees history as a universal and irresistible force, but at that point he steps outside the process and in the same paragraph he observes:

> Yet this feeling of inevitability, if we were to submit to it, would make our life perfectly empty; we should become conscious ciphers in a historical process whose intentions are not ours but its own; and our thoughts, our affections, our most intimate life, would be mere illusions to amuse or distract us.[4]

A purely historical view of existence would deny mankind his humanity, but an alternative view would have to be sustained by an usually powerful source in order to counter not only the sense of historical inevitability but also inevitability at a personal level, that intense apprehension of mortality, that sense of time as a corrupting element, which is a theme of *The Three Brothers*, *Poor Tom*, and some of the early poems. In Muir's case the source of the alternative view is faith, and his poems on the subject of time show him moving towards that source.

In his earliest poem on the subject, 'Betrayal',[5] from *First Poems* of 1925 beauty, personified in rather ambivalent terms as 'One with a foolish lovely face' and 'scattered moon-struck air', is betrayed by time: 'in her flesh/Small joyless teeth fret without rest', and her invisible gaoler 'inly wastes her flesh away'. The poem concludes: 'He who entrapped her long ago,/And kills her, is unpitying Time.' Time is a corrupting element bringing death to the individual and the race in this simple ballad, but when Muir returns to the subject in *Variations On A Time Theme* in 1934 he views it with a new complexity.

Variations On A Time Theme is the most sustained expression of Muir's preoccupation with time. The ten variations, not all of which are primarily concerned with time, open with the fall of man, which brings with it the beginning of consciousness and the beginning of time.[6] In the variations that follow, Muir tries to penetrate the mystery of time as part of his attempt to penetrate the wider mystery of existence.

Variations II,[7] first published in 1933 as 'The Riders', is a visionary poem with an ambiguous yet persuasive symbolism of horses and riders, and an early expression of some of the features that appear in Muir's great poems of reconciliation: the overall pattern of the poem presents existence as a time-journey, the origin and end of which lie beyond time, and the poem includes a sense of timelessness that one associates with mystical experience. Although *Variations* II is incompletely realised it is an important poem. Muir gave an explanatory comment on it in a letter to Gwendolen Murphy, editor of the anthology, *The Modern Poet*. He writes: 'The Horses, as I see them, are an image of human time, the invisible body of humanity on which we ride for a little while. . . .' And he adds: 'Yet the steed—mankind in its course through time—is mortal, and the rider is immortal.'[8]

The opening question of the poem: 'At the dead centre of the boundless plain/Does our way end?' extends the questions of *Variations* I and asks if existence is merely a finite, temporal journey. The horses, 'Like steeds for ever labouring on a shield', are on a journey that will never be completed; the riders are on the same journey but their 'hearts have flown so far ahead they are lost/Long past all finding'. The riders—perhaps one generation of mankind in the 'invisible body of humanity'—imagine a future stage of the time-journey, or a stage beyond the journey, and yet they remain trapped in time, 'staring at the same horizon'. Muir reinforces this sense of imprisonment when he speaks of 'generation after generation' on an incomprehensible 'sad stationary journey', and then in a vast leap of time he imagines a future generation reaching their goal:

> Suppliantly
> The rocks will melt, the sealed horizons fall
> Before their onset—and the places
> Our hearts have hid in will be viewed by strangers
> Sitting where we are, breathing the foreign air
> Of the new realm they have inherited.

The melting of the rocks, the falling of the horizons, and the line, 'Of the new realm they have inherited', suggests that the time-journey ends in a dimension beyond time.

Towards the end of the poem Muir creates another image of timelessness in a trance-like sequence that is like a form of mysticism:

> We still remember, when our limbs were weightless
> As red leaves on a tree, and our silvery breaths
> Went on before us like new-risen souls
> Leading our empty bodies through the air.

In his letter to Gwendolen Murphy, Muir explained this image:

I think this is an attempt to suggest those isolated moments of pure vision which have a feeling of timelessness (and are often called timeless). My feeling about these moments (which are a common experience, though most people are unconscious of them) has always been that they do not *go into* Time; . . . At the moment when we are aware of them we are released from the presence of Time.[9]

At that point in the poem Muir seems to dismiss the vision as 'A princely dream', but a few lines later he writes equivocally: 'and we who fall so lightly,/Fall so heavily, are, it is said, immortal.' And although the poem ends on a genuinely agnostic note—

> So we must mourn or rejoice
> For this our station, our inheritance
> As if it were all. This plain all. This journey all.

—it confirms the impression that Muir's conflict with time is a spiritual quest. *Variations* II raises questions of faith, and particularly the question of immortality, that preoccupy Muir through the 1930s until he experienced that moment of revelation early in 1939.[10] And the poem is an attempt at a vision of existence that finds its fullest expression in Muir's great poem of the time-journey, 'The Journey Back'.

When he resumes the direct conflict with time in *Variations* VII[11] Muir's vision narrows to a series of paradoxes in which he becomes increasingly aware of the temporal nature of existence. The opening line, 'Ransomed from darkness and released in Time', reads like a statement of liberation but it is immediately contradicted by the second line, 'Caught, pinioned, blinded, sealed and cased in Time'. The contradictions continue until the first stanza ends: 'Buried alive and buried dead by Time'. The image of entombment, which suggests both spiritual and physical death, dominates the second stanza, and the antithetical pattern of the first stanza with its alternating lines of triumph and defeat gives way to a growing sense of resignation. If there is 'no escape from Time', no way of finding 'The pure and trackless day of liberty', and 'Nothing in earth or heaven to set us free', then, the poet concludes:

> Imprisonment's for ever; we're the mock of Time,
> While lost and empty lies Eternity.

The poem ends with a sense of loss that is close to despair, and yet the final line opens another paradox. Muir's conclusion is not that eternity does not exist but that it is 'lost and empty'; the mystery—and the conflict—is to find a way from time to eternity, to find a vision of existence that transcends the temporal, to find a faith that will make these things imaginable, expressible.

The search continues in *Variations* VIII,[12] which is itself a set of variations. Muir presents a series of metaphors for time and then, by a process that strikes the reader as a combination of free association and literary contrivance, he practises his variations. The poem is self-consciously ingenious and literary, and one feels that this—linguistic and literary ingenuity—becomes the real purpose of the poem and that the attempt to penetrate the mystery of time is forgotten. Even so, the poem expresses a sense of conflict and anguish.

In the first stanza Muir associates man's mortality in time with the martyrdom of St Sebastian, which he expresses in the tragi-comic image: 'this cruel plumage, stagy and absurd,/Of a plucked angel or half-naked bird'. Man in the grip of time is 'A plucked angel', stripped of his wings, his immortality. The third stanza is a more explicit statement of Muir's longing for immortality. He wants to sail the sea of time until he finds 'Eternity's unhidden shore'—the eternity that was 'lost and empty' in *Variations* VII— but he realises that this train of thought, the voyage on the sea of time, is a willed and superficial fantasy, that there is no escape, and that time will 'dredge the very heavens'. The final stanza, the starting point of which is the metaphor, 'Time's a fire-wheel', has another reference to immortality in the unintentionally absurd image of 'that fireless kingdom in the sky', and the poem ends with the resigned, rhetorical question: '"Who shall outsoar the mountainous flame of Time?"'

Variations VII and VIII show Muir twisting and turning in his search for an escape from time and mortality, but these two poems, like *Variations* II, are also attempts to penetrate the mystery of time so as to find a meaning for man's existence; Muir strives for a vision of the human condition that will transcend the temporal and the mortal and thus resolve the conflict. The sustaining element in such a vision, the element that might bring with it the longed-for meaning of existence, is faith, but at the time of writing the *Variations* in the early 1930s Muir's faith could not sustain the vision, nor the vision the faith. The search fails and the poems end on a double note of frustration and fatalism. But gradually, out of a disillusionment that is sometimes close to despair—and almost as if that state of mind were a necessary stage in the development of the vision—comes the beginning of hope.

'The Human Fold',[13] first published in 1939 and subsequently in *The Narrow Place* of 1943, has its origin in a dream. Muir recalls the occasion in *The Story And The Fable*:

> The voice spoke from behind and a little above me, and said: 'I lean my cheek from Eternity for Time to slap'. At the same time I had a faint image of someone in white—a dim impression of a shroud—pushing his or her cheek against some transparent thin substance, slightly crinkling it; a feeling of an insubstantial displacement. I am certain I could never have framed that sentence except in sleep, though it seems so wonderful to me now, awake.[14]

Muir says he could never have framed the sentence except in sleep, but in the same account he says the line came to him when he was in that state between sleep and walking, and one feels that the line brings together the timelessness of the unconscious and temporal consciousness. And the imagery of the dream—someone as if in a shroud, that is, from beyond death, making 'an insubstantial displacement' in time—allows the interpretation that the dream could be one of Muir's earliest intimations of Christ's incarnation or resurrection.

The feeling of wonder Muir felt at the time of the dream is present in the poem but it is surrounded by a sombre fatalism. In the opening lines of 'The Human Fold' it is as if the conflict with time has been lost and the poet has long since accepted his imprisonment in time:

> Here penned within the human fold
> No longer now we shake the bars,
> Although the ever-moving stars
> Night after night in order rolled
> Rebuke this stationary farce.

In the next line the poem momentarily changes direction: 'There's no alternative here but love', but it is a conditional, uncertain love: 'So far as genuine love can be/Where there's no genuine liberty'.

As the first stanza develops Muir juxtaposes two sets of opposing forces—life and death—in expressly religious terms, but unlike the contradictions of *Variations* VII the forces are now in equilibrium:

> The heavenly and the hellish town,
> The green cross growing in a wood,
> Close by old Eden's crumbling wall,
> And God himself in full manhood
> Riding against the fall.

It is, one feels, a vision that assembles the various elements—heaven and earth and hell, past and present and future, the crucifixion and the incarnation and the fall—without quite unifying them. The vision falters and the poet returns to earth and mortality, to human faces in misery. And then as he looks at the faces he says:

> I read this burden in them all:
> 'I lean my cheek from eternity
> For time to slap, for time to slap.
> I gather my bones from the bottomless clay
> To lay my head in the light's lap'.

The human faces have eternal origins and—'To lay my head in the light's lap'—a destination of more than earthly radiance.

The second stanza seems more deeply pessimistic. It speaks of a long journey into a present in which there is 'no memory and no grace/To furnish evidence of a soul'; it speaks of a journey on which faith and community—'Altar', 'shrine', 'boundary stone', 'legends'—have been lost; it offers the prospect of a future in which man's existence in time is as meaningless as a 'shadow-dance' on a wall. And at that despairing point in the poem Muir repeats the refrain: ' "I lean my cheek from eternity . . . To lay my head in the light's lap" '.

'The Human Fold' is a perplexing poem. It is a lamentation, not so much a cry of despair as a statement uttered with a weariness of spirit that is beyond despair, and yet at the same time it offers an intimation of immortality. The contradictions of hopelessness and hope seem absolute, and yet in reading the poem one is more aware of a continuity from one state to the other than of the contradiction. Muir achieves this effect partly through his technical consistency in the use of language and imagery, tones and rhythms, and partly through his new attitude to time. The poem is written in a spirit of submission rather than of conflict, or acceptance rather than defiance, and paradoxically in this acceptance of the fallen, mortal human condition lies the beginning of Muir's mature vision of the time-journey.

When Muir returns to the theme of time in 'The Recurrence' and 'The Wheel'[15] in *The Narrow Place* is is clear that the conflict is almost at an end. 'The Recurrence' is a rejection of Nietzsche's theory but the greater part of the poem consists of an extended and increasingly persuasive vision of a Nietzschean, capriciously predestined universe that leads to the inevitability of the lines:

> What is ill be always ill,
> Wretches die behind a dike,
> And the happy be happy still.

Ironically, Muir presents the Nietzschean case so effectively that his denial of it in the brief closing section of the poem seems almost ambivalent; the reason for this, one feels, is that the presentation has the force of poetry whereas the denial is a statement of belief: 'And the heart and mind know,/What has been can never return'. And there is a mechanical quality in the paradox and ambiguity in the final lines of 'The Recurrence' so that the poem simply comes to an end rather than to the conclusion that is required by the over-all structure:

> What is not will surely be
> In the changed unchanging reign,
> Else the Actor on the Tree
> Would loll at ease, miming pain,
> And counterfeit mortality.

Although these lines are not outstanding as poetry, they give a firm expression of Muir's developing faith, and when one recalls the passage in the *Auto-biography* that clarifies the ambiguity of the last three lines of the poem then one begins to see the nature of the faith.

In the *Autobiography* Muir gives an account of a dream he had during the period of his psychoanalysis:

> I dreamt that I was in a crowd watching a crucifixion. I expected the crucified man to be bearded like Christ, but saw with surprise that he was clean-shaven

except for a heavy moustache. It was undoubtedly Nietzsche; he looked as if he
had usurped the Cross, though like many a usurper he appeared simultaneously
to be perfectly at home on it. He stared round him with an air of defiant
possession, as if this were the place he had always been seeking, and had now,
with deep astonishment, found—or, rather, conquered—at last; for he was like
a man who had violently seized a position which belonged to someone else.[16]

A few lines later Muir offers the interpretation: 'I slowly began to realize that
Nietzsche's life had been a curious kind of self-crucifixion, out of pride, not
out of love'. The interpretation can be taken further. Muir had looked to
Nietzsche and his ideas for the meaning of existence, even for salvation; the
dream shows not only that Nietzsche's life was a form of self-crucifixion but
that Muir's adoption of his ideas, and his adoption of Nietzsche as saviour—
although necessary for a time—was mistaken. Nietzsche had usurped a
position that belonged to someone else, and as early as 1919 when he was
being psychoanalysed Muir knew that the 'someone else' was Christ, but it
was the late 1930s before this awareness began to take the form of faith, and
a few years later still before the faith began to find expression in the poems.
In 'The Recurrence' the Actor on the Tree is, one suggests, both Nietzsche
and Christ, but it is perfectly clear where Muir's faith lies.

'The Wheel' confirms this position. The opening line, 'How can I turn this
wheel that turns my life?', suggests the wheel of time and the associated idea
of Eternal Recurrence, and the first section of the poem speaks of the poet's
need for a new vision that will free him from the loves and hates of 'the
acrimonious dead'. It is as if Muir has resumed the old conflict with time and
mortality, but in the opening lines of the second stanza he speaks not of
escape but of coming to terms with the condition through a form of renewal,
almost of re-dedication: 'How can I here remake what there made me?' A
purely historical view of existence is not enough since 'Nothing can come of
history but history', and the concept of historical inevitability brings chaos
rather than order:

> The jangling
> Of all the voices of plant and beast and man
> That have not made a harmony
> Since first the great controversy began.

And then with a naturalness and calm assurance he reaches the conclusion
that the vision of harmony cannot be achieved

> Unless a grace
> Come of itself to wrap our souls in peace
> Between the turning leaves of history and make
> Ourselves ourselves, winnow the grudging grain,
> And take
> From that which made us that which will make us again.

The concept of grace, which Muir alludes to in 'The Human Fold' and

'The Recurrence', is still expressed as a possibility rather than a present reality but it is now more openly stated. Muir is clearly using the word in the religious sense of a divine intervention that brings atonement for man, and this impression is confirmed by the image of harvesting that leads to a rebirth. 'The Wheel' is one of Muir's more important minor poems; it re-states the conflict with time and then, more fully and explicitly than before, it resolves the conflict in religious terms—grace, peace, a harvesting and a rebirth— that show Muir's emerging faith and the beginning of his great vision of reconciliation. The poem is a work of art in which complex issues are expressed in a highly rhythmical, almost incantatory way so that the 'argument' of the poem emerges not as doctrine but as personal experience that is transmuted by the imagination into the beginning of a transcendent vision of existence.

Muir's mature vision brings together the natural, the human, and the divine orders in a harmony that is incompatible with the concept of historical inevitability. He sees the world of natural forces, a world of continuous regeneration, as one that man must respect rather than conquer; he is aware of the continuity of ancestral elements in the human condition, of the re-enactment of mythological dramas in the life of modern man, of the survival of archetypal man; and in the mature vision the central archetype is the Christ-image, whom Muir sees as the power that unifies the human and divine orders, the temporal and the eternal.

Faith is the essential element that resolves the conflict with time and penetrates the mystery of existence, but finding or being found by faith is itself a process of confusion and bitter conflict.

CONVERSIONS

As an adolescent Muir found a temporary faith in the religious conversions he experienced at revivalist meetings in Kirkwall and Glasgow. The first conversion took place when Muir was fourteen years old, just before he left Orkney, and in the *Autobiography* he writes:

> Then one dark cold night—how it happened I do not know—I found myself in the crowd which marched after the preacher, all the length of Kirkwall to the mission hall . . . I remember nothing of it; I probably did not listen, for I was filled with an impatience which did not have anything to do with the words the preacher was saying; all round me people were bursting into sobs and loud cries, as if they too felt the same agonized anticipation; and when Mr Macpherson stopped at last and asked those who had accepted Christ to rise in their places the whole audience rose, lifting me with them, and I found myself on my feet with a wild sense of relief . . . When I got up at last, dazzled, an involuntary smile of joy on my face, and returned to my seat with the others, all the faces of the congregation melted into one great maternal face filled with welcome and wonder, and I felt I was walking straight into a gigantic pair of loving arms.[1]

The language in which Muir recalls the event makes it clear that what he found, and what he was probably looking for at that time, was emotional security. He says of the event that it was 'more a natural than a spiritual cleansing, and more a communal than a personal experience', and that it was not a genuine religious conversion since he was unaware of the religious issues involved.

Muir deals with his later conversion in Glasgow in a less detailed way, and after a brief account he comments that when he had a closer knowledge of these revivals he became disillusioned with them.[2] But although he came to see a spurious element in the revivalist meetings he does not totally reject the central experience. Of the Kirkwall conversion he says: 'a sort of purification had taken place in us, and it washed away the poisonous stuff which had gathered in me during that year.'[3] He recalls too that 'the change itself was so undeniable that it astonished me. I was not trying to be changed; I was changed quite beyond expectation.'[4] The Kirkwall conversion remained so vivid a memory—Muir could recall it in detail forty years later in *The Story And The Fable*, and later still in *An Autobiography*—that one feels it may have been a living memory during that period.

As a young man in Glasgow Muir became disillusioned with Christianity some time after his second conversion. He began to adopt new faiths, social-ism and later Nietzsche, and in the *Autobiography* he notes the similarity between his acceptance of socialism and the earlier religious conversion in Kirkwall:

> By now I was twenty-one, and although I did not know it, my conversion to Socialism was a recapitulation of my first conversion at fourteen. It was not, that is to say, the result of an intellectual process, but rather a sort of emotional transmutation; the poisonous stuff which had gathered in me during the past few years had found another temporary discharge. I read books on Socialism because they delighted me and were an escape from the world I had known with such painful precision.[5]

One accepts that the political conversion was a recapitulation of the religious one, but at the same time one feels that Muir is being too severe with himself in his attempt to establish a critical distance between the younger and the older Muir. His conversion to socialism might have been 'a sort of emotional transmutation' and nothing else, a search for security after the misery of the first few years in Glasgow, but even so the resulting political attitudes with their evangelical, at times millenial, overtones are valid. Most conversions, either religious or political, include an element of emotional need as well as intellectual choice. Muir clearly feels that he deluded himself about the nature of his political commitment, but the Glasgow chapter of the *Autobiography* shows that his adoption of socialism was not simply a personal escape, as he suggests, but an entirely reasonable response to the conditions in the city at that time. He denies that the conversion was the result of an intellectual process but at the same time he states that he studied the principles of the new faith, believing them to hold an answer to Glasgow's problems of poverty and ignorance and disease.

On reflection Muir sees the two experiences—the Kirkwall conversion and the conversion to socialism—as expressions of the same universal experience. He says in the *Autobiography*:

> The realization of the Fall is a realization of a universal event; and the two purifications which I have described, the one in Kirkwall and the one in Glasgow, brought with them images of universal purification. After that night in Kirkwall I felt that not only myself but everyone was saved, or would some time be saved; and my conversion to Socialism had a similar effect. It was as if I had stepped into a fable which was always there, invisibly waiting for anyone who wished to enter it.[6]

A symbolic expression of the purification and of stepping into the fable is Muir's account of his first May Day procession in Glasgow. The *Autobiography* offers a summary of the event but the same experience is presented in more detail in *Poor Tom*. Mansie Manson joins the procession, and Muir writes:

> And immediately he was enclosed in peace. It was as though he had stepped out of a confused and distracted zone into calm and safety, as though the procession had protectively enfolded him, lifted him up and set him down again on the

further bank of a tranquil river among the multitude who like him had reached the favoured land . . . he was embedded in fold after fold of security.[7]

The similarity between this experience and the Kirkwall conversion, when he felt he was 'walking straight into a gigantic pair of loving arms', is striking, and the religious imagery of the May Day account—'the further bank of a tranquil river' and 'reached the favoured land'—underlines the similarity. Socialism, for which the May Day procession becomes the symbol in the novel and to some extent in the *Autobiography*, allows Mansie to escape from his personal misery but it also offers the positive release into a new vision of humanity:

> . . . for everything was transfigured . . . the rising and falling shoulders, even the pot-bellied middle-aged man by his side; for all distinction had been lost, all substance transmuted into this transmutation of everything into rhythmical motion and sound.[8]

For Mansie Manson, and for the young Edwin Muir, the political procession is a religious occasion, and as the march makes its way through Glasgow Mansie's joy intensifies into a form of ecstasy:

> He was not now an isolated human being walking with other isolated human beings from a definite place to a definite place, but part of a perfect rhythm which had arisen, he did not know how; and as that rhythm deepened, so that all sense of effort vanished in it, he no longer seemed even to be propelled by his own will but rather to be floating, and with him all those people in front and behind: the whole procession seemed to be calmly floating down a sunny river flanked with rocky cliffs on either side, floating like a long wooded island where the trees stand in orderly ranks and breathe out fragrance and coolness to either shore.[9]

In abandoning himself to the new faith of socialism Manson, and to some extent the young Muir, found a paradisiac vision of life in which the conflicts were resolved and in which there were moments of semi-mystical harmony.

Muir held some of his political attitudes—a liberal, non-doctrinal social-ism—until his last years but the euphoric vision of the May Day procession did not last long. The vision was false, Muir felt, because it was 'earthly and nothing more', yet paradoxically the accounts in the *Autobiography* and *Poor Tom*, with the words 'purification', 'transmutation' and 'transfiguration', are accounts of religious experiences. Muir was trying to find in socialism more than it contained; he was trying to invest it with spiritual power in addition to its social and economic content, trying to find in socialism not just the promise of a more just social order but also a faith that would give meaning to existence.

When he was converted to socialism Muir rejected religion,[10] and one can see why the two faiths seemed incompatible to him as a young man in Glasgow at the turn of the century. Some thirty years later, in 1934, he made a tour of Scotland and published his impressions in the following year as

Scottish Journey. His return to Glasgow revived memories of the time he had lived in the city, including the memory of the great difference between the behaviour of the professing Christians and that of the trades union leaders he had known. Recalling a type of Christian he had known, Muir writes:

> He professed a Christianity which had no connection even with the means by which he contrived the feat of living, that is his daily business; a concern for the good of society which permitted him to do the same things that an inveterate enemy of it might have done with equal reason; and a patriotism, for the Empire or for Scotland or for both, which was merely a pleasant and warmth-giving emotion. In other words, he professed a great number of moral sentiments, but the most important part of his life, the part he spent at work, was quite uninfluenced by moral considerations, being ruled merely by considerations of legality. As most of the men I am speaking of were professing Christians, one cannot help thinking that the Scottish Church, by its weak or politic or merely worldly policy of trimming, has been largely responsible for this false state of things.[11]

What Muir is recalling here is a social order with no spirit of community, a religion without a faith, Christianity without Christ. In contrast, he says of the trades union organisers:

> Now among the trade union workers whom I met there did not exist this accepted and complacent division between profession and practice; and their relation to one another was not merely a self-seeking relation cloaked in moral sentiments, but a real moral relation. Their obligations to one another were obligations for which if necessary they had to make sacrifices. They were pledged neither to take advantage of their neighbours, nor to rise in the world at their expense. These are moral principles, and, socially speaking, among the most fundamental of moral principles. The remarkable thing is that these trade unionists not only held them, but also practised them.[12]

The trades union leaders lived their ideals as the Christians did not, they had a compassionate vision of society, or a part of society, that the Christians lacked and, unlike the Christians, they acted as if they had responsibility for the welfare of their neighbours. It is understandable that Muir as a young man felt himself under a moral pressure to make a choice between socialism and Christianity. His decision for socialism, however, is as much a religious as a political choice, and it is characteristic of Muir that he should choose the faith that seemed at the time to be the more compassionate.

It was at this time that Muir, deeply preoccupied by the question of faith and by the dilemma of whether the faith should be expressed in political or religious terms, made a comparative study of two extreme forms of ideology in his essay, 'Bolshevism And Calvinism'. He makes it clear that he is not identifying one with the other 'but only suggesting a parallelism'; even so, the similarities are so many and so striking, and the essay is so precise and objective an analysis of the two ideologies that it is worth quoting in some detail.

He begins by examining Calvinism, isolating those features of it that are also found in communism:

> First, it was a deterministic theory holding that certain changes were inevitable and that its own ultimate triumph was assured. Secondly, to concentrate its forces it possessed one central scripture reinforced by a mass of guiding exegesis, and encouraged the unremitting study of that scripture, attributing to all secular literature, of whatever nature, a secondary importance. Thirdly, on the model of its scripture it set up a complete new system of life and created a new machinery which was designed to be at once theoretically sound and practically efficient. Fourthly, in its secular policy it was eminently realistic, employing the pretext of liberty, as all young movements do before they attain power, but using the same weapons as its enemies; that is, repression and discipline within, and craft and force without. Fifthly, while in its triumph still hostile to literature and other forms of traditional culture, it showed an extraordinary enthusiasm for education and an almost fanatical belief in its efficacy. Sixthly, it essentially sought and secured the victory of a class which was at the same time under a stigma, for 'the elect' were roughly the new commercial stratum which was already beginning to rise to the top. Seventhly, once it had triumphed it set up a dictatorship by committees and preferred the claims of the mass to those of the individual, exercising a strict control over people's private affairs. Eighthly, it revolted against the traditional conception of love and marriage, and while disgusted by the romantic attitudes of chivalry, made divorce easier, at once rationalizing and loosening the marriage tie. And finally, it was in its policy international and revolutionary, from a convenient centre encouraging rebellion against the old order in other countries.[14]

This dissection of Calvinism, one of the most clinically succinct passages in Muir's prose writings, is equally true of communism, and Muir suggests that the strongest point of similarity between the two is their exclusiveness.[15] He reacts against their rigidly determinist attitude to life and states his conviction that there is 'a possibility of achieving a humanly satisfactory society without giving up the existing advantages of tradition and without having recourse to the machinery of Marxian determinism'.[16] He suggests that the change can be made through 'the theory of Social Credit associated with the name of Major Douglas'. The theory is not examined in 'Bolshevism And Calvinism', but Muir returns to the subject in *Social Credit And The Labour Party*, a booklet published in 1935.[17]

In *Social Credit And The Labour Party* Muir affirms his socialism, even to the extent of expressing his belief in Marx and the class struggle,[18] an assertion of a merely residual or token belief, one suspects, especially since Muir appeals against revolution and singles out the Reformation in Scotland as proof of the lasting damage caused by violent change.[19] The nature of the political faith Muir professes in this booklet is best summarised by two quotations:

> Socialism is not a mere Utopian ideal founded on moral precepts, but the final realization of all the good inherent in the development of society from its beginning.[20]

And:

> . . . you must trust mankind and distrust mankind, recognising man's poten-
> tialities for good if you are not to despair, and recognising his limitations if you
> are not to be lost in infatuated hopes.[21]

Clearly, Muir is less concerned with the class struggle than with the timeless struggle between good and evil, less concerned with the power structure of a new social order than with its moral basis and, as the millenial language of the first quotations suggests, he is still looking to socialism to provide the faith that would resolve many of the conflicts in the human situation and would satisfy the spiritual and emotional need that Muir had felt since his childhood.

THE IRON TEXT

The few books in Muir's childhood home in Orkney included the Bible and *The Pilgrim's Progress*, and there was the weekly journal, *The Christian Herald* and the monthly *The Scots Worthies*, biographies of Reformers and Covenanters. Muir writes that he was reading this material when he was nine years old.[1] He recalls too that his mother taught him hymns and the story of Jesus,[2] and that his father conducted a little service in the farmhouse each week:

> Every Sunday night he gathered us together to read a chapter of the Bible and kneel down in prayer. These Sunday nights are among my happiest memories; there was a feeling of complete security and union among us as we sat reading about David and Elijah. My father's prayer, delivered in a sort of mild chant while we knelt on the floor, generally ran on the same lines; at one point there always came the words, for which I waited, 'an house not made with hands, eternal in the heavens'.[3]

Throughout his childhood Muir was happily assimilating this Christian influence and practising the simple Christian pieties. Later, during his aimless adolescence in Kirkwall, there was the religious conversion; and later still in Glasgow there was the second religious conversion after which, he writes: 'I carried about with me a pocket edition of the New Testament which I was always reading, tried hard to practise self-renunciation, and was always doing some useless embarrassing service for the people I knew.'[4] Even with his conscious rejection of religion and acceptance of socialism, the religious preoccupation remained, and in 1919 some archetypal features of Christianity were rediscovered and accepted when his psychoanalysis by Maurice Nicoll revived his belief in the immortality of the soul.

In the late 1920s the question of religion demanded his attention in a different way. The publishers, Cape, for whom he was acting as a reader, commissioned him to write a biography of John Knox,[5] and the book, *John Knox—Portrait Of A Calvinist*, was published in 1929. Knox and Calvinism presented Muir with a form of Christianity and an image of God that he found abhorrent; in reaction he began to clarify his own attitudes, and the double process of opposition and clarification continued throughout his life. The process is expressed as an almost obsessive, sometimes morbid concern in the novel, *The Three Brothers* (1931), which is set in sixteenth-century Scotland and in which Knox is featured; the concern breaks through again

in the following year in *Poor Tom*; there is the closely argued case against Calvinism in the 1934 essay, 'Bolshevism And Calvinism', and in two publications of 1935, *Scottish Journey* and *Social Credit And The Labour Party*; opposition to Knox and the Reformation is central to his argument in *Scott And Scotland* in 1936, and ten years later in the illustrated booklet, *The Scots And Their Country* Muir renews the attack; and there is implicit rejection of Knox and Calvinism in the two autobiographies, *The Story And The Fable* and *An Autobiography*.

Muir's attitude is unequivocally hostile; Calvinism, Knox and the Reformation arouse a combative element in him as almost nothing else does, and he attacks the movement with an anger that is rare in his work. The frequency of the attacks shows that he was in continuous conflict with this form of religion for at least a quarter of a century, from the publication of *John Knox* in 1929 until *An Autobiography* in 1954, and probably for a longer period than this.

The nature of the faith that Muir opposed so forcefully is analysed in *John Knox*, where Muir writes of Calvin:

> He built his system on two realities: the Bible and human nature. Looking at the world as it was he could not but see that some men were well wrought and others warped; that some went the way of life and others the way of destruction; that some turned their faces towards God and others lived in blind indifference to Him. But if God had once revealed Himself to these, if they had seen His glory and been assured of the eternal happiness which they were to share with Him, was it conceivable that they should have remained indifferent? If it were a matter to be decided by man's will merely, would anyone consent to be damned? It was inconceivable; and therefore the irresistible conclusion followed that God only chose whom He willed, and voluntarily left the rest to darkness in this world and torment in the next. This was Calvin's reading of human destiny, but the Bible supported it, and the Bible was his infallible guide. There he found that in the beginning God had chosen one people alone out of many to be His elect to everlasting; there he found, too, as Luther had done, that God was omnipotent, omniscient and just. Being omnipotent, however, God had fashioned the world to His complete desire; being omniscient, His foreknowledge of all things was in complete agreement with his fore-ordination of them; and being just, His election of certain souls and His damnation of others was necessarily in accordance with an equity which it was blasphemy to question. But God was eternal as well, and therefore He had already ordained Adam's fall before He created him; He had ordained, in addition, all the consequences which ensued; His will had damned all the multitudes of the lost and chosen every member of the elect before the foundations of the world were laid.[6]

Muir writes that Calvin went on to assert that once a soul was elected it was God's forever; that the elect never lost the faith that would save them, even if they lost all consciousness of that faith; and that children of the elect were themselves elected, inheriting salvation like a genetic trait. And Muir brings out the enormity, the gross assumption of righteousness, that underlies all this:

Calvinism has been condemned as a gloomy religion, and its view of the world as one of almost unrelieved horror; but to do so is to overlook the fact that the one gleam of hope in that world was confiscated by the Calvinists as their own. To a soul convinced that he was ordained to burn in everlasting fire such a view would indeed be terrible, and if the Calvinists had believed in their own damnation, all the opprobrium which their enemies have cast upon them would be merited. But the Genevan religion was founded by a man who considered himself certain of his election, and the supporters it drew to itself had of necessity the same cheerful assurance. No healthy-minded Calvinist could think for long that he was a vessel of wrath; no one at all could be adopted by the Genevan communion who was fixedly of that opinion. Yet, as doubts were bound to arise, some step had to be taken; and it was to neutralize these that Calvin built up his impregnable line of defence around the certainty of election. The great aim of Calvin's theology was, in short, to instil certitude, confidence and strength into its adherents.[7]

In the Genevan theocracy this spiritual regime was reinforced by civic repression; the social order was seen as the expression of the spiritual order, and persons who did not conform could be imprisoned, tortured, or executed.[8] Although Knox did not succeed in establishing a theocracy in Scotland—some of his demands, for example, that idolatry and adultery be treated as capital offences, were rejected by parliament—he exerted a powerful inhibiting influence on Scottish life. Writing of Knox's Calvinism, Muir says its main feature was 'above all, a consciously virtuous determination to compel and humiliate people for the greater glory of God'. He adds:

> Its most fundamental idea was the corruption of man's nature, and its policy had necessarily, therefore, to be a policy of espionage and repression. Its sole instrument for keeping or reclaiming its members was punishment. The ministers had to correct their congregations; the elders had to correct the ministers; the congregations had to correct the elders. A Church such as this, held together by universal and reciprocal fault-finding, could not but have something ambiguous in its piety, and could not but encourage the self-opinionative and the censorious at the expense of the sensitive and the charitable. It did more, however; it substituted for the particular tyranny of the priest a universal and inescapable tyranny.[9]

The nature of the faith was determined to some extent by the personality of its founder. A man who re-interprets doctrine so radically that he formulates a new religion which he then uses as his justification for enforcing a new social order—such a man is driven by exceptionally powerful forces. At the same time the severity of Calvinism, its demand for rigid conformity of thought and action, was prompted by the insecurity of its exposed and isolated position. Having deserted the mother church and abandoned the security of its traditions, rituals and doctrines, the Calvinists had to assert an independent identity and safeguard it against the possibility of counter-reformation, a possibility that remained in Scotland for more than a century after the Reformation.[10]

Under such a regime there was no place for the expression of doubt, but

Muir experienced recurring doubt in his search for faith, and he knew that doubt may be of greater spiritual value than an assertion of belief. In the third section of *The Three Brothers* there are long theological arguments in which the dogmatic certainties of the Calvinists, the Anabaptists and the Roman Catholics seem to contradict the faiths they proclaim and are presented less sympathetically than the doubt of David Blackadder or even the agnosticism of his father. At a critical point in the novel the dying Sandy Blackadder, the oldest of the three brothers, tells David:

> Take your time, and dinna be over-confident that you're right until ye feel sure within yourself, and be humble and doubtful, and ask God's guidance; and dinna think it's His guidance if it tells ye anything that's proud or cruel or that does anybody a hurt.[11]

And Muir makes a similar point in *Poor Tom* when Mansie Manson, longing for a sure faith that would give meaning to life and redeem the misery of Tom's death, shies away from certainty, 'seeing that the penalty for certainty in any faith, heavenly or earthly, is some form of predestination, involving election and damnation'.[12]

Calvinism demanded total conformity and tried to suppress individual thought and expression; it silenced the poets and musicians in a general suppression of the arts—singing was a crime in Calvin's Geneva—and it excluded the arts from the new church. In *Scott And Scotland*, published in 1936, Muir writes:

> I have often wondered why the Scots, who have shown themselves in the past to be a theological and speculative race, should have produced scarcely a single verse of good religious or metaphysical poetry.[13]

One of the reasons, he says, was 'the strict Calvinism of the Scots, which was adverse both to the production of poetry, and to poetry itself'. In particular, Calvinism killed poetic drama in Scotland, and Muir writes:

> This matter of dramatic poetry, indeed, or rather the lack of it, was probably crucial for Scottish literature; and if that is so, then the Reformation truly signalized the beginning of Scotland's decline as a civilized nation.[14]

Later in the book Muir returns to this theme, referring to the poetry of Alexander Scott and arguing that before the Reformation 'there must have existed in Scotland a high culture of the feelings as well as of the mind: a concord which was destroyed by the rigours of Calvinism, so that hardly a trace of it has been left'.[15] Muir's point about the lost culture is confirmed by Professor John MacQueen who shows that much poetry and song in sixteenth-century Scotland was composed by men in church and court circles—for example, by Alexander Scott at the Chapel Royal in Stirling—and when church and court were reformed the poems and songs ceased. Professor MacQueen writes:

For the most part, however, the old culture withered, and after 1568 its disappearance is emblematized by the transformation of Robert Semple to a verse-pamphleteer and by the silence, for whatever cause, of Alexander Scott.[16]

This loss of the arts, of the old culture, and of the community, the family of Scotland is expressed in the poem, 'Scotland 1941',[17] in *The Narrow Place* of 1943. The poem is a lament for the loss and also an angry denunciation of the new culture, Calvinism, that replaced the old. The opening lines suggest a golden age; a sense of unity is given by the image of the 'simple sky' that seems to cover the whole people protectively, and a sense of fulfillment is given by the image of harvesting, 'The busy corn-fields':

> We were a tribe, a family a people.
> . . .
> A simple sky roofed in that rustic day,
> The busy corn-fields and the haunted holms,
> The green road winding up the ferny brae.

But with the arrival of Knox and his followers the scene is transformed. The Reformers, and Covenanters like the hysterical Sandy Peden, are seen as part-predators, part-scavengers, preying on the land and the people and bringing famine and disease; the golden age gives way to a fall:

> But Knox and Melville clapped their preaching palms
> And bundled all the harvesters away,
> Hoodicrow Peden in the blighted corn
> Hacked with his rusty beak the starving haulms.

The image of spiritual fulfilment is distorted under the influence of the new religion to an image of spiritual atrophy, and the first section of the poem leads with a growing sense of inevitability to the line: 'Out of that desolation we were born'.

In the second section the desolation spreads. The internal conflicts of Calvinism along with the repressive nature of the regime take the national qualities of courage and defiance and pervert them to the cause of national self-destruction:

> We with such courage and the bitter wit
> To fell the ancient oak of loyalty,
> And strip the peopled hill and altar bare,
> And crush the poet with an iron text,
> How could we read our souls and learn to be?

The remainder of the poem answers the question; Muir's conclusion is that the influence of Calvinism prevented us from reading our souls, prevented us from being. As the poem moves from past to present, Muir traces the legacy of Calvinism, implying that Calvinism made possible the worst excesses of capitalism:

> We watch our cities burning in their pit,
> To salve our souls grinding dull lucre out,
> We, fanatics of the frustrate and the half,
> Who once set Purgatory Hill in doubt.
> Now smoke and dearth and money everywhere.

The people who once had a whole culture and whose artists had a wholeness of vision now celebrate Burns and Walter Scott, 'sham bards of a sham nation'; and the result of all the ideological blood-letting inspired by Calvinism—the hanging of Covenanter Hugh Mackail, the intrigue and carnage of Montrose and Argyle—was 'to carve out/This towering pulpit of the Golden Calf'. The poem ends with a three-line section that expresses the futility of the loss and the hope that out of such waste there might come peace:

> Such wasted bravery idle as a song,
> Such hard-won ill might prove Time's verdict wrong,
> And melt to pity the annalist's iron tongue.

'Scotland 1941' tells of a nation remorselessly pursuing its Calvinist destiny—its own self-destruction. The language of the poem—'hacked', 'robbed', 'strip', 'crush', 'burning', 'grinding', 'twisted'—expresses Muir's view of Calvinism and its legacy with brutal perfection.

This mercilessness, Calvinism's inability to forgive, is something Muir stresses in *John Knox*:

> But though it had a place for the strong and the weak, the learned and the simple, the humble and the arrogant, the ascetic and the sensual, it had no place at all for the merciful or the generous. It could no more have produced a figure like St Francis than it could have produced one like Socrates. Judged by the best in humanity, its figures seem narrow, sick, and almost pathological.[18]

Later in his life Muir sees the same mercilessness in communism: 'The religious man is bound to forgive; the ordinary man forgives easily. Without forgiveness our life would be unimaginable.'[19] It is unimaginable for Muir because throughout his life he sees forgiveness as an act of reconciliation, a healing of the separation between man and his fellow men, a healing of the division within the self. Any faith that did not allow the act of reconciliation was unacceptable, and neither Calvinism nor communism had a place for forgiveness.

When Muir thinks of the end result of the merciless years of Calvinism he sees modern Scotland as a barren winter landscape. The poem, 'Scotland's Winter', appears in *Scottish Journey*[20] where Muir says it expresses his feelings about the contrast between Scotland's legendary past and its tawdry present. The poem opens with a chillingly beautiful and heraldic image of the season and the land:

> Now the ice lays its smooth claws on the sill,
> The sun looks from the hill

> Helmed in his winter casket,
> And sweeps his arctic sword across the sky.

As the poem develops the beauty gives way to a brief passage of lament for
all that has been lost:

> And all the kings before
> This land was kingless,
> And all the singers before
> This land was songless.

The monarchs and the poets and the musicians represent a nobility, a lyricism,
a capacity to create and celebrate that Scotland has lost. At this point Muir
turns from past to present, from the lost culture to 'This land that with its
dead and living waits the Judgement Day', and in the closing lines Muir
imagines the Scottish people as refugees in their own land, indifferent to their
destitution, a lost people who

> do not know
> Whence they come or where they go
> And are content
> With their poor frozen life and shallow banishment.

They—or rather, we—now walk without purpose or hope or faith, without
even identity, because these aspects of the human spirit have been lost in the
spiritual repression that is Calvinism.

Muir's attack goes even further than this. The Reformation corrupted not
only the spirit of the Scottish people but also the spirit of the faith it claimed
to represent. Muir comes to see not only that Calvinism lacked charity, that
it restricted freedom of thought and expression, that it suppressed the arts,
and that at worst it was a form of totalitarianism, but that in addition to this
it denied an essential element of Christianity itself.

In *The Story And The Fable* Muir records a dream:

> Curious dream last night about the Roman Catholic Church. I thought of it as
> something fluid, growing, and yet contained, like a lake. But then I said to
> someone that the Protestants were always writing letters to each other, pouring
> themselves out, and now the Protestant Church was *nothing*; there was nothing
> left there at all; it was a mere fiction.[21]

Muir comments: 'This seemed very profound in the dream. Not so now.' The
symbolism may not be 'very profound' but it shows the correspondence
between the themes that emerge from Muir's dream imagery and his conscious
attitudes towards religion. The Roman Catholic Church is seen as a living
faith and perhaps also a source of faith; Protestantism, in contrast, consists
of endless letter writing as a result of which the Protestant Church has poured
itself out until there is nothing left. The Roman Catholic lake, a reservoir of
faith—and a symbol of the unconscious mind—is replaced by the Protestant

Word, but since there is nothing but the Word in the Protestant Church of Muir's dream, the Word is 'a mere fiction'. The Protestant Word represents consciousness cut off from the unconscious, ideology cut off from faith.

In *An Autobiography* there is a passage that echoes the dream of Roman Catholics and Protestants in *The Story And The Fable*. Muir recalls the imagery of the Incarnation that he had seen everywhere in Rome and he contrasts this with the church he had attended as a child:

> But it was the evidences of another Incarnation that met one everywhere and gradually exerted its influence. During the time when as a boy I attended the United Presbyterian Church in Orkney, I was aware of religion chiefly as the sacred Word, and the church itself, severe and decent, with its touching bareness and austerity, seemed to cut off religion from the rest of life and from all the week-day world, as if it were quite specific thing shut within itself, almost jealously, by its white-washed walls, furnished with its bare brown varnished benches unlike any others in the whole world, and filled with the odour of ancient Bibles. It did not tell me by any outward sign that the Word had been made flesh.[22]

Since this, the Word made flesh, is an essential element of Christianity, the Protestant emphasis on the Word and nothing but the Word seems to Muir to be a denial of the incarnate Christ. The Word without the flesh becomes logotheism,[23] the 'iron text' of 'Scotland 1941'.

Muir's most passionate attack on Calvinism is the poem, 'The Incarnate One' in *One Foot In Eden*, 1956.[24] The opening lines have a harshness of sound that echoes the mercilessness of the Word and a bleakness of landscape that reflects the spiritual wasteland of a country dominated by Calvinism:

> The windless northern surge, the sea-gull's scream,
> And Calvin's kirk crowning the barren brae.

Muir turns immediately from this Calvinist arrogance, and from the irony of the kirk 'crowning' the land, to another version of Christianity:

> I think of Giotto the Tuscan shepherd's dream,
> Christ, man and creature in their inner day.

The contrast between a religion that reduces faith to the tyrannical code of the Word and a religion that brings the divine, the human and the natural orders into harmony—'Christ, man and creature in their inner day'—the contrast is so great that the poet sees these two versions of Christianity as quite separate religious, one of which has protested the living Christ out of its doctrine:

> How could our race betray
> The Image, and the Incarnate One unmake
> Who chose this form and fashion for our sake?

The second stanza goes beyond the bitterness of 'Scotland 1941' to show that Calvinism perverted Christianity, transforming it from a loving faith into a totalitarian social order, a system that Calvin achieved and his successors maintained by themselves supplanting Christ:

> The Word made flesh is here made word again,
> A word made word in flourish and arrogant crook.
> See there King Calvin with his iron pen,
> And God three angry letters in a book,
> And there the logical hook
> On which the Mystery is impaled and bent
> Into an ideological instrument.

Muir's rejection of the 'ideological instrument', a code without faith or vision, is absolute. He states: 'There's better gospel in man's natural tongue', and says the people who saw the crucifixion as a human act—'The archaic peoples in their ancient awe,/In ignorant wonder'—had a 'truer sight' of Christ than had Calvin and his followers; that is, human values and emotions, untouched by Christianity but with the power to wonder, are a better basis for faith than is Calvinism.

The fourth stanza opens with the lines:

> The fleshless word, growing, will bring us down,
> Pagan and Christian man alike will fall.

And here one feels that Muir is speaking not only of the 'iron pen' of Calvin but also the steel pen of Stalin, of the power of men who devise and impose impersonal, inhuman systems that lead to:

> Abstract calamity, save for those who can
> Build their cold empire on the abstract man.

In the final stanza Muir suggests that the impulse that drives man to impose impersonal, abstract systems is a continuing battle waged against generations of men:

> The bloodless word will battle for its own
> Invisibly in brain and nerve and cell.
> The generations tell
> Their personal tale

It is the struggle between the 'iron pen' and the 'natural tongue', between the 'ideological instrument' and the 'ancient wonder', and Muir concludes that the longer this struggle continues the longer it will be before a faith founded on the incarnate one can put an end to conflict: 'the One has far to go/Past the mirages and the murdering snow.'

The 'One' of these closing lines is perhaps less precise than 'The Incarnate One' of the title and the first stanza; it is as if in the last two stanzas Muir is thinking not only of the antithesis of the Calvinist Word and the incarnate Christ but also of the conflict between totalitarian systems and the people these systems try to subjugate, a conflict that continues while a vision that is prompted by an archetypal rather than a doctrinal Christ-image waits to be realised. And the conclusion, 'the One has far to go', is as true of Muir's personal life as the human condition generally. Muir's preoccupation with the One and his search for a faith that will sustain his vision find expression in the universal myth of the Way.

The Journey

THE ROAD

In his autobiography, *World Within World*, published in 1951, Stephen Spender said of his meetings with Muir over the years:

> To see him in his Hampstead home, or later at St Andrews, Edinburgh, Prague or Rome, where successively he worked, was to add gratefully to my appreciation of him, without feeling that the years between these journeys were an interruption to our steadily growing friendship. On each occasion I was struck by the integrity of purpose in his work and life, which made him seem a pilgrim from place to place rather than a wanderer like myself. Indeed, he had the purpose which converted a life of shifting jobs into a spiritual pilgrimage.[1]

Ten years after Muir's death H Harvey Wood, who was responsible for Muir's first appointment to the British Council in Edinburgh in 1942, offered an apparently different comment on Muir's journey. In a radio broadcast in 1969 Harvey Wood recalled some of his impressions of Muir at work in his office in Melville Street in Edinburgh during the war and then at Charles University in Prague between 1945 and 1948:

> Edwin looked no less at home, and no more at home, than he had done in Edinburgh. Indeed, I came to the conclusion that he never felt, or was, completely at home anywhere—that the most quintessential part of him was always withdrawn and remote.[2]

Understandably, since Muir seldom lived in any one place or one country for more than a few years at a time, Spender and Harvey Wood saw his life as a journey, but what strikes them is not so much the geographical as the spiritual nature of that journey, not simply Muir as traveller but as pilgrim and exile. The sense of pilgrimage, says Spender, came from 'the integrity of purpose in his work and life', and Harvey Wood concludes that Muir was never quite at home anywhere because 'the most quintessential part of him was always withdrawn and remote'. These two sympathetic views of Muir express two of the main features of his spiritual journey. The physical journey—from Orkney to Glasgow, to various towns and cities in Britain and Europe, to Harvard and finally to Swaffham Prior near Cambridge—was prompted by chance and necessity but as the travels continued, and especially after the spontaneous religious experience in St Andrews in the spring of 1939, Muir's search for a faith that gives meaning to life and allows a growing vision of reconciliation in his life and his work transforms the physical journey into a pilgrimage.

It is not the act of travelling but the spiritual quest of the traveller, however uncertain and intermittent the quest may be, that turns the journey into a pilgrimage. And the pilgrim is also an exile, never completely at home anywhere since his life is a re-enactment of the mythological journey from eternity to eternity, from the paradise of unconscious childhood before the fall to the immortality of the soul that Muir believed lay at the end of the journey. Between the beginning and the end of the journey there may be occasional resting places but as long as the traveller is concerned to sustain a faith that can support a vision of wholeness and reconciliation, as long as the quest continues, there can be no home. Almost inevitably the preoccupation of the spiritual quest leads the pilgrim to some extent to disregard or even distrust a purely physical and historical view of the world. For the Christian pilgrim, even as idiosyncratic and non-doctrinal a Christian as Muir, there is a transcendent order of reality in which life is seen against the background of eternity. It may not be too fanciful to suggest that Muir's pilgrimage invites comparison with the *peregrinatio* of the Celtic saints whose voyaging, both geographical and metaphorical, was a search for resurrection.[3]

The image of life as a mythological journey runs through Muir's poetry from 'Ballad Of The Soul' in *First Poems* to the posthumously published 'Dialogue' ('Returning from the antipodes of time'), and the volume, *Journeys And Places*, includes the explicitly titled 'The Mythical Journey'. As Muir's work develops, the mythological journey becomes the spiritual journey, an exile and a pilgrimage, until in the great poems of *The Labyrinth* and *One Foot In Eden* Muir's vision of the journey ranges from its origin in the fall of man to its end in man's resurrection. The theme of the journey emerges clearly from the poems, not as a continuous progress but as a vision of life that gradually clarifies until it is expressed with a radiance that is close to mysticism. The completeness of the journey, from bewilderment through exile and pilgrimage to grace, is the greatest achievement in Muir's poetry, and in completing this cycle of fulfilment from fall to resurrection Muir is one of the most deeply satisfying poets of the twentieth century. And yet there are occasions when Muir is uncertain of the nature of the human journey, even in a poem that is prompted by the great story of exile, penance and pilgrimage, the Biblical myth of Exodus.

Section VI of *Variations On A Time Theme*,[4] which first appeared in 1933 as a separate poem, 'In The Wilderness', speaks of the Israelites' forty years in exile. Almost surprisingly, given the mythological starting point, the poem is not itself mythological, and in contrast to other sections of the *Variations* where the mode is variously visionary, metaphysical or paradoxical, Section VI is essentially a lyrical narrative spoken in the collective, representative but uncomprehending voice of a member of the tribe. The poem is one of Muir's rare attempts at technical virtuosity: the assymetrical stanza patterns, the widely variable lines, the changing rhythms and above all the sensuously detailed language and imagery combine to give the impression of a long and painful journey broken by mysterious incidents and apparitions.

In the opening stanza the travellers are aware only of the physical act of travelling through 'Sharp rock, soft dust, a land/Choked in sand'. The state of exile has become an endless, almost meaningless penance but the pain is sometimes interrupted by frightening and beautiful things, joys and torments that are part of the same story of the journey. In the second stanza there is the recollection of the stream that 'leapt from the smitten rock' to tantalise the travellers for a time; in the third stanza there is 'the bright cloud' and 'the bright and shadowy hill' of Sinai; and in the fourth stanza the sweaty sensuality of 'The brazen calf, the naked youths and men'.

The fifth stanza, the memory of the destruction of Pharaoh's army, shimmers in their mind like a mirage in the desert:

> All that is now a memory,
> Burning, burning,
> With Pharaoh's body floating on the sea
> Among his wide-robed seers, his men and cavalry,
> And the dim desert slowly turning,
> And the evening shadows
> On temple-mirroring Nile, the wells and shining meadows.

There are times when the travellers forget the purpose of the journey, 'Something once tender and green', and see instead 'Pale whirlwinds racing round like spectral hounds' on the horizon, an agitation on the edge of consciousness.

Only in the final stanza does Muir treat the journey in terms of pilgrimage: 'There is a stream/We have been told of. Where it is/We do not know. But it is not a dream'. The pilgrimage, however, is a fatalistic journey to a predestined end: 'We cannot miss/The road that leads us to it'. And the force that leads to deliverance is not faith but 'Fate' so that the religious awe of the final line, 'And enter the unknown and feared and longed-for land', seems as incongruous in a stanza that speaks of predestination as that stanza does in a poem of such lyrical intensity. Indeed, the final stanza distorts the figure of the poem; until then the travellers are uncomprehending, unaware of or forgetful of the purpose of their journey and the meaning of the signs and events. The device of the uncomprehending traveller is superbly controlled until the end when the narrative voice and viewpoint become those of the poet who intervenes so that the poem might have a universal interpretation. (Eliot's 'Journey Of The Magi', published in 1927, maintains the travellers' incomprehension throughout and is the more persuasive poem).

Section VI of the *Variations* is best seen as a hauntingly beautiful descriptive account of the exilic myth rather than a re-creation of the myth, and as one of those rare occasions that show Muir as a poet at play, conjuring a series of intensely visual and musical images from the wilderness.

Although the spirit of pilgrimage is missing from Section VI, the poem—and the journey it represents—has an overall cohesion, a shapeliness and a lyrical consistency. Muir's most sustained prose statement on the subject of the journey expresses such confusion about the nature of his personal journey that the statement is, by Muir's standard as a writer of prose, almost incoherent. Towards the end of *The Story And The Fable* in a passage that is an attempt at metaphor rather than myth Muir brings together ideas of identity, of the conscious and unconscious mind, of conflict and of time within the overall framework of the journey. The metaphor develops with an almost mechanical facility and in a language that lacks the particular autobiographical quality one thinks of as Muir's—the depth of insight expressed in humility, the sense of human experience as a distillation of sensation and intuition and reflection—until one suspects that Muir is simply following the impetus of the metaphor. One suspects too that the metaphor may be Kafka's rather than Muir's own.

His essay, 'Franz Kafka', and his translation of Kafka's *America* both appeared in 1940, the year in which *The Story And The Fable* was published. The essay, reprinted in *Essays On Literature And Society* in 1949, is similar to the passage in *The Story And The Fable*, and one suggests that Muir adopts Kafka's version of the metaphor of the journey because at this crucial stage in Muir's life—although the mythological journey, and the journey as exile and pilgrimage, was emerging from the poems—the myth of the poems did not yet inform his daily life. Muir writes:

> I am not one man, but two. Yet I have only one road, intended for me, not for the other. If it were not for him I should never have left that road, and should still be walking along it. But it is not wide enough for two. So my companion keeps looking about for more convenient and wider roads, and, as it happens, there is one at every few yards. He inconspicuously edges me into one of these, talking all the time to distract my attention; for he is a great talker, a wonderful story-teller. When we have gone along some particular road for a while I come to myself, accuse him of deceiving me, and start back for the original road again. But then he begins to manufacture excuses, flings himself down, says he is tired: why not take a rest? And when we have struggled back to the right road—the return journey is always much harder than the first one; great boulders, even dangerous chasms, appear in it, though it had seemed perfectly smooth before— when we have struggled, or rather straggled back (for my companion loiters and complains all the way; sometimes I have actually to carry him on my back), I am so tired that I have to rest for a long time. And what is gained by resting on a road, even if it is the right road, when I should be energetically striding along it?[5]

The experience referred to in the opening statement, 'I am not one man, but two', is the familiar tug of war within the self between the good angel and the bad, between conscience and the fiend, duty and distraction. But here Muir sees his other identity not as evil but as absurd, the archetypal trickster figure,[6] the whimsical, petulant infant who survives in adult man and who makes nonsense of man's most serious purposes.[7] The real purpose, Muir feels, is that he should be 'energetically striding along', as if the journey were a continuous progression, and Muir reinforces this sense of the journey as a linear process when he introduces the concept of time at this point in the same passage:

For my road only suits me, is only mine, if I reach various stages at the right hour. Otherwise I am merely an unwanted stranger at every stage. And my companion, who recovers far more quickly than I do once we get back, soon manages to distract my attention again, so that I am very likely lured along the first by-road that comes. And then the smooth journey covering miles in a few minutes, and the long and rocky and laborious climb back again. What hope of reaching the various stages in time, or even, in this way, the next stage?

Here the traveller is neither exile nor pilgrim but simply Western man in a hurry, filled with dismay at any check in his advance, any disruption to the time-table and itinerary.

At this point Muir attempts to change the nature of the metaphor from the absurd to the millenial:

> As I speak of it the road may seem a single, unrelated road. It is single, but not unrelated. If every man and woman took his or her road and stuck to it without listening to anyone the march of mankind would be one triumphant march to a glorious end. There would be millions of friends on either side of me, and nothing but friends. For my companion, in spite of his incomprehensible passion for all roads, is not really friendly; he is merely gregarious and inconsiderate.

The 'one triumphant march to a glorious end'—with the inherent contradiction of millions of friends who stick to the road without listening to anyone—is an echo of those other occasions in Muir's life, the boyhood march through the streets of Kirkwall and the May Day procession through the streets of Glasgow, but here it is so brief an allusion that it does not change the nature of the journey Muir is describing. The passage from *The Story And The Fable* ends as it begins with Muir speaking of his travelling companion, the trickster figure who is part of Muir's own identity:

> He wants to come across people, in every sense of the phrase, not to walk in unity with them. So, in spite of his engaging smile, he gets into countless quarrels, and drags me into them as well. And this confuses everything and wastes much time.
>
> If my road were wide enough for two, would he behave any better? I know him too well to think so. For though he may not be wicked, he is quite incorrigible. He has never learned a single thing in his whole life.

This insistent, almost obsessive concern to make continuous progress along the right road reads like an expression of personal and professional anxiety rather than a spiritual quest, while the conflict of wills between the purposeful traveller and the trickster suggests an acute and unresolved personal crisis rather than a crisis of faith. Even so, this passage from *The Story And The Fable* contains an element of pilgrimage, however absurd, in its urgent sense of purpose, its conviction that there is a right road, and in its determination to hold to that road despite the trickster's continual disruptions.

When Muir turns from this metaphorical account of his personal road to the image of the road in Kafka's work he turns from the absurd to the mysterious. In a radio essay, 'A Note On Franz Kafka', broadcast in September 1951 Muir said:

> Imagine a sort of *Pilgrim's Progress* written like Bunyan's in the conviction that there is a right way and that it leads to salvation. Imagine at the same time that the hero has no real knowledge on which he can depend, does not know anything about 'the ways of God to men', and has to find out everything for himself; and you will have a rough and ready notion of Kafka's greatest allegorical novel, *The Castle*. Christian at least had sign-posts to guide him on his journey; but the sign-posts in Kafka's story are equivocal, may have several meanings, may even be put there to deceive the pilgrim. The very roads themselves are deceitful. The hero sets out one winter day for the Castle, the stronghold of salvation, but finds that though the road seems to be making for it, he never comes any nearer. In that little touch you have the quintessence of Kafka.[8]

The explicit comparison with Bunyan's *The Pilgrim's Progress* makes it clear that Muir sees *The Castle* as a great religious allegory, a work in which the realities of the road and the castle are the physical expression of the quest for an ultimate truth. But K's search is an agnostic quest. Pilgrim advances in a spirit of righteousness; indeed, an essential part of the drama of *The Pilgrim's Progress* is that the hero is persecuted because of his faith and that his salvation is a prize for valour. In contrast to this K has no faith; he cannot even trust the physical evidence on his journey, the ambiguous sign-posts and roads, but 'has to find out everything for himself'. K's journey, like long stretches of Muir's, is not just a search for the eternal order against which the temporal order can be seen but also a search for the temporal order itself; it is a pilgrimage on which the traveller is more aware of the penance of exile than the possibility of salvation.

In 'Franz Kafka' in *Essays On Literature And Society* Muir discusses the image of the road in Kafka's work:

> The image of a road comes into our minds when we think of his stories; for in spite of all the confusions and contradictions in which he was involved he held that life was a way, not a chaos, that the right way exists and can be found by a supreme and exhausting effort, and that whatever happens every human being follows some way, right or wrong.[9]

Here Muir moves immediately from the image of the road to the universal symbolism of life as a way, and then to the concept of 'the right way'. Muir and Kafka, responding independently to their separate experience, arrive at a vision of life—or rather, the belief that such a vision may exist—that is central to the great religions, Judaism, Christianity, Buddhism, and Islam.[10]

Muir continues:

> The road then is there; we may imagine beside it a wayside inn from which an anonymous figure is just emerging. He looks ahead and sees, perhaps on a distant hill, a shape which he has often seen before in his journey, but always far away,

and apparently inaccessible; that shape is justice, grace, truth, final reconciliation, father, God.[11]

Clearly, this comment on Kafka's work is equally true of Muir's own. In many of Muir's poems, especially in *Journeys And Places*, an anonymous figure looks ahead and sees a landscape re-defined by the concept of the way. But in these poems of the 1930s Muir has not yet gained a clear vision of the way, and the result is a series of poems that speak of yearning and disorientation. Some of the poems—'The Mountains', 'The Hill', 'The Road', 'Tristram's Journey', 'Hölderlin's Journey', 'The Solitary Place', 'The Unattained Place'—are so uncertain of the way that their landscapes are emblematic rather than symbolic or allegorical, static and ornamental views that lack the urgency of purpose of Muir's later poems on the journey. A feature that Muir detects in Kafka's work—the hero's uncertainty as to whether he is actually travelling or has become a fixed point in the landscape—is present in the poems in *Journeys And Places* and *Variations On A Time Theme*, and the interpretation Muir offers for Kafka is equally true of his own work:

> But the hero can neither reach it nor escape it, for it is enveloped in a mystery different from the ordinary mystery of human life, and he does not know the law of that mystery.

The further interpretation that Muir offers in the Kafka essay is yet again one that fits Muir's own work and also goes some way towards defining that element of uncertainty in the poems of the 1930s:

> The frustration of the hero is an intrinsic part of Kafka's theme; and it is caused by what in theological language is known as the irreconcilability of the divine and human law; a subtle yet immeasurable disparity.

It is this disparity between the human and the divine, the temporal and the eternal, that makes the shape on the distant hill—'justice, grace, truth, final reconciliation, father, God'—apparently inaccessible to Kafka and to Muir. In the comic drama of the road in *The Story And The Fable* the disparity is so great that the traveller loses sight of the shape on the hill and of the hill itself. But that passage was written before the moment of spontaneous revelation Muir experienced in the spring of 1939. The moment of revelation gradually became a lasting experience that informs many of the later poems, and a crucial stage in the long process of assimilation and acceptance can be traced in letters Muir wrote to friends in the 1940s after the publication of *The Story And The Fable*.

Writing to Alec Aitken, Professor of Mathematics at Edinburgh University, Muir discusses with remarkable clarity and detachment what he considers an incompleteness in his view of life:

> I find with some dismay, after going over my life, that I have no philosophy—here am I, a middle-aged man and a professional writer, and I have no philosophy. I had a philosophy when I was 27, but it was not my philosophy. I have no

philosophy now—that is no rational scheme for accounting for all the time I have lived in the world, or comprehensively for life itself. And this lack—which I must share with several million people—really does dismay me in some part of me, and gives me a troubling sense of insecurity. I believe that I am immortal, certainly, but that in a way makes it more difficult to interpret *this* life (in another way it makes it easier: I would be the last to deny that: if life were *only* this life, I would find it virtually impossible to find a meaning in it—moral or aesthetic).[12]

The immortality Muir speaks of is of course the immortality of the soul, and one can understand his dismay, his 'troubling sense of insecurity', at being so calmly assured of an afterlife while being uncertain about how to view his temporal life. But even as he confesses his confusion he begins to move towards an understanding of time and eternity, life and immortality. The understanding does not amount to a philosophy, nor does it, despite his faith, amount to a doctrine; rather it expresses the attitude of acceptance that makes possible the encompassing vision. The letter continues:

I suppose what I mean when I say I have no philosophy is that I have no explanation, none whatsoever, of Time except as an unofficial part of Eternity— no historical explanation of human life, for the problem of evil seems insoluble to me: I can only accept it as a mystery, and what a mystery is I do not know. All these thoughts have been roused (and clarified a little in my mind) by writing my life: there is very little in the book itself about them.

Here in the letter to Aitken, Muir is becoming aware of some of the attitudes of acceptance and acts of integration that underlie his mature poetry: the concept of time as a unofficial part of eternity, his acceptance of the fact that he has no historical explanation for human life, and his acceptance of the mystery. As the letter continues, Muir speaks of the central element of his faith, a force that is both creative and reconciling:

All I can say I have, confronted by these things, is faith, and I think that perhaps my faith is a little too easy, considering the enormity of these things. But faith can produce a sentence like: 'I am the resurrection and the life'. (It seems to me the most sublime sentence ever uttered, especially the order of the terms, the resurrection preceding the life, as if a real life only began with a resurrection, even in this world (and I believe this).) So that there may be something more in faith than we can account for, a source of energy and reconciliation which philosophy cannot reach. I do not know: I wish my mind were more single and clear.

The wish for a mind 'more single and clear' is an echo of the more urgently expressed longings discussed in the chapter, 'Against Time', but the letter to Aitken makes it clear that the acute crises of the earlier years have been resolved through the discovery, or re-discovery, of a faith that contains the belief that a real life in this world only begins with a resurrection.

Four years later, in March 1944, Muir raises some of the same issues in a letter to Stephen Spender. When he speaks of immortality now he does so with the quiet confidence of one for whom immortality is the unquestioned order of reality within which all other temporal orders are contained. Muir writes:

> I shall stick to my belief in immortality, I feel that it is involved with so many of our instinctive feelings, especially the feeling that we have free will, which is simply, I think, the feeling that, in spite of the fact that all our actions and thoughts are obviously determined by all the things around us, and by our position in time, we are not completely contained by these things, therefore that there is something else in us not dictated to by time. This may appear unconvincing to you; perhaps it is only convincing if one believes in immortality as I do.[13]

In the 1940 letter to Aitken, Muir raised a note of doubt and wished that his mind were more single and clear; here in the letter to Spender he rejects a certain kind of religious or philosophic clarity and instead accepts the problems of existence:

> The problems are terrifying, as you say. The religions exist, I suppose, to provide an explanation of them. I can't accept any religious explanation that I know of, any more than you. I would rather have the problems themselves, for from an awareness of them and their vastness I get some sort of living experience, some sense of communion, of being in the whole in some way, whereas from the explanations I should only get comfort and reassurance and a sense of safety which I know is not genuine.

Muir rejects the comfort, the reassurance and the safety in favour of the problems themselves, and through his acceptance of their vastness he gains a sense of communion. The communion he speaks of here, one feels, is not the abandonment of the May Day procession, not the ecstasy of merging one's identity in a joyful mass of humanity, but the communion of a man who, writing in a time war and with a knowledge of the horrors of war, identifies himself with the sufferers and sees that community of suffering, that common expression of the problem of evil, as more genuine and more acceptable than any religion that might explain the problem. This painful paradox of a communion in suffering that is part of the wholeness and continuity of the human journey is present in Muir's second poem on the theme of Israel in exile.

Moses, from *The Voyage* (1946),[14] again takes the exilic myth as its starting point, but in contrast to Section VI of the *Variations* it is a poem of awesome solemnity. It opens with Moses' vision of Canaan, a vision of ultimate fulfilment after the years of exile:

> He left us there, went up to Pisgah hill,
> And saw the holiday land, the sabbath land,
> The mild prophetic beasts, millenial herds,
> The sacred lintel, over-arching tree,
> The vineyards glittering on the southern slopes,
> And in the midst the shining vein of water,
> The river turning, turning towards its home.

Promised to us. The dream rose in his nostrils
With homely smell of wine and corn and cattle,
Byre, barn and stall, sweat-sanctified smell of peace.
He saw the ribes arrayed beside the river,
White robes and sabbath stillness, still light falling
On dark heads whitened by the desert wave,
The Sabbath of Sabbath come and Canaan their home.

The deliverance is complete in Moses' vision of a physical and spiritual homecoming in which the people inherit 'the sabbath land', 'millenial herds' and the 'sweat-sanctified smell of peace'. It is as if the wider state of exile that began with the fall is at an end; through penance and pilgrimage mankind has arrived at a second Eden.

But it is Moses' vision only. The people see instead the brutal realities of the time: 'The battle for the land, the massacres,/The vineyards drenched in aboriginal blood'. And then, in a natural, almost inevitable extension of the story, the Israelites become the Jews and at the same time the narrator, the characteristic collective voice, becomes the timeless victim and observer of the suffering:

We did not see and Moses did not see,
The great disaster, exile, diaspora,
The holy bread of the land crumbled and broken
In Babylon, Caeserea, Alexandria
And on a splendid dish, or gnawed as offal.

The story extends into the present century: 'the ghetto rising,/Toledo, Cracow, Vienna, Budapesth', and includes an image of the pilgrimage reduced to the hopelessness of the dispossessed 'wandering countless roads,/And not a road in the world to lead them home'.

These lost pilgrims in 'Moses', which first appeared in *The Listener* in November 1945, are almost certainly prompted by the memory of people Muir saw earlier that year when he drove across Europe to Prague. In *An Autobiography* he writes:

When we reached Germany there seemed to be nothing unmarked by the war: the towns in ruins, the roads and fields scarred and deserted. It was like a country where the population had become homeless, and when we met occasional family groups on the roads they seemed to be on a pilgrimage from nowhere to nowhere. In the towns and far out in the countryside we met them pushing their belongings on hand-carts, with a look of dull surprise on their faces. Few trains were running; the great machine was broken; and the men, but for the women and children following them, might have been the survivors of one of the mediaeval crusades wandering back across Europe to seek their homes. Now by all appearances there were no homes for them to seek.[15]

There is a profound irony, perhaps unintentional, in transposing the suffering and homelessness of the Germans in this passage in *An Autobiography* to the Jews in 'Moses'.

The closing lines in 'Moses', like those in Muir's other treatment of the exilic myth in Section VI of the *Variations*, speak of the inevitability of the suffering: 'All this was settled while we stood by Jordan/That first great day, could not be otherwise'. Here the inevitability is not only that of doctrinal predestination but also the narrator's resigned acceptance of evil as part of the human condition.

The final lines of 'Moses' briefly re-state the promise of Moses' vision:

> But now it stands becalmed in time for ever:
> White robes and sabbath peace, the snow-white emblem.

The suffering is contained within the peace, the problem of evil encompassed by the vision of eternity. The journey of the Jews in 'Moses' is a pilgrimage from one eternity to another, and yet the pain of the journey is so prolonged and intense that it threatens to overwhelm the closing image of peace that gives the pilgrimage its purpose and meaning. The state of grace and final reconciliation that Muir saw as the goal of Kafka's hero is not a permanent state but one that has to be rediscovered again and again throughout the journey. Similarly, the faith Muir found that evening in 1939 is not a fixed condition but one that comes and goes regardless of the will of man.

THE LOST WAY

Muir's vision of life is sustained by his faith in the immortality of the soul. His faith in turn is made possible by grace, the mysterious force which in Christian terms is seen as a divine intervention that reconciles the temporal and the eternal, the human and the divine, and in so doing reconciles man to his world, his fellow men and to his own self. But grace is unpredictable and beyond the control of man, and when grace is absent then faith ebbs and the vision fades. The human journey becomes the 'pilgrimage from nowhere to nowhere', a journey without purpose or destination through an incomprehensible landscape; the traveller feels lost and alone, spiritually and emotionally dispossessed.

The despair of the lost way is as inexplicable as the faith of the pilgrimage. It can be partly understood in terms of the failures and indignities and pains an individual may suffer, those patterns of experience that lead man to feel separate from his world, his fellow men and even from himself. Muir was aware of this separation and of the wider separation between time and eternity, but even when one tries to take account of these factors in Muir's experience of the lost way the essential nature of the experience, the encircling sense of irredeemable loss, is not finally explained. One can only conclude that the lost way—the loss of vision, faith and grace—is an inescapable and perhaps necessary stage on the journey. It is certainly a recurring stage in Muir's life and work.

In the first chapter of *An Autobiography* Muir recalls on occasion from his early childhood:

> And I had actually gone away into a world where every object was touched with fear, yet a world of the same size as the ordinary world and corresponding to it in every detail: a sort of parallel world divided by an endless, unbreakable sheet of glass from the actual world. For though my world was exactly the same in appearance as that world, I knew that I could not break through my fear to it, that I was invisibly cut off, and this terrified and bewildered me. The sense that I was in a blind place was always with me; yet that place was only a clear cloud or bubble surrounding me, from which I could escape at any moment by doing something; but what that was I did not know. My sister, playing in the sun a few feet away, was in that other world; my brothers cut and gathered the hay in it, the ships passed, the days followed one another in it. I could not reach it by getting close to it, though I often tried; for when my mother took me in her arms and laid my head on her shoulder she, so close to me, was in that world, and yet I was outside.[1]

The familiar has become the foreign. The figures who were the primary landmarks in the child's world—mother, sister, brothers—are inaccessible even in those moments of closest physical contact. The child is completely isolated and cannot find his way back into the family from which he is estranged.

Muir describes this childhood experience as a 'passion of fear and guilt', and he associates these feelings with a sack of poisonous sheep dip his father had left in a field and with his father's warning that the sack must not be touched. The idea that he may have touched it accidentally, thus disobeying his father and also running the risk of poisoning himself, seems inadequate to explain the intensity of the fear; the child's sense of separation is like that of someone who has become the bearer of a terrible secret, shameful, incommunicable to others, and inadmissible to himself. One imagines that what Muir experienced was an extreme version of an otherwise normal childhood crisis, an abrupt extension of consciousness with a loss of some of the innocence of unconscious childhood. Incommunicable and inadmissible, the knowledge was like a taboo secretly broken, dividing him from his family and, since he did not have enough conscious experience to allow him to assimilate the knowledge, dividing him from himself.

Muir's sensation of being isolated and overwhelmed by the enormity of his fear is not simply a childhood experience. Some twenty years later when he was working in the bone factory in Greenock, the Fairport of the *Autobiography*, he experienced a similar version of the fear:

> During my years in Fairport I had experienced now and then an anxious vague dread which I could not explain or attach to any object. Its real cause, I feel pretty certain, was my work in the bone-yard. This state now grew worse, or I became more conscious of it, realizing that it was bound up with my feeling of separation and yearning . . . It was as if I could grasp what was before my eyes only by an enormous effort, and even then an invisible barrier, a wall of distance, separated me from it. I moved in a crystalline globe or bubble, insulated from the life around me, yet filled with desire to reach it, to be at the very heart of it and lose myself there.[2]

The separation and the loss may have been caused partly by Muir's work in the bone factory, and partly by the grief and anxiety he still felt after the deaths of his parents and his brothers, but one suggests that the essential experience cannot be explained in purely biographical terms. The lost way is the common, recurring experience of fallen man and may be felt more acutely by those who have a sense of the right way, a sense of the journey as pilgrimage.

The lost way of the child on the island of Wyre and of the young man in Greenock is the same as that of Jeremiah who cried:

> He hath set me in dark places, as they that be dead of old. He hath hedged me about, that I cannot get out: he hath made my chain heavy. Also when I cry and shout he shutteth out my prayer. He hath inclosed my ways with hewn stone, he hath made my paths crooked.[3]

And a similar experience is recalled by Traherne, whose views of childhood Muir came to share.[4] In section 23 of the Third Century Traherne writes:

> Another time, in a Lowering and sad Evening, being alone in the field, when all things were dead and quiet, a certain Want and Horror fell upon me, beyond imagination. The unprofitableness and Silence of the Place dissatisfied me, its Wideness terrified me, from the utmost Ends of the Earth fears surrounded me. How did I know but Dangers might suddainly arise from the East, and invade me from the unknown Regions beyond the Seas?[5]

Traherne's account begins in dismay but ends in faith: 'I was made to hold a Communion with the Secrets of Divine Providence in all the World: that a Remembrance of all the Joys I had from my Birth ought always to be with me.' Jeremiah too is certain of his salvation but Muir is always closer to doubt than to certainty, and he is never far from the experience of the lost way.

One of his poems on this theme briefly recalls that early childhood crisis. 'The Solitary Place',[6] which first appeared in 1935 as 'I and not I', opens with one of Muir's characteristically pastoral images of fulfilment, an image that is probably prompted by memories of childhood and also anticipates the great image of fulfilment in the later poem, 'Moses'. In 'The Solitary Place' Muir writes:

> I have known
> The mead, the bread,
> And the mounds of grain
> As half my riches.

It is only half the poet's riches because the vision is incomplete:

> But I can never
> See with these eyes the double-threaded river
> That runs through life and death and death and life,
> Weaving one scene.

The unity of vision cannot be attained, the poet suggests, because he, or more generally mankind, is trapped in his incomplete identity, the 'I and not I', which prevents him from giving full recognition to others and to the world and so makes communion impossible:

> If all that I see,
> Woman and man and beast and rock and sky,
> Is a flat image shut behind an eye, . . .
> O then I am alone,
> I, many and many in one.

And in the closing lines of 'The Solitary Place' there is the memory of the terrible isolation of the waking nightmare he experienced as a child:

A lost player upon a hill
On a sad evening when the world is still,
The house empty, brother and sister gone
Beyond the reach of sight, or sound of any cry,
Into the bastion of the mind, behind the shutter of the eye.

The poem opens with an image of fulfilment drawn from Muir's childhood in Orkney, and ironically it closes with an image of solitary desolation drawn from the same period. The solitary place of the title is clearly the incomplete self of the poet who cannot achieve communion with the world, and the incomplete vision that cannot see the 'double-threaded river', that is, the force that brings the temporal and the eternal into unity.

In the Introduction to the collection, *Journeys And Places*, in which 'The Solitary Place' appeared in 1937, Muir wrote: 'The Journeys and Places in this collection should be taken as having a rough-and-ready psychological connotation rather than a strict temporal or spatial one.'[7] But Muir discussed the poem in rather different terms in his letter to Stephen Spender in September 1935:

The theme of the poem, especially of the second part of it ('if there is none else to ask reply', etc.) was, as I consciously saw it, the modern historical view of the world, in which there is no reality except the development of humanity—humanity being in that case merely an I and not I, a sort of long and interminable monologue of many. This view of the world has always repelled me very deeply and even horrified me—though I have only recently been able to explain partially to myself why. The question I ask myself in the poem is whether there is not some reality outside this I and not I (that is humanity in its historical development). My own deepest feeling is that there is . . . My own feeling is that in allowing ourselves to adopt a purely historical view of human life we are losing half of it; for history too is a sort of substitution of the technique of existence for the content.[8]

The letter expresses Muir's continuing quest for a vision of existence that encompasses more than the historical, and the letter indicates—'My own deepest feeling is that there is'—that he has begun to find the faith that might sustain such a vision. But although the letter reflects Muir's preoccupation at a critical period in the development of his faith, it does not fully represent the poem. The abstract, impersonal language of the letter contrasts with the physical imagery of the poem and with the intensely human nature of the drama in which the poet directly confronts the problems of identity, communion and vision. And the letter clearly suggests a possible resolution of the crises through the adoption of a suprahistorical vision whereas the poem ends with the poet isolated and trapped in the lost way.

Towards the end of the letter Muir writes: 'This is a long rigmarole to set down in explanation of my poem; but the poem is only part of an argument that I hope to carry on, if I have good luck.' The argument in which he is engaged is no less than the dialogue between the historical and the eternal, the human and the divine, in an attempt to unify these orders. The argument continues, but the good luck Muir hopes for is as elusive and unpredictable as faith. The next stage of the argument—finding a route from the lost way of the solitary place to the right way of the pilgrimage—proves to be a painful and dangerous experience.

THE BRIDGE OF DREAD

'The Solitary Place' brings together the questions of identity, vision and communion, suggesting that the incompleteness of man's identity, and of Muir's individual identity, is associated with an incompleteness of vision that prevents man from seeing the unity of the temporal and eternal orders of being, and this double incompleteness of self and of vision prevents man from establishing a true communion even with the temporal world. Answering the question of identity becomes essential for the continuation of the journey and for any study of Muir.

Muir was acutely aware of unanswered questions of identity and knew the incompleteness was not a uniquely personal circumstance but a wider human condition. Some events in his life—the dislocation of the move from Orkney to Glasgow followed by the deaths of his parents and brothers—prolonged and intensified the crisis, but the previous chapter of this study suggests that the first episode of the crisis occurred in his early childhood at a time of emotional security. The problem of self cannot be expressed in purely biographical or causal terms; the problem is the common inheritance of mankind, so common that it may go undetected by many people and accepted as a normal condition by others. Few people, one suspects, ever solve the problem for any length of time so as to achieve a wholeness of self that they can recognise as their familiar state of being. Solving the problem is not a matter of will or determination but rather, as Muir came to believe, the healing power of grace or, in psychological terms, the healing power of the unconscious mind.

Just such terms were used by the man who psychoanalysed Muir in 1919.[1] At the time he was treating Muir, Maurice Nicholl had just published *Dream Psychology* and was already preparing the second edition in which writes:

> Finally, I believe that we find in the unconscious material—in the dream—a typical doctrine or tendency, which is not unrelated to the central teaching of many religions. I believe that doctrine or tendency to be relative to the necessity of the development of individuality—the rebirth of self from collective values to individual ones.[2]

Nicoll makes the link between the unconscious and the rebirth of self, and he makes the further link between the psychological concept of the rebirth of self and 'the central teaching of many religions'. Nicoll does not specify the central teaching but his statement seems to imply a doctrine of resurrection or immortality. (His reference to religion is in contrast with the recollections of Muir[3] and Willa Muir[4] who say that Nicoll dismissed and even ridiculed a possible religious content in Muir's dreams.) Later in *Dream Psychology* Nicoll speaks of the unconscious as an 'entelechy', a power that brings a condition to its realisation, even to perfection, and he goes on to say of the unconscious: 'It has an aim that is corrective, healing or developmental, just as the forces governing the physical body have these aims.'[4]

Like Jung, whose influence he acknowledges, Nicoll is more concerned with the therapeutic than the pathological qualities of the unconscious, and the Jungians openly speak of the unconscious in mythological and religious terms. But even psychologists who offer a less numinous interpretation of dreams than Jung also find the therapeutic force at work. J A Hadfield writes of the unconscious 'process of restoration', of sleep and dreams 'working towards a state of readjustment and equilibrium', of 'the urge to completeness', and that 'the process of readjustment goes on quite apart from our being conscious of our dreams or from any interpretation'.[5]

If one accepts Nicoll's view that the unconscious 'has an aim that is corrective, healing and developmental', and Hadfield's view that there is an unconscious 'urge to completeness', then one may accept that even on the most bewildering stretches of the lost way the unconscious may retain a sense of direction and purpose, that this may reveal itself to the traveller through sleep and dreams, and that this healing purpose, even if it is not revealed to the conscious mind, may still exercise an influence on the traveller's destination. The occasion on the evening in February 1939, when Muir found himself reciting the Lord's Prayer,[6] suggests that such a force was at work in him.

Out of the crisis in his life comes the new vision of the journey, as if an image of the way has been forming unconsciously in his mind and is induced into consciousness by the crisis. This is the pattern of the poems, 'The Narrow Place', 'The Grove', 'The Escape' and 'The Bridge Of Dread', where the increasing desolation of the lost way leads to the turning point at which, sometimes inexplicably, the right way presents itself.

This is the poet's hope in 'The Narrow Place',[7] the title poem of the 1943 collection, which has the same 'rough-and-ready psychological connotation' as some of the poems in *Journeys And Places*. The poem expresses a state of mind and spirit rather than a landscape. The opening image is one of constriction: 'How all the roads lead in', and to this is added the desolation of the lines: 'For nothing comes and goes/But the bleak mountain wind'. The later line: 'And no road goes by', confirms the impression that 'The Narrow Place' is another poem of the lost way, and then, with the introduction of the image of the tree—'Only one little wild half-leafless tree', but one that will grow to become a powerful symbol in Muir's later work—he introduces a suggestion of comfort and hope as the people of the lost way sleep underneath the tree.

In the final section of the poem Muir reaches towards an understanding of the problems of self and vision:

Sleep underneath the tree.
It is your murdering eyes that make
The sterile hill, the standing lake,
And the leaf-breaking wind.

It is this negative vision of life, a vision based on consciousness only, that shuts out the world and shuts in the traveller. And the poem ends with this possibility:

Then shut your eyes and see,
Sleep on and do not wake
Till there is movement in the lake,
And the club-headed water-serpents break
In emerald lightnings through the slime,
Making a mark on Time.

The new vision that will allow him to escape from the lost way will come through sleep and the unconscious. The image of agitation, the 'movement in the lake', suggests a stirring in the unconscious mind; the water serpents that break through the slime can be taken to represent a crossing over from the unconscious to consciousness, so that the serpents symbolise a different form of knowledge or wisdom; and the 'emerald lightings' suggest a new energy and brilliance. All this will make 'a mark on Time' because a timeless element in the unconscious mind will become part of the traveller's consciousness; the temporal will be transmuted by the eternal.

The symbolic argument of 'The Narrow Place' is that the journey within the journey, the pasage through the narrow place of the mind and spirit, is a stage that must be undergone if the traveller is to have any chance of finding the vision that will transform the journey into a pilgrimage. This route from the lost way is a rite of passage, a psychological and spiritual ordeal that precedes the pilgrimage.[8] But the ordeal is not a single, once-and-for-all event; it is a recurring, symbolic act in several poems on the theme of the journey within the journey.

In some poems the ordeal is a more positive act of confrontation than the sleep of 'The Narrow Place'. 'The Grove', as the title indicates, stages the confrontation in a wood; 'The Escape' proceeds from images of the lost way, the maze and the web to a symbolic encounter at a border between two states; 'The Bridge Of Dread' ends with the crossing of that border. The symbols change from poem to poem but a common factor in each is that the traveller has reached a critical stage in his journey and that he can advance only by risking everything in the ordeal. This critical stage in the psychological journey can be seen as the act of acknowledging the 'personal unconscious', that area of repressed desires and guilts and impulses that may be amoral rather than actively evil; in religious terms it may be seen as the renunciation of personal will and personal identity in the attempt to discover a divine will and identity. The great risk is that the person who crosses over from a purely conscious identity to the unconscious does not know what he may find on the other side and does not know if, having seen the other side, he can return safely to his original state, or return at all. But the risk has to be taken because paradoxically it is personal identity, the features that make the person an individual, that separate him from his fellow men, from his god and from dimensions of his own self.

Of this passing through the personal unconscious Jung writes:

> The meeting with oneself is, at first, the meeting with one's own shadow. The shadow is a tight passage, a narrow door, whose painful constriction no one is spared who goes down to the deep well. But one must learn to know oneself in order to know who one is.[9]

The shadow is the narrow place, the grove, the border, the bridge of dread that Muir must cross in order to draw from 'the deep well' that is the healing power of the unconscious. On the way to the well he must acknowledge much that his conscious mind would normally deny, and 'The Grove'[10] makes this acknowledgement.

The poem moves immediately into the world of the unconscious:

> There was no road at all to that high place
> But through the smothering grove,
> Where as we went the shadows wove
> Adulterous shapes of animal hate and love.

The 'high place' of the first line, a recurring landmark in Muir's poems of the journey, is the vantage point that would allow the traveller a wider view of the journey, that is, an elevated spiritual state that brings with it a new clarity of vision. But the only way to achieve this vision is to pass through 'the smothering grove' in which the shadows and the 'shapes of animal hate and love' are aspects of the traveller's own shadow, his personal unconscious. Entering the grove, the traveller steps into a splendid, glittering world:

> The scarlet cardinals,
> And lions high in the air on the banner's field,
> Crowns, sceptres, spears and stars and moons of blood.

But the grove of the scarlet cardinals, the golden dukes, the silver earls, the curvetting knights and the silk-tunicked eunuchs is also a world marked by 'The first great Luciferian animal', and animals are equal inhabitants of the grove:

> The well-bred self-sufficient animals
> With clean rank pelts and proud and fetid breath,
> Screaming their arrogant calls,
> Their moonstone eyes set straight at life and death.

The cities and civilisations that exist 'deep in the forest', the powers and dominations, are not the achievements of man but are:

Like shapes begotten by dreaming animals,
Proud animal dreams uplifted high.

In making his way through the grove the traveller enters his personal unconscious where he finds a world of animal impulses and a civilisation with an
animal ancestry. In acknowledging the co-existence of the two, the animal
and the human, plutonic and historic, Muir admits the inadmissible and
breaks the power of the secret. A sense of guilt and separation may recur,
but the traveller has endured the ordeal of the passage from a world of time
and consciousness to the unconscious realm on the edge of time.

Muir's grove is a version of the sacred mythological grove. In Frazer's
account of the myth of the Grove of Nemi, whoever killed the priest of the
grove became himself the priest.[11] Although the original myth may contain
other symbolic elements—a trace of totemism or even parricide[12]—it is clear
that the myth contains the ideas of confrontation and ordeal, of death and
regeneration. In Muir's grove the poet confronts his animal ancestry and the
animal impulses that survive in his personal unconscious; he briefly sacrifices
his consciousness and humanity, and when he emerges from the grove he
knows that he has completed a necessary stage on the journey within the
journey, the route that leads to the pilgrimage.

The release from the grove of the poem is unexplained:

We trod the maze like horses in a mill.
And then passed through it
As in a dream of the will.

Although the final section of 'The Grove' is less satisfying as poetry than the
vivid, disturbing earlier sections, the closing lines are psychologically true;
the poet's necessary ordeal is to make his way through the grove of the
unconscious, and the successful completion of the ordeal brings release into
consciousness and light. The final lines of the poem express the knowledge
that only through ordeal can there be release:

We know
There was no road except the smothering grove.

A later poem of crisis, 'The Escape'[13] from *The Voyage* of 1946, opens with
the traveller in a landscape that lies between the despair of the lost way and
the impending decision of the narrow place or the grove. The second stanza
reads:

The endless trap lay everywhere,
    And all the roads ran in a maze
Hither and thither, like a web
    To catch the careless days.

One notes again the image of the maze, an ancient symbol of the lost way
and of the penitential element of pilgrimage; the image reflects the physical

reality of certain stages of the journey and also the traveller's state of mind. Paradoxically, visual images of the maze can be similar to images of the Christian rose or the Buddhist mandala, symbols of completeness and perfection; it is as if the maze, once it has been negotiated, can be seen as the rose. Indeed, Christian ritual once included the walking of a maze to symbolise pilgrimage.[14]

In the third stanza of 'The Escape' the landscape becomes familiar, with features that Muir uses elsewhere as symbols of fruition, but here in 'the enemy's vast domain' the symbols have lost their meaning:

> There was no promise in the bud,
>   No comfort in the blossoming tree,
> The waving yellow harvests were
>   Worse than sterility.

The poet's sense of alienation from the landscape reminds one of the experiences of separation he records in the *Autobiography*; here he goes further and suggests that the harvest is the enemy's harvest, the fruit of time, and since it cannot be enjoyed it is worse than sterility. At the centre of the poem the traveller seems to approach the ordeal and steels himself for the decision:

> And when I reached the line between
>   The Occupied and the Unoccupied,
> It was as hard as death to cross . . .

The pattern of development in this poem and others leads one to believe that the 'death' will be followed by a rebirth, but the poet finds 'no change on the other side./All false, all one.' The moment of false decision leads to the indecision of 'What is escape? and What is flight?' until the poet realises that the 'frontier line' lies 'Beyond the region of desire'. In that ultimate region beyond the reach of human will 'There runs a wall of towering flame'. But even the wall of flame is not the ordeal, and the poem ends:

> I must pass through that fiery wall,
>   Emerge into the battle place,
> And there at last, lifting my eyes,
>   I'll see the enemy's face.

'The Escape' operates at a level between metaphor and symbolism. It suggests that man's existence in time is fugitive, like that of someone seeking escape from enemy territory. Although there are pleasing landscapes in that territory the fugitive is so obsessed with the need to escape that he cannot enjoy these places. His wilful attempt at the ordeal and escape is followed by greater confusion and indecision until he realises that at some extreme limit of experience—'the very frontier line'—there will be a painful and dangerous encounter that leads not to the longed-for escape and the encompassing vision that unifies time and eternity but rather to a simpler clarity of vision that will allow him to face the reality of his temporal condition. The escape of the title is not release *from* the world but *into* it.

The later poem, 'The Bridge Of Dread'[15] from *The Labyrinth* of 1949, opens with the traveller on the very edge of the ordeal:

> But when you reach the Bridge of Dread
> Your flesh will huddle into its nest
> For refuge and your naked head
> Creep in the casement of your breast.

Despite his shrinking fear, the traveller continues across the bridge, observing his own progress with the slow-motion awareness of autoscopic detachment—like Hector in 'Ballad Of Hector In Hades'—as the mind seems to disengage from the body at the moment of greatest danger:

> While dazed you watch your footsteps crawl
> Toadlike across the leagues of stone.

The object of the fear and the real nature of the ordeal is unknown; 'bodily terror' in the form of 'Great knotted serpents' would be accepted 'as a grace' instead of the nameless dread. It is at that moment of extreme fear, and with the pivotal line, 'You would accept it as a grace', that the traveller sees the mysterious sign, as if the extremity of his fear along with the words 'accept' and 'grace' had induced the sign:

> Until you see a burning wire
> Shoot from the ground. As in a dream
> You'll wonder at that flower of fire,
> That weed caught in a burning beam.

The vision of the 'flower of fire' is like the vision Moses experienced during his time in Midian:

And the angel of the Lord appeared unto him in a flame of fire out of the midst of a bush: and he looked, and, behold, the bush burned with fire, and the bush was not consumed.[16]

For Moses the burning bush symbolises the angel of the Lord; Muir's flower of fire is less explicit as a symbol, but for Muir as for Moses it is an intimation of deliverance that brings the ordeal in 'The Bridge Of Dread' to an end:

> And you are past. Remember then,
> Fix deep within your dreaming head
> Year, hour or endless moment when
> You reached and crossed the Bridge of Dread.

Once again the resolution of the crisis in unexplained. The phrases, 'As in a dream' and 'your dreaming head', seem almost too decorative to suggest the powers of the unconscious mind and yet—since 'The Grove', 'The Escape' and 'The Bridge Of Dread' all end with the traveller finding himself inexplicably released from the crisis—one must conclude that these elliptical endings express the nature of the transformation as Muir experiences it. The change is not a conscious process of transition that can be analysed and explained but rather a change of state like an awakening.

The act of crossing the bridge takes the traveller to the other side of the crisis and so takes him to a further stage on the journey within the journey than the point he reaches at the end of 'The Escape'. The bridge of the poem is the symbolic passage from one state of mind, one state of being, to another, and it is a bridge of dread because the new state is the unknown. The crossing of the bridge is a crucial stage on the route from the lost way to the pilgrimage, from the incomplete self to the possibility of wholeness. The transformation is more adequately expressed in symbols than in explanation, and Muir's symbol of the bridge of dread with its connotations of a last judgement and the link between life and death—the symbol and the connotation probably borrowed by Muir, who knew the ballads well, from 'A Lyke-Wake Dirge'— express both the momentous and inexplicable nature of the transformation.

It is almost certain that Muir knew the 'Brig o' Dread' in 'A Lyke-Wake Dirge'; he may also have known Freud's comment[17] on the bridge symbol in *The Interpretation Of Dreams*: 'In the same way many landscapes in dreams, especially any containing bridges or wooded hills, may clearly be recognised as descriptions of the genitals.'[18] The Jungian psychologist Gerhard Adler, one of the editors of Jung's *Collected Works*, offers the more helpful comment that the bridge symbol indicates an impending decision.[19] But a more revealing comment comes from an apparently remote source.

In *The Story And The Fable* Muir writes: 'There is surely no writing about the soul more wonderful than some of the *Upanishads*.'[20] And in one of the *Upanishads*, the *Chandogya*, appears the passage:

There is a bridge between time and Eternity; and this bridge is Atman, the Spirit of man. Neither day nor night cross that bridge, nor old age, nor death nor sorrow.

Evil or sin cannot cross that bridge, because the world of the Spirit is pure. This is why when this bridge has been crossed, the eyes of the blind can see, the wounds of the wounded are healed, and the sick man becomes whole from his sickness.

To one who goes over that bridge, the night becomes like unto day; because in the worlds of the Spirit there is a Light which is everlasting.[21]

The bridge of the *Chandogya* is Muir's bridge of dread. It is the spirit of man, his soul, his greater self, which unifies time and eternity. In the new spiritual state on the other side of the bridge the blind can see, the wounded man is healed and the sick man made whole; the negative vision of the incomplete self is cleansed and clarified so that things unknown become part of his consciousness as 'night becomes like unto day'; and in the 'Light which is everlasting' the unity of the temporal and the eternal, of the human and the divine, is revealed to the traveller.

Muir's poems, his *Autobiography* and to some extent his letters show that the act of crossing the bridge of dread is not a single event but a recurring ordeal in his life. His work shows too that on the other side of the bridge he did not enjoy an immediate and permanent transformation into the new state of being; instead, he had to rediscover that state—either by searching for it or through the equally demanding discipline of waiting patiently for its return—many times in his life. But it is only when he crosses the bridge that he achieves his great vision and his great poetry.

THREE MYSTERIES

On the other side of the bridge of dread Muir sees that his personal journey is part of the continuum of the human journey that spans time and space from origin to end. This extended vision of the journey is most fully expressed in the great prophetic poem, 'The Journey Back', in several sections of which the vision is transcendental and teleological, expressing a mythological and at times a mystical journey from its eternal origin to its eternal end. But Muir never loses sight of the actual, temporal journey, and he remains fascinated by the patterns of pilgrimage, both individual and archetypal, that emerge from his own life.

In his prose too he searches for an idea of the journey in which the personal biographical pattern can be seen in terms of the evolution of the race. And throughout his prose, from *We Moderns* to *The Estate Of Poetry*, Muir's idea of the journey brings together the moral and prophetic elements, the concern for the nature of man's existence in the temporal world as well as for the immortality of man's soul. At an early stage in *An Autobiography* he writes:

> Our minds are possessed by three mysteries: where we came from, where we are going, and, since we are not alone, but members of a countless family, how we should live with one another. These questions are aspects of one question, and none of them can be separated from the others and dealt with alone.[1]

This statement of the three mysteries follows an account of a dream in which a Christ-like figure summons the sleeping Muir to join 'a confused crowd of other men and women in curious or ragged clothes' to a field filled with animals that 'raised their heads with the inevitability of the sun's rising, as if they knew, like the sun, that a new day was about to begin.' Muir says of the dream, one of many he experienced at the time of his psychoanalysis:

> There were Millenial airs in that dream, or, in the analyst's words, themes from the racial unconscious. But there was also in it something of my first few years; the hills were the little green hills of childhood; the figure who appeared by my bedside was a childish image of Christ; and the event itself, the Millenium, had often been discussed by my father and mother at the Bu after a reading of the Reverend Doctor Baxter, while I listened and almost without knowing it fashioned my own delightful pictures, long since forgotten.[2]

Here in the autobiography, written more than thirty years after the dream,

Muir reveals an assimilation process that is at once both natural and extremely complex. His sense of himself contains the child near the beginning of life, and the young man who was the dreamer of the dream, and the old man who recalls the dream some five years before his death. The setting of the dream is the millenium, the end of the earthly journey and the beginning of an eternal one, and yet the setting is also the Orkney landscape that was the beginning of Muir's personal journey. In the dream, and more importantly in his conscious recalling and interpreting of it, all these things are assimilated. The origin and end of the race, the death and resurrection of mankind, the association of humans and animals in one congregation, and a clear image of himself as a participant in these events—all this is expressed in the account.

On the other side of the bridge of dread Muir can see the end of the journey both as *finis* and *telos*,[3] death and resurrection; the dread of mortality and the obsession with time is over, and the idea of the greater journey prevails. But the mystery of where we are going, says Muir, is inseparable from the mystery of where we have come from.

This search for origins is one that begins in his first book, *We Moderns*, where in a long examination of the concept of original sin he writes:

> Or again, may not the myth be an attempt to glorify Man and to clothe him with a sad splendour? And not Original Sin, but Original Innocence is the true reading of the fable? Its *raison d'etre* is the Garden of Eden, not the Fall? To glorify Humanity at its source it set there a Superman. The fall from innocence—that was the fall from Superman into Man. And how, then, is Man to be redeemed? By the return of the Superman! Let that be our reading of the Myth![4]

The sense of urgency in this passage, with its prose style of short sentences, questions and exclamations, is partly the urgency of the author urging ideas on himself as a willed belief. The Muir of *We Moderns* longed for some intervening power that would glorify man and clothe him in splendour, even sad splendour, and for a time Muir thought he had found that power in the Nietzschean Superman. But the passage is more than a piece of wishful thinking by the young Muir. He expresses a genuine sense of intellectual excitement and discovery as he argues that the real purpose of the Biblical myth is to show that man has his origins in the innocence and timelessness of Eden rather than in the fallen world outside Eden.

The first Superman in the passage from *We Moderns* is of course Adam who, as a result of the fall, is transformed from an archetypal being into a mortal. The second Superman is Nietzsche's, the monstrous hero-figure created from a deification of the will and a rejection of those qualities that make man vulnerable and truly human. But a year after the publication of *We Moderns* Muir was freed from Nietzsche's influence. His marriage, his move to London, the psychoanalysis that released the healing power of his unconscious mind and gave him the insights that became part of his growing vision of life—these changes helped Muir to accept his humanity and to begin his gradual acceptance of Christianity. In his dream of the millenium he sees that if man is to be redeemed from the fall then it will not be 'By the return of the Superman' but by the arrival of a Christ-like archetype.

Even with its Nietzschean elements, the passage in *We Moderns* suggests that Muir sensed that man's origin and end were inseparable mysteries. On the same page of *We Moderns* in a brief section titled 'The Use Of Myth' he links the mysteries yet again:

> In the early world myth was used to dignify Man by idealizing his origin. Henceforward it must be used to dignify him by idealizing his goal. *That* is the task of the poets and artists.[5]

Here again the language has an almost religious intensity. The glory and the dignity Muir speaks of in these two passages, the idealising of man's origin and end, is an expression of Muir's longing for the restoration of dignity in his personal life which had been made almost meaningless by the enormity of his loss during the years in Glasgow, but at the same time the two statements show the universal scope of his imagination as he reaches to the extremes of the human journey that can be expressed only in mythological terms.

Much of *We Moderns* reflects Muir's search for a meaning in his own life and in the temporal existence of mankind. Even at this early stage he sees that a meaning can be found only in the context of a myth that will 'glorify humanity at its source' and idealise man's origin and goal; that is, man will find meaning in life only when he sees life as a stage between one form of perfection and another. It is a search not just for dignity but for a complete pattern that encompasses the origin and destination of the race, a search that is an underlying theme in the novel, *The Three Brothers*, of 1931 and to a lesser extent in the autobiographical novel, *Poor Tom*, published in the following year.

Muir began to see the outline of the pattern when he wrote the first version of his autobiography, *The Story And The Fable*. Shortly after its appearance in 1940 Muir published the essay, 'Yesterday's Mirror—Afterthoughts To An Autobiography', which is both an extension of *The Story And The Fable* and a fascinating insight into autobiography as a form. The essay begins:

> I wrote my autobiography some time ago. While I was working at it I tried to make clear the pattern of my life as a human being existing in space and moving through time, environed in mystery.[6]

The phrase, 'environed in mystery', shows that Muir believes the pattern extends beyond the limits of time and space. But the pattern is difficult to trace, and he adds:

> After I had finished I went over the manuscript many times, seeking to make the pattern clearer, and felt like a man with an inefficient torch stumbling through a labyrinth, having forgotten where he entered and not knowing where he would come out.

The obscurity of the pattern prompts the metaphor of the labyrinth, which in this case represents the complex literary and emotional task of editing a life into an autobiography as well as the confused journey from beginning to end. Muir seems to admit defeat when he continues:

> To write a book describing one human being is strictly an impossibility; for what we require for real self-knowledge is the power to stop the sun and make it revolve in the opposite direction, taking us back stage by stage through manhood and youth to childhood, missing nothing until it conducts us to the mystery from which we started.[7]

The impossibility Muir speaks of is the double one of throwing time into reverse and of taking the final backward step from childhood to 'the mystery from which we started', from biography to myth.

It is a step Muir takes many times in the poems, including the early poems, and yet in *The Story And The Fable* and in 'Yesterday's Mirror' he writes as if he were unaware of what he has achieved in poetry or as if he were unwilling in his prose work to acknowledge that as a poet he has begun to penetrate the mystery. There are times when it seems that Muir's poetic imagination, which is always open to the wisdom of dreams and the unconscious mind, is familiar with realms that are less well known to the rational intellect of Muir the prose writer. With the publication of *An Autobiography* in 1954 the knowledge becomes admissible, although the admission seems strangely delayed.

Muir and his wife lived in Dresden for a few months in 1922, and in the autobiography he recalls:

> There during the hot, idle summer I seemed at last to recover from the long illness that had seized me when, at fourteen, I came to Glasgow . . . I went over my life in that resting space, like a man who after travelling a long, featureless road suddenly realizes that, at this point or that, he had noticed almost without knowing it, with the corner of his eye, some extraordinary object, some rare treasure, yet in his sleep-walking had gone on, consciously aware only of the blank road flowing back beneath his feet . . . so that life I had wasted was returned to me.[8]

As the Dresden idleness continued, Muir found more and more of his life returned to him in a healing process of self-discovery:

> I looked, and what I saw was myself as I had lived up to that moment when I could turn my head. I had been existing, to use Holms's phrase, merely as something which consisted of 'the words with which one tries to explain it'; so that when at last I looked back at that life which, whatever I might think of it, was the life I knew best, it seemed to me that I was not seeing my own life merely, but all human life, and I became conscious of it as a strange and unique process.[9]

The vision extends from the personal to the universal, from the individual self to the self as everyman, and as the process of restoration continues so the vision extends from the temporal to the timeless:

> In turning my head and looking *against* the direction in which time was hurrying me I won a new kind of experience; for now that I no longer marched in step with time I could see life timelessly, and with that in terms of the imagination. I felt, though I had not the ability to express it, what Proust describes in *Le Temps Retrouvé*. 'A moment liberated from the order of time' seemed actually to have re-created in me 'a man to feel it who was also freed from the order of time.'[10]

Recalling in the 1950s that Dresden summer of 1922, Muir achieves what he describes as impossible in *The Story And The Fable*: he reverses the order of time until he moves back from biography to myth, from time into timelessness, from childhood to 'the mystery from which we started'. This act of the imagination is itself a mystery that fascinated Muir; he refers to it as 'a mind within our minds which cannot rest until it has worked out, even against our conscious will, the unresolved questions of our past'.[11]

He is speaking of the healing power of the unconscious mind that takes no account of space or time, makes no division between history and myth or between the individual and the race. It operates, Muir says, 'even against our conscious will', but one feels that the power operates effectively to grant its wisdom only to those conscious minds that recognise the value of some of the messages from the unconscious. These relevations from the mind within the mind are so powerful, Muir writes, that they give meaning to life:

> These solutions of the past projected into the present, deliberately announced as if they were sybilline declarations that life has a meaning, impress me more deeply than any other kind of experience with the conviction that life does have a meaning quite apart from the thousand meanings which the conscious mind attributes to it: an unexpected and yet incontestable meaning which runs in the teeth of ordinary experience, perfectly coherent, yet depending on a different system of connected relations from that by which we consciously live.[12]

In his prose accounts of three mysteries, especially the mysteries of man's origin and end, Muir offers an interpretation of experience; in the poems of origin and end he offers the experience itself. Although some poems lack the elegance and authority of the prose they convey an immediacy and authenticity of experience, even in their occasional awkwardnesses. This is not to argue that Muir is less of a craftsman in his poems nor that his approach to poetry is always different from his approach to prose, but in the two forms— poetry and prose—he seems consistently to operate at different levels of the imagination; where the prose offers a considered recollection of a dream or a reflection on a myth, the poems re-create the dream and participate in the myth.

The outstanding example of this participation without apparent reflection is the mythopoeic poem, 'Ballad Of The Soul'; Muir returns to the mysteries of man's origin and end in 'The Stationary Journey', 'The Mythical Journey' and 'The Fall' in *Journeys And Places* in 1937, and in two of his great poems, 'The Labyrinth' and 'The Journey Back' in *The Labyrinth* in 1949.

The opening lines of 'The Stationary Journey'[13] express the obsession with time that tormented Muir throughout the 1930s. He feels he might be released from the tyranny of time if he could only see far enough back into the past, and in the following stanzas he retraces history—Charlemagne, Saint Augustine, the Pharaohs—until he imagines himself on the edge of time-lessness:

> So, back or forward, still we strike
>> Through time and touch its dreaded goal.
> Eternity's the fatal flaw
>> Through which run out world, life and soul.

The journey back leads paradoxically not to the origins of time but to 'its dreaded goal', and when Muir compounds the paradox by describing eternity as 'the fatal flaw', then origin and end are inseparably but ambiguously linked since these lines could mean either that 'world, life and soul' issue from eternity or that they disappear into it.

In the next stanza Muir seems to admit a momentary failure of vision in the phrase, 'there in transmutation's blank', a blank that he fills with the surrealist symbolism of 'Blue wave, red rose, and Plato's head'. The symbolism is contrived but it is partly effective since it breaks the stasis, clarifying Muir's vision and leading to the stanzas that penetrate the mystery of time and eternity. (The blue wave may suggest the depths of the unconscious mind, the red rose suggests a form of perfection, while Plato's head may suggest a realm of ultimate truths.)[13]

Within the same transmutation's blank sleeps 'Immortal Being' but the absoluteness of this concept prompts a change in the direction of the poem:

> To the mind's eternity I turn,
>> With leaf, fruit, blossom on the spray,
> See the dead world grow green within
>> Imagination's one long day.

The 'mind's eternity' is man's intellectual ability to abstract himself from time and it is also the timelessness of the unconscious, the two sets of forces coming together to form the eternal present of 'Imagination's one long day' in which fruit and blossom, completion and regeneration, co-exist. And at the centre of imagination's one long day is the perfection of:

> There while outstretched upon the Tree
>> Christ looks across Jerusalem's towers,
> Adam and Eve unfallen yet
>> Sleep side by side within their bowers.

The blossoming tree of the previous stanza becomes the tree of the Cross and the tree of Eden, the tree of life as well as the tree of the knowledge of good and evil, the tree of death and resurrection, of the end and the beginning. Christ appears as an archetypal figure in the same living myth as Adam and Eve, and he is also the doctrinal Christ whose death and resurrection bring the hope of immortality and the restoration of prelapsarian innocence to fallen man. In *We Moderns* Muir called for the return of a Nietzschean Superman to redeem the fallen Superman, Adam; here the returning Superman is a Christ who is both historical and supra-historical, the Christ of the New Testament and also a Christ-figure taking shape in Muir's unconscious to emerge as an archetype in Muir's mythology.

The last three stanzas of 'The Stationary Journey' are an anti-climax but they cannot diminish the moment of perfection when Muir's imagination and his growing faith allow him a vision of the eternal origin and end of the journey.

When Muir resumes his search for origins in the poem, 'The Mythical Journey',[14] his approach is strikingly different. The poem begins not in myth or even history but in Muir's personal past, and the journey is the geographical return to the Orkney of his childhood:

> First in the North. The black sea-tangle beaches,
> Brine-bitter stillness, tablet-strewn morass,
> Tall women against the sky with heads covered

The opening lines have a sharply defined imagery, a physical intensity and a rhythmic urgency that capture the particularity of place, but the Orkney of the poem, which is the Orkney of Muir's childhood, is the place where the ordinary and the fabulous co-exist. The tall women are actual women and also archetypes, and in the same stanza the 'roofless chapel' and the 'twice-dead castle on the swamp-green mound' are topographical features of the island of Wyre and also the features of a fable. The lines: 'Darkness at noonday, wheel of fire at midnight,/The level sun and the wild shooting shadows', speak of natural phenomena—the midwinter darkness and the aurora borealis of northern latitudes—and at the same time they add a supernatural drama.

'How long ago?', the question that opens the second stanza, suggests that the Orkney years are being seen not only as part of his life but as part of a greater past. And the voyage north, a voyage Muir made several times as a young man when he lived in Glasgow and Greenock and took his summer holiday in Orkney,[15] is like 'sailing up to summer/Over the edge of the world' towards a destination that is both geography and myth, towards 'The towering walls of life and the great kingdom'.

Inside the great kingdom the poet's journey is a pilgrimage: 'Where long he wandered seeking that which sought him'. But the object of the pilgrimage is uncertain:

> One whose form and features,
> Race and speech he did not know . . .

And whether at all on earth the place of meeting,
Beyond all knowledge.

This ambiguous pilgrimage is like the *peregrinatio* of an early Celtic saint seeking the place of his resurrection without knowing where that place might be or even if it can be found. But Muir's search is more than Christian pilgrimage; it is a search for a presence—divine, or ancestral, or perhaps the pagan presence that is the spirit of the place—communion with which will bring a sense of the continuity of mankind and a sense of meaning to life. Muir searches the kingdom:

> Turning, returning, till there grew a pattern,
> And it was held. And there stood both in their stations
> With the hills between them. And that was the meaning.

Unlike the moment of revelation in 'The Stationary Journey', the 'pattern' and the 'meaning' of 'The Mythical Journey' are unrealised abstractions. Even so, the vision seems assured until, in one of those changes in direction and tone that is a recurring feature of Muir's poetry, he writes: 'And then the vision/Of the conclusion without fulfilment'. But the lines that follow this denial are of such beautiful elegiac music that they create a mystical vision of an afterlife:

> The plain of glass and in the crystal grave
> That which he had sought, that which had sought him,
> Glittering in death. And all the dead scattered
> Like fallen stars, clustered like leaves hanging
> From the sad boughs of the mountainous tree of Adam
> Planted far down in Eden.

These are lines of lamentation, but the dead, like the fallen stars or the leaves on the tree in Eden, have their origins in eternity. And the closing lines of this section of the poem—lines that Muir repeats in his great poem, 'The Labyrinth'—bring the eternal and the temporal together:

> And on the hills
> The gods reclined and conversed with each other
> From summit to summit.

In the final section of the poem Muir repeats the phrase, 'Conclusion/Without fulfilment', but the vision that emerges from the poem is one of conclusion *and* fulfilment, *finis* and *telos*. Indeed, 'The Mythical Journey' is an early expression of Muir's mature vision, a vision that penetrates the mysteries of man's origin and end and yet retains a human uncertainty along with a complex attitude of acceptance that reconciles the temporal and the eternal, the human and the divine, while still seeing them as separate orders. 'The Mythical Journey' ends with the lines:

> The living dream sprung from the dying vision,
> Overarching all. Beneath its branches
> He builds in faith and doubt his shaking house.

Throughout 'The Fall',[16] another search for origins in the volume, *Journeys And Places*, there is the underlying assumption of the timeless continuity of mankind. In contrast to the gradual approach of 'The Stationary Journey' or the more biographical approach of 'The Mythical Journey', 'The Fall' plunges directly into myth in its opening line, 'What shape had I before the Fall?', and into cosmogonic myth in the following stanzas. 'The Fall' is similar in outline to 'Ballad Of The Soul' but it lacks the vast scale and violent intensity of that early poem in which Muir expresses and to some extent resolves a great psychological crisis. Here Muir speaks calmly of the creation of the universe: 'Did our eyes . . . See Heaven and Earth one land, and range/Therein through all of Time and Space?' and 'Did I see Chaos and the Word,/The suppliant Dust, the moving Hand . . . ?' He imagines a stage in the evolution of life when 'I walked/By rivers where the dragon drinks', and in lines of brightly coloured, childlike simplicity he asks:

> Did I see there the dragon brood
> By streams their emerald scales unfold,
> While from their amber eyeballs fell
> Soft-rayed the rustling gold?

Writing in *An Autobiography* of the dragons and monsters of his dreams, Muir says: '. . . the strange thing about these monsters was that they did not terrify me; instead I felt in a curious way at home with them.'[17] And so it is in 'The Fall' where the dragons are creatures of innocence, a state in which man and the animals calmly co-exist, but as soon as Muir creates this effect he contradicts it in the lines:

> But this side Eden's wall I meet
> On every twisting road the Sphinx.

And then 'The Fall' repeats the grotesquely absurd conflict of 'Ballad Of The Soul' until man in the form of a winged spirit emerges from the sphinx-like creature.

The poem is brought to a double conclusion, neither of which is satisfying. Muir offers the antithetical cleverness of 'And so I build me Heaven and Hell/To buy my bartered Paradise', and concludes with the ambiguous stanza:

> While from a legendary height
> I see a shadowy figure fall,
> And not far off another beats
> With his bare hands on Eden's wall.

The second figure can be seen as Adam—and by extension as mankind—in his fallen state; the first figure might also be Adam, and man, in the act of falling from Eden, or it could be Satan in his archangelic form as Lucifer falling from heaven to earth. The effect of the ambiguity is to bring the poem to an inconclusive end, and it has to be said that the complete poem, with a rhetoric that is neither the language of myth nor of rational consciousness, fails to satisfy as a work of art. But through elements of cosmogonic myth and the myth of human and animal evolution it briefly penetrates the mystery of man's origin, and through the symbolism of transformation from the sphinx-like creature to a winged spirit the poem offers a vision of the goal of mankind.

'The Labyrinth',[18] the title poem of Muir's 1949 volume, is only indirectly a comment on the three mysteries of where we came from, where we are going, and how we should live with one another. It is not a search for the origin and end of the human journey but an expression of three states of being in which man exists simultaneously.

Muir commented on the poem in a radio broadcast in September 1952:

> 'The Labyrinth' . . . started itself in a castle in Czechoslovakia which had been presented as a home for writers by the Benes government after the War. This was a year or two before the Communists came into power. Thinking there of the old story of the labyrinth of Cnossos and the journey of Theseus through it, I felt that this was an image of human life with its errors and ignorance and endless intricacy. In the poem I made the labyrinth stand for all this. But I wanted also to give an image of the life of the gods, to whom all that is confusion down here is clear and harmonious as seen eternally.[19]

In fact the poem offers two images of human life, the underworld of the labyrinth and another human world of goodness and light and lovely mobility:

> To the world, the still fields swift with flowers, the trees
> All bright with blossom, the little green hills, the sea,
> The sky and all in movement under it,
> Shepherds and flocks and birds and the young and old.

This bright world, an idealisation of the ordinary, appears early in the poem when the narrator is recalling his ordeal in the labyrinth so that the effect is that of the labyrinth surrounding and containing 'its enemy,/The lovely world'. The memory of the past experience of the underworld, and the narrator's vision of the life of the gods that appears later in the poem, are expressed more powerfully and extensively than the present reality of the bright world. The three orders of reality exist simultaneously, but it is an uneasy co-existence in which the middle order is almost overwhelmed by the other two.

In his radio broadcast Muir described the first of these orders, the world of the labyrinth, as 'an image of human life with its errors and ignorance and endless intricacy', but in the course of the long and ingeniously labyrinthine opening sentence the symbol of the labyrinth takes on several meanings.

The starting point of the poem is the myth of Theseus killing the Minotaur in the labyrinth of Cnossos. The symbolic killing of the bull or the man-bull—there must also have been actual killings in the Cretan labyrinth[20]—and the re-emergence of Theseus represents a great cultural shift. It suggests the end of a form of totemism in which a man, perhaps a king, was identified with a bull, and the rejection of animal gods in favour of new sky gods; it suggests the ending of the practice of human sacrifice and perhaps the introduction of animal sacrifice. Theseus's safe return is a release from plutonian values—the world of the personal unconscious that Muir explores in 'The Grove'—into the world of consciousness and rational thought. In more general terms the killing of the bull in Muir's poem—'After the straw ceased rustling and the bull/Lay dead'—represents the defeat of the powers of darkness, and the 'twilight nothingness' of the underworld contrasts with the brightness of the world above ground and the other world of the gods who are 'bright as clouds'.

But the main feature of Muir's labyrinth is its sheer labyrinthine complexity and the disorientation this causes:

> . . . deceiving streets
> That meet and part and meet, and rooms that open
> Into each other—and never a final room—
> Stairways and corridors and antechambers

In terms of Muir's myth of the journey, the labyrinth is the lost way, and that long opening sentence expresses the meaninglessness, and the search for meaning, more effectively than most of the poems of the lost way. Even above ground the narrator has the recurring fear that ' "there's no exit, none, . . . and you'll end where you are,/Deep in the centre of the endless maze." '

It is at this point that Muir introduces his vision of the life of the gods, a vision prompted by the same dream that appears in 'The Mythical Journey', but here the first part of the vision is the gods' view of the earth, that middle order to which the narrator returns in astonishment and delight earlier in the poem. The gods converse

> While down below the little ships sailed by,
> Toy multitudes swarmed in the harbours, shepherds drove
> Their tiny flocks to the pastures, marriage feasts
> Went on below, small birthdays and holidays,
> Ploughing and harvesting and life and death,
> And all permissible, all acceptable.

This idealized vision of the human order is contained within the vision of the gods—'this our life/Was a chord deep in that dialogue'—whose 'eternal dialogue was peace'. But the earlier vision of the human order was contained within the world of the labyrinth so that the complex figure of the poem shows the middle order, the world of goodness and light, in uneasy equilibrium with the underworld and the world of the gods.

In the closing lines of the poem Muir achieves an ambiguous harmony of the three orders. As he thinks of the labyrinth, 'the wild-wood waste of falsehood' he asserts his freedom and his faith: 'I'd be prisoned there/But that my soul has birdwings to fly free', but the final lines of the poem suggest that it is an uncertain freedom and faith:

> Last night I dreamt I was in the labyrinth,
> And woke far on. I did not know the place.

It would be comforting to interpret 'The Labyrinth' as the triumph of light over darkness and the affirmation of a human order that participates in and is protected by the divine, but the pattern of the poem presents the more disturbing truth of a complex and equivocal order of existence in which goodness and light, meaning and faith, are synchronous with meaninglessness and unknowing.

THE GOLDEN HARVESTER

Muir's most satisfying and yet bewildering expression of the theme of the journey is the long poem, 'The Journey Back'.[1] In it he penetrates the three mysteries of man's origin, his end and his earthly existence, and he celebrates these mysteries in a sublime delight that is a form of mysticism, a participation in the ultimate harmony of all things. 'The Journey Back' is the prophetic vision of a mature artist at the height of his powers.

The opening lines seem to suggest a simple search for ancestors, but this is followed by a metaphor that shows the search will be more than is normally implied by a search for kindred:

> I take my journey back to seek my kindred:
> Old founts dried up whose rivers run far on
> Through you and me.

The metaphor expresses Muir's concept of the continuity of mankind, a concept that has become an integral part of his faith and his vision. His ancestors are the old founts that have gone dry, or appear to have gone dry, for the rivers continue mysteriously to flow from these seemingly exhausted sources in the past, running through the present generation and far into the future. The theme of continuity is confirmed and extended in the first stanza of Section 1 when Muir writes that into 'the riverless future . . . myriad tributaries' will flow from the present generation when its 'live patchwork land of green and brown' has withered. Humanity is symbolised by the continuous river of life that links past and future generations, and as Section 1 develops, so this faith in the continuity of mankind becomes associated with human identity in its double sense of individuality and community.

This association of the continuity and identity of man is a recurring theme in Muir's prose[2] as well as in his poetry, and is expressed with urgent simplicity in Muir's final prose work, the posthumously published *Estate Of Poetry* where he writes:

> We are bound to the past generations by the same bond as to our neighbours, and if only for the sake of preserving the identity of mankind we must cherish memory.[3]

In the second stanza of 'The Journey Back' Muir restates the theme of the search, and when he thinks of his personal past he sees the value of his inheritance:

152

My hands grow firm, my father's farmer's hands,
And open and shut on surety while I walk
In patient trust.

But this is only the beginning of the realisation of his total inheritance, only 'the first friendly station / On the long road'; the poet knows that in his search for the indentity of mankind he must accept the brutal and the primitive as well as the good, 'must lodge in dark and narrow skulls' and, in the first indication of the universal visionary quality of the poetry that is to come, he sees he must 'Be in all things.' And in the remainder of the third stanza he enters those other lives—the madman, the hero, the murderer and others—admitting them to the continuity of mankind, admitting them as kindred because he knows from his own painful experience that these identities are part of his own identity.

This admission, which is both confession and acceptance, is a dramatic expression of the admission he makes in the autobiography of those 'unacknowledged failures and frustrations causing self-hatred and hatred of others'.[4] In Muir's case the admission led to a new unified sense of himself in communion with others:

> I saw that my lot was the human lot, that when I faced my own unvarnished likeness I was one among all men and women, all of whom had the same failures and frustrations, the same unacknowledged hatred of themselves and others, the same hidden shames and griefs . . .[5]

But Muir is not simply rehearsing a psychological theory in Section 1 of 'The Journey Back'. When he writes of 'emptiness and dirt and envy,/Dry rubbish of a life' he is re-living such periods in his own life, the years in Glasgow and Greenock, or the post-war years in Prague when he witnessed one brutal regime replaced by another. And when he sees his hands, once his father's farmer's hands, become 'the officious tools/That wash my face, push food into my mouth' without thinking or caring, then he is re-living those times of extreme impersonality in his own life when he felt possessed by indifference as if by a fiend. The fourth stanza ends with the multiplicity of opposing identities coming together to form the composite identity of the 'hapless Many in One', but the many do not form a unity and the fifth stanza opens with the line, 'In all these lives I have lodged, and each a prison.' For a moment the imprisonment—the limitations of personality and identity, or of man's temporal existence—seem unbearable and Muir says he would give up the search, 'break my journey/Now, here'. But he is sustained by a belief:

> I know I shall find a man who has done good
> His long lifelong and is
> Image of man from whom all have diverged.

Professor Peter Butter, one of Muir's most sympathetic critics, suggests that the man is Christ[6] but Muir himself does not identify the figure as Christ.

(And Muir's lower case spelling of 'a man' and 'man' imply that the figure is not the historical or doctrinal Christ.) 'The Journey Back' is not a Christian poem, and although the man who appears in the closing lines of Section 1 could be a Christ-figure who represents the goal of one stage of the journey, a more appropriate interpretation in terms of the complete poem may be to see the man as an archetypal ideal with whom Muir was familiar from his reading not only of the *New Testament* but of Plato and the *Upanishads*. The encounter with the archetypal ideal lies in the future, perhaps in an afterlife, but something of the timeless ideal has entered the present when, in the final lines of Section 1, Muir re-assumes his personal identity which is now both self and soul:

> To my sole starting-point, my random self
> That in these rags and tatters clothes the soul.

Between the first and second sections of the poem there is a great leap of the imagination. The poetry changes from the recognisably autobiographical material to the mythical, from the story to the fable, and the viewpoint changes from that of the poet speaking in his own voice and looking from the present into the past, to that of a discarnate primal spirit in an order of existence that is infinitely remote in space and time:

> Through countless wanderings,
> Hastenings, lingerings,
> From far I come,
> And pass from place to place
> In a sleep-wandering pace
> To seek my home.

Muir creates an effect of hypnotic lyricism partly through his use of language, imagery and rhyme, and through the 'falling' rhythm of the third and sixth lines, but the effect comes largely from the completeness of the mythological conception. A spirit travels from an origin so incalculably distant as to be indistinguishable in time and space from the celestial accident that was the creation of the stars:

> I wear the silver scars
> Of blanched and dying stars
> Forgotten long.

This section of the poem is of a similar cosmogonic scale and presents a similar mythology of evolution to those of 'Ballad Of The Soul' and 'The Fall' but here the myth is more coherently and purposefully expressed as part of an assured vision. It is also more tranquilly expressed; the spirit sways to a serene music, and the home the spirit seeks is humanity on planet earth, so that the countless wanderings, hastenings and lingerings that open and close this section of the poem form a cosmic *peregrinatio*.

And when it arrives on earth the spirit is at one with primeval mythological creatures. Peter Butter suggests that the dragon in the third stanza may be 'the dragon of Christian tradition overthrown at the Crucifixion'[7] but Muir's purpose is not to overthrow the dragon but to identify with it. The dragon is the same creature as the 'well-bred animal/With coat of seemly mail' which 'Was then my guide.' It is also the same creature as the dragon of 'The Fall'. And when the dragon dies Muir writes: 'I trembled in my den/With all my kindred'. In the opening lines of Section 1 of the poem Muir takes his journey back to seek his 'kindred'; now in a mythological evolution he finds his kindred amongst dragons. The death of the dragon marks the passing of an evolutionary period so far back in time that even after the creature's death the spirit that is the narrator of this section—the essence or potential that is evolving towards humanity—is still in animal form:

> Before the word was said
> With animal bowed head
> I kept the laws.

The line, 'Before the word was said', suggests a time before language had evolved rather than the word of God, confirming the impression of a mythological rather than a doctrinal pilgrimage. The element of pilgrimage survives the brief disorientation of 'The mountains as in play/Dizzily turn/My wild road round and round', lines that can be read literally as a physical upheaval on the geological time-scale and as a seriously playful echo of the lost way. But the way is sure, and Section 2 of the poem ends with the conviction that the goal of the journey, although a 'secret place', will inevitably be reached:

> Nearer I come
> In a sleep-wandering pace
> To find the secret place
> Where is my home.

The effect of this section of the poem with its starting point set many light years in the past is to extend the myth of the journey and the concept of man's origin far beyond the limits that Muir has previously established, and the combination of the celestial music and the trance-like inevitability with which the section unfolds reflect a new assurance in Muir's vision, a conviction that the journey will be completed and the destination reached.

Section 3 reaches a new stage on the evolutionary journey:

> And I remember in the bright light's maze
> While poring on a red and rusted arrow

The 'red and rusted arrow' suggests a violent past, and Muir implies a ritual violence, perhaps human sacrifice, in the lines that follow. He also re-introduces the question of identity so that the narrator is at once the sacrificial victim, the killer and the observer:

> How once I laid my dead self in the barrow . . .
> And stood aside, a third within that place,
> And watched these two at their strange ritual

Butter suggests that 'these two' may be Cain and Abel,[8] and although the religious element in this section of the poem makes the Biblical interpretation acceptable, one feels that here again Muir's purpose is even wider than this. He may have been prompted by a knowledge of the neolithic funeral mound of Maeshowe at Stenness in Orkney, one of Orkney's many neolithic burial chambers.[9] This section speaks of people who are recognisably human but it is a limited form of humanity in which 'the poor child of man' is not the archetypal ideal but rather natural unregenerate man 'Not knowing the resurrection and the life'. Instead of the continuity of mankind and the promise of eternal continuity through resurrection, primitive man is 'Shut in his simple recurring day' in a repetitive, meaningless existence: 'A million leaves, a million destinies fall'. And then, just when Muir has established this sense of hopeless recurrence he transforms it into one of regeneration:

> And over and over again
> The red rose blooms and moulders by the wall.

Section 3 opens with the symbol of violent death, 'a red and rusted arrow', recalls a ritual death and the death-in-life of primitive man, and then through the symbolism of the rose the section restores the sense of perpetual renewal that is expressed in the symbol of the river in Section 1.

The rose, with its associated symbolism of perfection and spiritual fulfilment, prepares the reader for another change of direction on the journey back, but even so the imaginative leap between Sections 3 and 4 is astonishing in its completeness. Section 4 opens with the mystery of

> And sometimes through the air descends a dust
> Blown from the scentless desert of dead time

And as this section of the poem evolves the mystery intensifies into mysticism. The descending dust is the clouding of consciousness that precedes the unconscious revelation, and the scentless desert of dead time suggests both the actual desert or deserted place to which the mystic would withdraw in order to experience the vision, and also the non-sensory nature, the placelessness and timelessness of the mystical vision. The vision is an absolute form of experience that is beyond the senses and the intellect, beyond language and imagery. Muir writes:

> Do not put your trust
> In the fed flesh, or colour, or sense, or shape.
> This that I am you cannot gather in rhyme.

The true nature of this ultimate experience is inexpressible, says Muir, but what follows is clearly the great religious experience of losing and finding, of withdrawing from the world and entering into a communion with the infinite:

> And here escape
> From all that was to all,
> Lost beyond loss.

It is a detachment of the spirit from the body so that the mystic seems to move in the air like the dust; it is a losing of identity, a symbolic losing of life itself—'the last power used'—because only by losing all that can be named does the visionary find the ultimate wholeness and harmony of all things:

> The last form found,
> And child and woman and flower
> Invisibly fall through the air on the living ground.

The child, woman and flower that appear in the two lines of Section 4 are the transfigured forms of the rose and of primitive man's 'child and wife' in the previous section.

The ultimate experience of the mystical vision in which all is found suggests that Muir has realised the origin and goal, and that his journey is complete, but the section that follows presents another dramatic contrast. After the mystical unity of Section 4 Muir speaks again in his own voice, and after the transcendental placelessness he returns to a world:

> Where good seemed evil and evil good
> And half the world ran mad to wage
> War with an eager heart for the wrong,
> War with a bitter heart for the right.

These lines may have been prompted by the destruction Muir saw when he travelled across Europe in 1945 and by the brutalities he learned of during his three years in Prague—'The Journey Back' was published in *The Listener* in August 1948 just after Muir's return from Prague—but the lines also have a universal truth. Muir's response to the madness in which good and evil seem indistinguishable is to call for 'Blessing upon this time and place' and 'upon the disfigured face' of humanity. The second stanza of Section 5 is a prayer for mercy, without which there is no hope for mankind:

> Blessing upon our helplessness
> That, wild for prophecy, is dumb.
> Without the blessing cannot the kingdom come.

It is like a Kyrie Eleison, a plea for a divine intervention that will save helpless man, except that Muir omits the Kyrie and begs mercy not from an exclusively Christian Lord but from whatever may be the source of mercy. (The 'kingdom' of the final line has the non-doctrinal lower case spelling.)

As if in answer to this prayer, Section 6 of 'The Journey Back' is a fully realised vision of the kingdom. The inhabitants of the kingdom are like the gods on the mountain tops in 'The Mythical Journey' and 'The Labyrinth', or like fallen man restored to paradise: 'They walk high in their mountainland of light', and in that world of light the 'winding roads' bring no confusion but are 'Paths that wander for their own delight'. It is a millenial vision of a divine order that is the origin and end of the journey:

> There they like planets pace their tranquil round
> That has no end, whose end is everywhere,
> And tread as to a music underground.

The sense of fulfilment is expressed not just in the meaning but in the form and texture of the poetry. The terza rima stanza pattern with its interlocking tercets gains a particularly melodic resonance from Muir's use of rhythm and rhyme, and musical imagery flows throughout this section: 'paths that wander for their own delight', 'music underground', the 'ever-winding and unwinding air', 'music's self itself has buried there', 'tongues in silence overflow', and 'That music only should be melody'.

Musical imagery is rare in Muir's poetry but here he creates a music of the spheres so that when he re-introduces the theme of the journey in the line, 'This is the other road, not that we know', then the other road—the transcendental origin and end of the journey—seems as natural and inevitable a part of the way as does the road we know.

At this point Muir gently disengages from the millenial vision and, in a figure that echoes the falling to earth in Section 4, he writes:

> This is the place of peace, content to be.
> All we have seen it; while we look we are
> There truly, and even now in memory.

The effect of this change of direction in the closing lines is not to break the vision but to make it part of the earthly journey. The millenial vision of the end of the journey has become part of the poet's conscious experience; to experience the vision is to experience eternity—'while we look we are/There truly'—and even the memory of the vision allows man to participate through his imagination. The section ends with a linked image of the temporal and eternal as a star falls from the millenial vision to guide man on his earthly journey: 'Here on this road, following a falling star.'

The link between the eternal and the temporal extends into the final section of the poem but the section begins in doubt. Here Muir speaks again in his own voice, and as he tries to relate the mysteries he has experienced to the perplexity of the earthly journey, the note of doubt comes into his voice:

> If I should reach the end, if end there was
> Before the ever-running roads began . . .
>   if there was ever a place
> Where one might say, 'Here is the starting-point'

The twists and turns of thought in the long opening sentence of Section 7 remind the reader of the labyrinthine sentence that opens 'The Labyrinth', but here in 'The Journey Back' there is no real sense of disorientation. Instead, the convolutions and paradoxes are like a form of serious play as the sentence and the train of thought move at an accelerating pace to the image of 'that deafening road,/Life-wide, world-wide, by which all come to all'; the human journey, with that echo of 'From all that was to all' in the mystical vision of Section 4, is a version of the eternal journey. And the paradoxes are resolved in Muir's confident restatement of the mystery:

> But all with no division strongly come
> For ever to their steady mark, the moment,
> And the tumultuous world slips softly home
> To its perpetual end and flawless bourne.

And then the voice changes from 'I' to 'we' as Muir affirms the unity and continuity of mankind in the line, 'How could we be if all were not in all?'

In the opening lines of Section 1 the water-beds were 'Stone-white with drought' but now Muir sees that 'all around these fields are white with harvest', and in the final lines of the poem Muir imagines a symbolic day when the human journey and his personal journey reach a conclusion that is both *finis* and *telos*:

> But we have watched against the evening sky,
> Tranquil and bright, the golden harvester.

The golden harvester, the sun that brings things to fruition at the end of the journey, is also part of Muir's cosmogonic myth of the creation and of the origin of the journey. It shines like an intimation of immortality over the great harvesting of fields and lives and souls.

'The Journey Back' is Muir's greatest single statement, and his most complex, on the theme of the journey. Indeed, so great is the scope of the poem that it includes Muir's other great preoccupations, the myths of the conflict and the fall. Conflict occurs in Sections 1, 3 and 5 but in Section 5 when the conflict seems universal Muir rediscovers the only means to end the conflict, and in Section 6 he offers the millenial vision of existence beyond the reach of conflict. Sections 3 and 5 show the recurring fall of man but the mystical vision of Section 4 and the millenial vision of Section 6 redeem man from the fall and restore him to 'the place of peace'. The immensity of the task Muir tackles, and the intractability of his material, are partly concealed by the technical accomplishment with which he handles a variety of poetic forms and by his use of narrative modes that range from personal recollection to myth and mysticism. The effect of the organisation of the poem—the dramatic contrast between one section and another, and the overall harmony of the complete poem—is to show the journey as being both terrestrial and transcendental, temporal and eternal, man's story and his fable. 'The Journey Back' gathers the myths of the conflict, the fall and the journey into one great composite myth that offers a unique vision of the human condition.

Strange Blessings

REDEMPTION

Reconciliation is part of the theme of 'The Journey Back', and the theme of reconciliation is confirmed in the ordering and re-ordering of the vision through the seven sections into the final configuration of the finished poem, a form in which the number seven retains some of its symbolism of spiritual perfection, so that 'The Journey Back' is a great act of reconciliation. Clearly, 'The Journey Back' is a religious but not expressly Christian poem. If the 'Image of man from all have diverged' is a Christ-image then it is Christ as an archetypal ideal rather than Christ of the New Testament or of doctrine. But this ideal seems equally close to Plato's 'most completely perfect of intelligible beings . . . a single visible living being, containing within itself all living beings of the same order'.[1] And the closing image of the poem, 'the golden harvester', is not a Christian symbol nor even the symbol of a pagan sky god but rather a beautifully appropriate and characteristic way of showing the completion of the journey as both *finis* and *telos*.

The state of reconciliation in 'The Journey Back' is a creation of Muir's imagination, and so too is the implicit theme of redemption. The 'place of peace' in Section 6 of the poem is Muir's vision of the immortality of the soul at the end of the human journey; it is a place of Muir's own making rather than the Christian eternity. But just six months before 'The Journey Back' was first published (in *The Listener*, 19 August 1948) Muir's great poem of Christian redemption had appeared.

'The Transfiguration'[2] celebrates the redemption of fallen man through the divinity, the transfiguration, of Christ. The poem is prompted by the Gospel accounts[3] and expresses essential elements of Christian faith, and yet Muir says that in writing the poem 'I seem to have blundered into something greater than I knew'.[4] And when one considers the development of Muir's faith one sees that he arrives at Christianity, and his great Christian poems, by accident rather than by design.

Muir himself was aware of this; he omitted from the 1960 *Collected Poems* his four explicitly Christian poems in *One Foot In Eden*: 'The Christmas', 'The Son', 'Lost And Found', and 'The Lord',[5] only one of which, 'The Son', had been previously published in magazine form. In August 1958 when Muir was preparing the new edition of the *Collected Poems* he wrote to T S Eliot, his publisher at Faber and Faber, about the project, and in the course of the letter he states quite simply: 'I have decided to leave out four of the religious poems, which seem to me now to be quite inadequate'.[6] The decision seems right; the four pieces read like devotional exercises that express piety without imagination and faith without vision.

Eliot suggests in his essay published in 1935, 'Religion and Literature', that much religious poetry is 'a version of *minor* poetry', and he adds: 'What I want is a literature which should be *un*consciously, rather than deliberately and defiantly, Christian'.[7] Some of Muir's Christian poetry is unconscious in this and in a wider sense. An early chapter of this work, 'Versions Of Everyman', argues that the Christ-image took shape gradually in Muir's unconscious mind until it found conscious expression on that occasion in February 1939 when Muir broke into a spontaneous recitation of the Lord's Prayer. In any study of Muir's religious poetry it is important to see that he discovers—or rediscovers—Christianity through a process that was partly unconscious; that his faith, sometimes idiosyncratic and always personal rather than sanctioned by doctrine or institution, is partly an intuitive and imaginative achievement; and that his expression of faith in his writings is never codified or formulated but is always universal.

The crucial period in the process that led to Muir's mature acceptance of Christianity is the late 1930s. In 'Extracts From A Diary, 1937–39', the final chapter in *The Story And The Fable*, he records the dream:

> I was in a pub with some clamorous, hearty men who looked like racing men. They were discussing Christ in irritable voices, as if they knew him personally and could not decide what to make of him. At last one of them said: 'Well, at least you can bash his face in for him', and this seemed to be an original thought, a solution. Then Christ was there. He was a thin-faced man with an unhealthy, hectic-red complexion. He had on a shabby waterproof, and was wearing eyeglasses, which for some reason gave him a pedantic, opinionated expression. A huge clenched fist came out and struck him in the middle of the face, breaking his glasses: the hand was so huge that it covered most of his face. What can one make of such a dream?[8]

What one makes of the dream is that it identifies Muir with Christ. The description of Christ is almost certainly a description of Muir himself. The blow he receives is not only an absurd unconscious symbolism of the suffering and rejection of Christ but also of the difficulties Muir was experiencing in his personal and professional life in Scotland at that time.[9] The colloquial metaphor of a blow in the face is appropriate, and the fist covering the face may express the extent to which Muir felt himself being ignored and rejected, or perhaps the fact that he could not see the face of Christ at that time. Muir's unconscious mind presents him as Christ, and a conscious interpretation of the dream is that Muir is accepting Christ.

When Muir recalls these years in *An Autobiography* he writes of his recitation of the Lord's Prayer and adds:

> Now I realized that, quite without knowing it, I was a Christian, no matter how bad a one; and I remembered a few days later that Janet Adam Smith had told me, half-teasingly, while I was staying in Hampstead, that my poetry was a Christian poetry: the idea then had been quite strange to me. I had a vague sense

during these days that Christ was the turning-point of time and the meaning of life to everyone, no matter what his conscious beliefs; to my agnostic friends as well as Christians.[10]

He had become a Christian 'quite without knowing it', and he felt that Christ offered meaning to everyone's life 'no matter what his conscious beliefs'. The passage continues:

I read the New Testament many times during the following months, particularly the Gospels. I did not turn to any church, and my talks with ministers and divines cast me back upon the Gospels again, which was probably the best thing that could have happened. I had no conception of the splendours of Christendom; I remained quite unaware of them until some years later I was sent by the British Council to Italy.

But even in Rome when he was surrounded by these splendours Muir did not commit himself to any church. Indeed, his avoidance of institutions and denominations was an important part of his faith. In the last chapter of *The Story And The Fable* he writes of this:

Walking to the pier [at St Andrews] yesterday, I seemed to see that a Church which is not universal and all-inclusive is evil by virtue of that fact alone, for it rejects mankind. All Churches which do this are fond of the doctrine of Hell, and consign great multitudes to damnation.[11]

Willa Muir in a radio broadcast in 1964 commented on Muir's form of Christianity:

I would say he would regard the apparatus of ecclesiastic churches as being fairly irrelevant and otiose, and what he had was the essence of the Gospel itself, without any accretions. But he got the feeling that Christ had been a real, actual human being on earth in Rome very strongly. I should say that he would have made a very good early Christian.[12]

Rome gave Muir a sense of the incarnate Christ as a living presence, but in Rome he was aware too of older gods 'still present in a sense in the places where they once were'[13] and co-existing with the Christian God. In fact, Muir's mature faith and vision are not exclusively Christian, even in some of his expressly Christian poems. His belief in the importance of myth—the myth of his childhood and the childhood of the race, the myth of human continuity, Greek myth—is not a Christian belief; his deep and sometimes fearful delight in the natural world of this planet and the encircling cosmos is a form of faith; his concern for a harmony between the human and the natural orders has a religious intensity that is seldom Christian; above all, his belief in the power of the imagination and in the revelations of the unconscious mind is a form of faith from which most other forms originate. And when these unconscious revelations are shaped by the imagination into great mythopoeic acts—as in 'Ballad Of The Soul', some sequences of *Vari-*

ations On A Time Theme, 'The Journey Back'—the result is a visionary poetry which, like all great visionary poetry, transcends the beliefs of the age in which it is written to become its own form of religion. It is in this context that one reads 'The Transfiguration' and 'The Annunciation'.

In a radio broadcast in 1952 Muir seemed to confuse the provenance of 'The Transfiguration':

> Later on, when I was transferred by the British Council from Prague to Rome, I managed to write a more hopeful kind of poetry. I had always been deeply struck by the story of the Transfiguration in the Gospels, and I had felt that perhaps at the moment of Christ's transfiguration everything was transfigured, mankind, and the animals, and the simplest natural objects.[14]

But the poem first appeared in *The Listener* in February 1948, the month of the communist coup in Czechoslovakia, when Muir was still director of the British Council in Prague. His memory transfers this poem of redemption from Prague at a time when he was nearing a state of spiritual exhaustion to Rome where he experienced a resurgence of hope and faith. What puzzles the reader is not that Muir forgot the origin of the poem so soon after writing it but that so triumphant a poem was written in such bleak circumstances.

The poem opens with the disciples' recollection of Christ's transfiguration, which Matthew's Gospel reports in these terms:

> And after six days Jesus taketh Peter, James, and John his brother, and bringeth them up into an high mountain apart, and was transfigured before them: and his face did shine as the sun, and his raiment was white as the light . . . While he [Peter] yet spake, behold, a bright cloud overshadowed them: and behold a voice out of the cloud, which said, This is my beloved Son, in whom I am well pleased; hear ye him.[15]

In the poem this supernatural radiance that confirms the divinity of Christ becomes a living force that seems to rise from the ground and enter the veins of the disciples, transfiguring them too in a miraculous purification:

> The source of all our seeing rinsed and cleansed
> Till earth and light and water entering there
> Gave back to us the clear unfallen world.

With their new clarity and purity of vision the disciples see the world afresh in a momentary re-enactment of the creation, and the world they re-create is 'the clear unfallen world' restored to innocence through the divine intervention that transfigures Christ. The disciples enjoy a spiritual and physical radiance that is like a form of immortality, but after the first spontaneous surge of innocence they begin to doubt the nature of their experience. Was it a vision, they wonder, a projection of their religious ecstasy, or had they actually seen the divine transfiguring power as a physical reality:

> the unseeable
> One glory of the everlasting world
> Perpetually at work, though never seen
> Since Eden locked the gate that's everywhere
> And nowhere?

Muir, through the characteristically collective voice of the narrators, associates the transfigured world with the unfallen world of Eden, and in his extended image of that day when 'all/Was in its place' he offers an image that is at once prelapsarian and millenial and he draws again on the dream of the millenium that he records in the autobiography:[16]

> The lurkers under doorways, murderers,
> With rags tied round their feet for silence . . .
> Stepped out of their dungeons and were free.

The purifying force of the transfiguration liberates not only the murderers but all mankind in a universal redemption.

It is at this triumphant moment in the poem that Muir's vision seems to falter once again as he introduces a hiatus that breaks the spiritual momentum and disrupts the figure of the poem:

> But the world
> Rolled back into its place, and we are here,
> And all that radiant kingdom lies forlorn.

This discontinuity is a recurring and deliberate feature of Muir's poetry. Muir's purpose in these modulations—for example, in 'The Transfiguration', 'Moses', 'The Labyrinth' and others—is to show one order of time and reality juxtaposed with, or contained within, another, and to show man's fallen condition set against eternity. Similarly, a sense of discontinuity may be felt when Muir disengages from a dream or vision and thus changes the narrative mode or even the persona of the narrator within the poem. (A further possible explanation may lie in Muir's working methods: as he took a poem through various drafts or rehearsed it in his mind over a period of weeks, or months, or even years, so the intensity of imagination would inevitably change). Had 'The Transfiguration' ended at this point where the radiant kingdom 'blossoms for itself while time runs on', then the two orders, the human and the divine, would have remained separate and man would have remained fallen and unredeemed, but Muir reaffirms the vision of the first section of the poem and extends the theme of redemption in the second section, which tells of the second coming of Christ.

In these lines of the poem Muir introduces the other great act of redemption—the crucifixion—and through the image of the cross he links the timeless innocence of the second coming with that of Eden:

His agony unmade, his cross dismantled—
Glad to be so—and the tormented wood
Will cure its hurt and grow into a tree
In a green springing corner of young Eden.

The transfiguring power of the crucified Christ, who becomes 'Christ the uncrucified,/Christ the discrucified' through the second coming, is symbolised by the 'tormented wood' that is transformed into the tree of life, and also by the restoration of Judas to a state of childlike innocence. Even Judas, the archetypal betrayer, is redeemed.

'The Transfiguration' is partly a statement of faith and partly a visionary poem; the beliefs it expresses are not simply assertions of doctrine but rather discoveries made in the act of writing the poem. The poem opens with the miraculous purification of the world that follows the confirmation of Christ's divinity, and it concludes with the promise of redemption implicit in the crucifixion, a crucifixion contained within the prophecy of the ultimate redemption of Christ's second coming. 'The Transfiguration' evolves in such a way that the poem reads like a new and spontaneous vision of redemption.

For Muir the vision, and the near-mythology he makes of it, was new but he seems to have sensed that he was approaching some ancestral, universal experience. In his introductory comments to the radio broadcast of the poem in 1952, after he wrongly attributed the poem to his time in Rome, he went on:

> After the poem appeared in *The Listener*, I had a letter from a lady who had made a long study of the subject, and to my surprise I found that the idea which I had imagined in my own mind possessed a whole literature, and that in some of the Russian churches it was often presented pictorially. Perhaps in the imagination of mankind the transfiguration has become a powerful symbol, standing for many things, and among them those transformations of reality which the imagination itself creates.[17]

Muir's letter of reply to the woman, Miss Maisie Spens, also contains the idea that the transfiguration is not simply a Christian doctrine but a universal symbol in the imagination of mankind. He writes:

> I know nothing of the literature of the Transfiguration, and in writing the poem probably did not see where it was leading me. On the other hand I have always had a particular feeling for that transmutation of life which is found occasionally in poetry, and in the literature of prophecy, and sometimes in one's own thoughts when they are still. This, I think, is one of the things which have always been with me, or more exactly, which have persistently recurred to me, and I suppose in this poem it has found a point of expression . . . The idea of Judas going back into innocence has often been with me. But I seem to have blundered into something greater than I knew, though as it grew the poem became clearer and clearer in my mind.[18]

The broadcast comments and the letter to Miss Spens suggest that 'The

Transfiguration' falls into Eliot's category of literature that is '*un*consciously, rather than deliberately and defiantly, Christian'. It is this unconscious, intuitive faculty that allows Muir to blunder, as he himself says, into something greater than he knew and create a poem that ranges beyond the limits of his conscious knowledge and even beyond Christianity. The experience of purity, of transformation from substance to essence, from the corporeal to the spiritual, is a universal religious experience of the mystical state in which man participates in divinity, an experience symbolised by radiant light.[19]

When Muir recalled 'The Transfiguration' as having been written in Rome he was probably confusing that poem with another great Christian poem, 'The Annunciation',[20] which first appeared in *Botteghe Oscure* in 1950 under the title, 'From A Roman Bas-Relief'. In *An Autobiography* he recalls the bas-relief that prompted the poem:

> I remember stopping for a long time one day to look at a little plaque on the wall of a house in the Via degli Artisti, representing the Annunciation. An angel and a young girl, their bodies inclined towards each other, their knees bent as if they were overcome with love, 'tutto tremante', gazed upon each other like Dante's pair; and that representation of a human love so intense that it could not reach farther seemed the perfect earthly symbol of the love that passes understanding.[21]

In the poem as in the autobiography Muir speaks not of Gabriel and Mary but of the angel and the girl, and it is clear that the poem is prompted not by the first chapter of Luke's Gospel but by the little plaque. Muir's personal vision of the annunciation occurs in a city street, and this circumstance, this miracle-in-ordinariness of his encounter with the living Christian myth and the angel's encounter with the seemingly ordinary girl, becomes an antiphon that sounds its variations throughout this persuasively musical poem:

> The angel and the girl are met.
> Earth was the only meeting place.
> For the embodied never yet
> Travelled beyond the shore of space.
> The eternal spirits in freedom go.

There is an air of quiet inevitability in their meeting, and in their meeting on earth. And when Muir juxtaposes the eternal spirit and the embodied girl the effect is not so much the contrast between the divine and the human as the natural association of the two conditions.

The antiphonal figure is repeated in the second stanza, this time with an air of surprised recognition as if Muir begins to see the meaning of the encounter:

> See, they have come together, see,
> While the destroying minutes flow.

The phrase, 'the destroying minutes', is like the despairing language of some sequences in *Variations On A Time Theme* but here it serves to emphasise the epiphany: the angel has come to earth and into time to tell the girl she has been chosen, just as the later epiphany will mark the transfiguration of the girl's son. As the second stanza unfolds the angel seems as struck by the earthly girl as she is by him; each participates in the other's condition, the divine and the human, until the two conditions are as one:

> Each reflects the other's face
> Till heaven in hers and earth in his
> Shine steady there.

The angel has come to her 'From far beyond the farthest star' and yet he is so enchanted and feels such 'increasing rapture' that he trembles like a lover.

In the third stanza Muir reminds himself that his trance, like that of the angel and the girl, is happening in the world of time and the passing of time:

> Outside the window footsteps fall
> Into the ordinary day
> And with the sun along the wall
> Pursue their unreturning way.

At this point in the poem Muir omits from the later collected editions a line that appears in the poem in *One Foot In Eden* (1956) and in the 1952 *Collected Poems*: 'That was ordained in eternity'. It is as if Muir came to feel that the reminder, this further juxtaposition of time and eternity, was no longer needed since the miracle of divine intervention in human affairs has already been realised in the poem. And even in the closing lines of the stanza, when Muir sounds a deliberately harsh chord in the antiphony of time and eternity, the harmony between the two still holds:

> Sounds perpetual roundabout
> Rolls its numbered octaves out
> And hoarsely grinds a battered tune.

Muir stretches the harmony to its limits in the line, 'And hoarsely grinds its battered tune', but by this stage in the poem human life is so clearly linked to the divine, time and eternity are so clearly reflections of each other, that the effect of the third stanza is to extend rather than distort the vision. And in the final stanza the 'battered tune' of time becomes the timelessness of 'the endless afternoon':

> But through the endless afternoon
> These neither speak nor movement make,
> But stare into their deepening trance
> As if their gaze would never break.

The deepening trance that looks as if it will never break is, as Muir says in the autobiography, 'the perfect earthly symbol of the love that passes understanding'. And in the mythology of that love the annunciation is the prelude to the incarnation and transfiguration of Christ. For Muir the little plaque in the Via degli Artisti is confirmation of the indissoluble union of the divine and the human, and an assurance of redemption for fallen man. It is confirmation too of those other religious but not exclusively Christian elements in his vision: that temporal existence finds its meaning when seen against the background of eternity, and the human story its meaning when seen as the expression of the timeless fable.

THE EARTHLY SUCCESSION

The timeless fable contains Muir's myth of the continuity of mankind. It is a myth that emerges gradually from Muir's work—the autobiographies, the criticism, and the poems—and is fully realised only after he penetrates the mystery of the journey from its origin to its end, and the mysteries of divine intervention through the annunciation and the transfiguration. His vision of the cosmic journey and the promise of eternity allow him to see more clearly the earthly, temporal succession which in its ideal form is the continuous regeneration and fulfilment of life, but which also includes life's defeats and despairs. The great visionary and Christian poems speak of divinity, eternity and the immortality of the soul; the poems of the earthly succession speak of humanity and the temporal world, and speak of them with greater confidence and gratitude because Muir has experienced them within the context of the greater vision.

This difference, not of opposed visions but of the lesser contained within the greater, can be seen in some of Muir's prose statements. In *An Autobiography* he writes of immortality:

> I realized that immortality is not an idea or a belief, but a state of being in which man keeps alive in himself his perception of that boundless union and freedom, which he can faintly apprehend in time, though its consummation lies beyond time. This realization that human life is not fulfilled in our world, but reaches through all eternity, would have been rejected by me some years before as an act of treachery to man's earthly hopes; but now, in a different way, it was a confirmation of them, for only a race of immortal spirits could create a world fit for immortal spirits to inhabit.[1]

Here he writes of a state of boundless union and freedom, the consummation of which lies beyond time, of human life reaching through all eternity, and of mankind as a race of immortal spirits. But in the lecture, 'Poetry And The Poet' in *The Estate Of Poetry* (in the passage already quoted in the earlier chapter, 'The Golden Harvester') Muir argues that the preservation of our human identity depends on our acknowledging that we are 'bound to the past generations':

> We are bound to the past generations by the same bond as to our neighbours, and if only for the sake of preserving the identity of mankind we must cherish memory.[2]

Muir is not suggesting that through our imagination we should live in the past or even re-live the past but that the past itself is a living force that must be recognised if we are to retain our human identity. For Muir this is a personal as well as universal truth. Shortly after the appearance of *The Story And The Fable* in 1940 he published the essay, 'Yesterday's Mirror: Afterthoughts To An Autobiography', in the opening paragraphs of which he discusses the way we allow ourselves to be deceived 'by the importance of the present moment' while ignoring 'those past moments where we could recognize if we liked, by an effort of imagination and understanding, the self which has always been there through all the hours' changes.' And he concludes that

> There is a law by which the momentary self continuously ousts the permanent self. Consequently to know what we are we must cease for a time to be what we are. Otherwise we live in a perpetual bright oblivion of ourselves, insulated in the moving moment and given meaning only by the moment.[3]

Indeed, Muir begins to recognise this truth of the living past—that it is part of the identity of mankind and of individual man—as early as 1935 in his essay, 'Hölderlin's *Patmos*', reprinted in *Essays On Literature And Society*, when he writes of Hölderlin's treatment of the past:

> It widened the present in a striking and incalculable way; and this expansion gives us a sense of a vast whole, a universal dispensation which is the life of mankind from beginning to end.[4]

Muir writes this of Hölderlin's vision but it is already part of his own, and by the year 1955–56 when he delivered the lecture, 'Poetry And The Poet', at Harvard the vision was a familiar reality:

> The past is a living past, and past and present co-exist; that also the imagination tells us. It opens the past to us as part of our own life, a vast extension of our present. It cannot admit that anything that ever happened among the dead is dead for us, or that all men and women have done and suffered was merely meant to bring us to where we are.[5]

Muir's sense of the living past, like his sense of the immortality of the soul, is not an idea or a belief but a state of being. For him past and present form one indivisible order of experience in which he has communion with ancestral figures whose fate he feels being re-enacted in his own personal life. This sense of a unified contemporaneous order of past and present is expressed throughout Muir's prose and is an essential element in his vision of the human condition, a secular myth within the greater cosmic and sacred myths. The secularity, and also the re-enactment of the past-in-the-present and the present-in-the-past, is something to be accepted and even celebrated. In the late essay, 'The Poetic Imagination', Muir writes:

> Imagination tells us that we become human by repetition, that our life is a
> rehearsal of lives that have been lived over and over, and that this act, with all
> that is good and evil in it, is a theme for delighted and awed contemplation.[6]

There is no sense of dualism in Muir's reference to good and evil here; instead,
he sees good and evil as one condition, just as past and present are one
dimension, and all are part of the same act that is 'a theme for delighted and
awed contemplation'.

It is a theme that finds its supreme expression in the volume, *One Foot In
Eden*, but begins to emerge in the mature poems of the 1940s. The suffering
Muir refers to in 'Poetry And The Poet', the unity of good and evil, of past
and present, are seen in the poem, 'The Fathers'[7] in the 1946 volume, *The
Voyage*.

There is more of awe than delight in this poem, the opening lines of which
speak of a poverty that becomes more and more extreme the further the poet
looks into the past:

> Our fathers all were poor,
> Poorer our fathers' fathers;
> Beyond, we dare not look.

From all that Muir says about the past in his prose and poetry it is clear that
the poverty of 'The Fathers' is not spiritual but material and yet from this
bleak past the sons have inherited 'tarnished gold'—that is, an inheritance
of good and evil—'that gathers/Around us in the night'. But when the past
is understood and assimilated with the present then all 'Will open into the
light'. The same figure is repeated in the second stanza of the poem where
the suffering of past generations is seen as part of present reality. 'Archaic
fevers' afflict the living:

> The fathers's anger and ache
> Will not, will not away
> And leave the living alone.

The restless spirits of the dead torment the present generation, transforming
the 'sunny house' of the present into a 'Nightmare of blackened bone,/Cellar
and choking cave.' The sunny house is that 'perpetual bright oblivion of
ourselves' Muir speaks of in 'Yesterday's Mirror', an insulation in the moving
moment that excludes the truths of the past. And when Muir recognises this
in the third stanza the figure changes. 'Panics and furies'—mythological as
well as emotional presences—continue to 'fly/Through our unhurried veins',
but by acknowledging these forces from the past the poet achieves a state of
purification:

> Heavenly lights and rains
> Purify heart and eye,
> Past agonies purify
> And lay the sullen dust.

In the closing lines of the poem Muir makes it clear that the act of acknowledgement does not finally exorcise the restless ghosts and bring peace to the
living: 'The angers will not away.' The effect is not exorcism but an acceptance
of good and evil, past and present as inseparable truths of man's fallen
condition:

> We hold our fathers' trust,
> Wrong, riches, sorrow and all
> Until they topple and fall,
> And fallen let in the day.

This account of the unquiet dead who demand recognition from the living is
strikingly similar to a passage in Jung's autobiography, *Memories, Dreams,
Reflections* where, after recalling a crisis that he describes as an example of
'loss of soul', Jung writes:

> From that time on, the dead have become ever more distinct for me as the voices
> of the Unanswered, Unresolved, and Unredeemed . . . These conversations with
> the dead formed a kind of prelude to what I had to communicate to the world
> about the unconscious: a kind of pattern of order and interpretation of its general
> contents.[8]

Ten years after the first publication of 'The Fathers' Muir re-stated part of
the poem's theme more explicitly in a radio broadcast, 'The Inheritors'. The
programme, part of a series entitled 'Heritage', took the form of a Socratic
dialogue in which the beliefs of the principal narrator are clearly those of
Muir himself. The narrator recalls some of tragic episodes in Scottish history
and says:

> We are the descendants of the victors, but also of the defeated. The blood of
> both runs in our veins. We do not inherit only what we want to inherit.[9]

The defeated and the dead, says the narrator, cannot be denied but are with
us in the present and will travel with us into the future:

> They come back whatever we may do, and we can either welcome them or turn
> our backs on them. They come back without a thought for our new ideas, new
> movements, new policies, new inventions, and they go with us into the future.

And the narrator concludes that the dead are a necessary presence without
whom life loses its meaning:

> We can turn over a new leaf, but the dead will be there, or the new leaf will be
> a blank. If they are not there, we have lost our inheritance.

The radio broadcast of 1955 ended with a reading of Muir's poem, 'The
Debtor' from *The Labyrinth*,[10] a poem in which he speaks with gratitude and
delight of the completeness of his involvement in the world and of his debt

to the dead: 'On the backs of the dead,/See, I am bourne'. The poet acknowledges again his inheritance from both victor and vanquished, and its closing
lines speak of a communion with—almost of a possession by—the dead.

> The meadows of Lethe shed twilight around me.
> The dead in their silences keep me in memory,
> Have me in hold. To all I am bounden.

Muir is clearly alluding to his own death in that self-consciously poetic line,
'The meadows of Lethe shed twilight around me', but this is a minor point,
almost an aside, in the poem. What is more important in 'The Debtor', in
the radio dialogue about the dead, and in much of what Muir writes in his
prose and poetry about the dead and the past, is that he sometimes gives the
impression that he has experienced death and that his narrative viewpoint is
that of the dead. Muir's purpose is not to come to terms with his personal
death, although that is an incidental effect, but to see the dead as members
of the living continuity of the earthly succession. The living are enriched if
they acknowledge the dead, and the dead are fulfilled, redeemed, by this
recognition; the living, in turn, become part of this succession as their presences survive into future generations.

Here again Muir's vision is similar to Jung's. Writing of the mother archetype in *The Archetypes And The Collective Unconscious*, Jung says:

> The conscious experience of these ties produces the feeling that her life is spread
> out over the generations—the first step towards the immediate experience and
> conviction of being outside time, which brings with it a feeling of *immortality*.[11]

Jung refers to the experience as being essentially feminine whereas Muir sees
it as a common human experience. In the same paragraph Jung adds:

> This leads to a restoration or *apocatastasis* of the lives of her ancestors, who
> now, through the bridge of the momentary individual, pass down into the
> generations of the future. An experience of this kind gives the individual a place
> and a meaning in the life of the generations, so that all unnecessary obstacles are
> cleared out of the way of the life-stream that is to flow through her.

Jung's analysis—that the 'momentary individual' sees herself as the physical
embodiment and also the conceptual bridge that links past, present and future
generations—contains the essence of Muir's myth of the earthly succession.

The most satisfying expressions of the myth are some of the poems in *One
Foot In Eden*. The two linked poems, 'Abraham' and 'The Succession',[12]
extend the myth from an archetypal Biblical starting point into the present.

'Abraham' is a serenely lyrical first stage in the succession in which Abraham—literally, 'the father of multitudes'—leads his people

> With the meandering art of wavering water
> That seeks and finds, yet does not know its way.

And yet this random journey is one of continuous creation and fulfilment:

> He came, rested and prospered, and went on,
> Scattering behind him little pastoral kingdoms,
> And over each one its own particular sky.

'The Succession' is a sequel to 'Abraham' and Isaac the successor to Abraham, extending the succession to 'Other peoples, other lands. / Where the father could not go', and in the third stanza the succession is carried into the present:

> We through the generations came
> Here by a way we do not know
> From the fields of Abraham,
> And still the road is scarce begun.

The poem ends in a series of rather flat observations, and 'The Succession' is less effective than Muir himself may have felt; he thought of making it the title poem for his 1956 collection, *One Foot in Eden*, until he was dissuaded by Eliot.[13] The title, with its implicit theme of human continuity, may have led Muir to over-estimate the importance of the poem; but in the same volume two genuinely important expressions of the theme are 'The Difficult Land' and 'Into Thirty Centuries Born'.

'The Difficult Land'[14] begins in despair and then, partly through a painful re-affirmation of common humanity but mainly through communion with the dead, Muir re-discovers the sense of continuity that gives meaning to life and allows an attitude of acceptance. The difficult land of the title is a metaphor for the human condition but in contrast to the pastoral idyll of 'Abraham' this is an unyielding land where the efforts of the people are frustrated day after day, year after year until the land, their attempts to cultivate it, and life itself all become meaningless:

> Dust rising before us and falling again behind us,
> Slowly and gently settling where it lay.
> These days the earth itself looks sad and senseless.

What sustains the people of the difficult land is not faith or hope but a sense of their common humanity: 'We are a people; race and speech support us'; the lingering memory of their common inheritance: 'Ancestral rite and custom, roof and tree'; and above all their awareness of an indefinable and yet inextinguishable element in the human spirit that survives despite the hopelessness and despair: 'And something that, defeated, still endures'.

But even this element, the vulnerable and yet enduring essence of survival that remains when the will to survive has gone—the thing that sustains the soft round beast in 'The Combat'—even this is lost and there are times 'When name, identity, and our very hands,/Senselessly labouring, grow hateful to us'. At such times the possibility of an end to all the suffering becomes a mysteriously beautiful prospect, like the completion of a natural and almost inevitable cycle:

> And we would gladly rid us of these burdens,
> Enter our darkness through the doors of wheat
> And the light veil of grass (leaving behind
> Name, body, country, speech, vocation, faith)
> And gather into the secrecy of the earth.

They would gladly end their existence as a people but what makes them draw back is the other, intimately personal image of humanity: 'faces of goodness, faithful masks of sorrow', and 'The love that lasts a life's time' along with those qualities that give meaning to existence: 'Honesty, kindness, courage, fidelity'. But the people are drawn back from death not only by their love of the living and by their thoughts of the dignity and compassion that is part of the human condition, but also by their debt to the dead which only they, the living, can pay:

> And the dead
> Who lodge in us so strangely, unremembered,
> Yet in their place.

The living cannot renounce their own lives because the renunciation would cancel the past as well as the present and the future. The enormity of such a rejection, and the finality of it, would be greater than any despair the living have to endure:

> For how can we reject
> The long last look on the ever-dying face
> Turned backward from the other side of time?

The image of 'the ever-dying face' suggests the continuity of death and life, or death-in-life, and the phrase, 'from the other side of time' introduces the idea of timelessness into the continuity. Through this painfully earned re-discovery of the human succession the poet is able to accept his present human condition:

> And how offend the dead and shame the living
> By these despairs? And how refrain from love?
> This is a difficult country, and our home.

The theme of the succession runs throughout *One Foot In Eden*—sometimes implicitly as in the explorations of the myths of Prometheus, Orpheus, Oedipus and Telemachos—and it is the theme of several late, posthumously published poems, notably 'The Brothers', 'Dialogue' ('Returning from the antipodes of time'), and 'The Forgotten Dead'. The simple conclusion is probably true: as Muir approaches the end of his life he becomes more and more aware of death. But his faith allows him to see death not as a cessation but as fulfilment, and with the further promise of immortality. He sees death as part of the complete cycle of the individual and the race, and through his greater vision he sees that the dead can find fulfilment through their recognition by the living. This continuity is a form of earthly immortality, and this secular succession of common humanity is more central to Muir's vision than a concept of an apostolic succession of Christ and his saints.

Muir expresses the myth of the succession with a growing confidence and clarity in his last ten years, but during the same period he became increasingly aware of the great threats to the earthly succession, the threat of the nuclear holocaust and the other, more gradual but equally destructive threat of science and technology. The threat as Muir sees it is that science and technology might become powerful, almost irresistible forces that could bring about an impersonal and mechanistic order of existence in which man would be divorced from the natural world, from his fellow men and even from himself. The rapid changes introduced by science and technology, and the associated concept of progressive change as a universal ideal, would put an end to man's sense of the earthly succession. In Muir's vision of human continuity, past, present and future are equal elements in the same dimension of time, and time is seen against the background of eternity. But in contrast to this a technological regime necessarily rejects the past—and to some extent rejects human values—in favour of constant change within a context of change.

These fears are expressed in some of Muir's prose of the 1950s: the essay, 'The Decline Of The Imagination';[15] the Harvard lectures, particularly 'The Natural Estate' and 'Poetry And The Poet' in *The Estate of Poetry*; and the late essay, 'The Poetic Imagination' in the second edition of *Essays On Literature And Society* where Muir writes:

> We live in a world created by applied science, and our present is unlike the present of any other age. The difference between our world and the world of the imagination is growing greater, and may become so great that the one can hardly understand any longer the other. Applied science shows us a world of consistent, mechanical progress. There machines give birth to ever new generations of machines, and the new machines are always better and more efficient than the old, and begin where the old left off. If we could attribute sentience to a new machine, we should find that it simply did not understand the old, being too far ahead, in another world.[16]

There would be no understanding, and no continuity, between past and present. The paragraph ends:

> . . . when outward change becomes too rapid, and the world around us alters from year to year, the ancestral image grows indistinct, and the imagination cannot pierce to it as easily as it once could.

But between the opening and the conclusion of this paragraph Muir offers a contrasting image of life:

> But in the world of human beings all is different; there we find no mechanical progress, no starting where a previous generation left off; instead there is a continuity ruled by repetition. Every human being has to begin at the beginning, as his forebears did, with the same difficulties and pleasures, the same temptations, the same problem of good and evil, the same inward conflict, the same need to learn how to live, the same inclination to ask what life means. Conspicuous virtue, when this creature encounters it, may move him, or a new and saving faith, since the desire for goodness and truth is also in his nature. Nevertheless he will pass through the same ancestral pattern and have the same feelings, the same difficulties as generations long before he was born. All this may seem dull to the thinker, but it enchants the imagination, for it is an image of human life.

It is this image of life that Muir celebrates in the poem, 'Into Thirty Centuries Born'.[17] The opening lines express his unease at some aspects of the present that contrast with the reaffirmation of human identity that we get from the past:

> Into thirty centuries born,
> At home in them all but the very last,
> We meet ourselves at every turn
> In the long country of the past.

In this poem 'the long country of the past' is more fully realised than it is in 'The Difficult Land'. Here it becomes a realm of purification and redemption in which the dead, instead of simply being held in suspension as they wait for recognition from the living, experience a form of resurrection:

> There the fallen are up again
> In mortality's second day,
> There the indisputable dead
> Rise in flesh more fine than clay.

There is redemption too for the living as our broken identities are made whole:

> And the dead selves we cast away
> In imperfection are perfected.

The same sense of wholeness prompts the exclamation of delight: 'And all is plain yet never found out!' 'The poet sees himself, plainly but inexplicably, as part of the living mystery of the human succession in which past and present co-exist. And then Muir's vision intensifies so that, within the framework of co-existent time, the past seems to evolve against the flow of time and, like Judas in 'The Transfiguration', 'Old Priam shall become a boy/For ever changed, for ever the same'. It is a vision in which the poet's personal past with its images of 'The horses on the roundabout' and 'The gunboat in the little bay' are transformed from the condition of static emblems and become part of the living past of all mankind so that the poet's personal fable becomes part of the universal fable. It is a vision in which the past is not history but prophecy and in which the myth of original innocence, and the myth of the fall, become present, ordinary realities:

> And round a corner you may see
> Man, maid and tempter under the tree.

At this point in the second stanza, with that characteristic change of pace and direction that is a deliberate feature of Muir's narrative technique, he introduces a note of doubt. Is the vision mere self-delusion or is it a form of truth? And in asking the question Muir's concern is for 'the helpless dead' as well as for present or future generations:

> Is it fantasy or faith
> That keeps intact that marvellous show
> And saves the helpless dead from harm?

In the remaining lines of the poem, a reflection on the vision rather than an extension of it, the mystery is at first reduced to:

> Tomorrow sound the great alarm
> That puts the histories to rout;
> Tomorrow after tomorrow brings
> Endless beginning without end.

But the third stanza opens with the confident belief that the unity will extend into the future: 'Then on this moment set your foot,/Take your road for everywhere'. The human condition is uncertain, 'a place of hope and fear', of 'defeat and victory', but the strength of the vision in the first two stanzas convince the poet that it is also a condition in which faith can emerge even 'when hope is lost', and in which man is 'free/And bound to all'.

The closing lines of the poem recapture the intensity of the vision and restore the mystery:

> Time shall cancel time's deceits,
> And you shall weep for grief and joy
> To see the whole world perishing
> Into everlasting spring,
> And over and over the opening briar.

Time's deceits will be cancelled not by transcending time and achieving immortality but by time itself; fulfilment comes not through an escape from the human condition but by accepting its grief and joy, its cycle of death and resurrection. And in the act of acceptance Muir finds his symbol of fulfilment and perpetuity:[18]

And over and over the opening briar.

ONE FOOT IN EDEN

This act of acceptance, which is itself an expression of faith, is the force that prompts some of Muir's most joyful lyric poetry. Poems from the 1940s onwards—'The Transmutation', 'A Birthday', 'All We', 'In Love For Long', 'The Animals', 'The Days', 'The Late Wasp', 'The Late Swallow' and 'Sunset'—these poems and others are the responses of someone who is, as Muir said of himself, in love with the world. But they are even more than this; they are the poems of the traveller who has completed the pilgrimage and discovered the place in which he is accepted, the place of his resurrection. They are the poems of the pilgrim who knows that the place is not so much a particular location as a way of seeing, who knows that the end of the pilgrimage is a vision of acceptance and fulfilment. It is a vision clarified by faith, and the poems of that vision begin to appear after Muir's religious crisis of 1939 with his re-acceptance of Christ and the immortality of the soul. Through his faith and his vision Muir finds the meaning he has been seeking for much of his life.

In the early essay, 'Against The Wise', which first appeared in 1921 and was republished in 1924 in *Latitudes*, he writes:

> We desire to possess a wisdom which does not merely deny, but which transcends its denial; which not only creates the antithesis, thought and life, but also reconciles them; a wisdom not merely conscious, a form finally empty and void, but a wisdom both conscious and unconscious, fundamental, integral, the affirmation not in words merely, but in being, of all existence, the one and only real affirmation.[1]

Muir may have been recalling his experience of psychoanalysis in 1919 when he writes of a wisdom that comes from the integration of the conscious and the unconscious, and it is possible that as Muir moved towards this kind of integration he might have been able to make 'the one and only real affirmation' by achieving a unified state of mind. But the assimilation of conscious and unconscious is the basis of a much greater process of integration. Muir's belief in the wisdom of the unconscious and the healing power of dreams is a form of faith, and to this he adds those other elements of personal faith—in the natural world, in the living dead—and the faith he finds in Plato, the *Upanishads* and in Christianity. Part of Muir's mature wisdom is his ability to accept, and through accepting to understand, the suffering of persons and of nations; it is an understanding that owes much to his personal qualities of penetrating intelligence and rare humility that allow him to see meaning and pattern in the fragmentary affairs of mankind.

His imagination is greatly enriched by other men's visions, for example, Hölderlin's, Kafka's, and the anonymous authors' of the Scottish ballads, but a distinctive quality of Muir's imagination—his ability, and his willingness, to see no real distinction between the ordinary and the fabulous—is one that remains with him from his early childhood until his death. Muir was aware of these things and aware too of the continuous process, partly deliberate and partly involuntary, of assimilation. In a broadcast talk in 1952 he said:

> . . . for once the imagination is awakened it cannot stop until it tries to unite all experience, past and present, serious and trivial.[2]

The unity of experience Muir speaks of here, and the affirmation of being he writes of in *Latitudes*, are expressed in his radiant lyrics. One of the earliest of the poems of joy, 'The Transmutation'[3] from *The Voyage*, creates the effect of the unity of time and the redemption of the present by the living past and by the poet's delighted vision of time as an expression of eternity. The new vision brings a new sense of the mystery of a world poised between permanence and change, between eternity and time:

> That all should change to ghost and glance and gleam,
> And so transmuted stand beyond all change,
> And we be poised between the unmoving dream
> And the sole moving moment—this is strange.

Man fell into time and the corruption of time, but he also fell into 'this phantom ground', a spiritual order of existence as real as the physical:

> . . . that we who fall
> Through time's long ruin should weave this phantom ground
> And in its ghostly borders gather all.

A prelapsarian innocence is still available to fallen man: 'There incorruptible the child plays still', and to experience this innocence is to experience time as the expression of eternity:

> As in commemoration of a day
> That having been can never pass away.

With 'The Transmutation' Muir achieves the kind of affirmation he strives for in *Latitudes*, the fully realised expression of a state of being that can be made only in poetry. In his prose, and especially in the two autobiographies, Muir describes with a unique lucidity the mysteries that preoccupy him; in the poems he penetrates and re-enacts the mysteries. The prose accounts are descriptions of a state whereas the poems are re-creations of the state. This distinction between prose and poetry is not of course an absolute one, but it is a distinction Muir himself makes in his critical volume, *Scott And Scotland*, published in 1936. Muir makes the distinction with particular reference to Scottish literature, and then he speaks of the unifying power of poetry:

> Poetry is not spontaneous in the sense that it is restricted to the expression of simple and spontaneous feelings, but rather in the sense that it reconciles the antithesis of feeling and thought into a harmony, achieving with apparent effortlessness a resolution of subject-matter which to the ratiocinative mind is known only as a difficulty to be overcome by intense effort.[4]

Muir goes on to discuss the fragmentation of intellect and emotion in Scottish literature, referring to 'that reciprocally destructive confrontation of both for which Gregory Smith found the name of "the Caledonian antisyzygy".' (The antisyzygy was never a problem for Muir personally; his early poem, 'Ballad Of The Soul', offers a vision of the syzygy restored). In the same paragraph in *Scott and Scotland* Muir suggests that this confrontation and others can be resolved through poetry and the imagination:

> The mere assertion of life in its most simple form is an act of reconciliation. And the mark of great poetry, as Coleridge said, is that it reconciles all opposites into a harmony.[5]

Such a reconciliation is Muir's achievement in 'The Transmutation' and the other poems of joy. The volume, *The Voyage*, ends with three poems that form a trilogy of delight: 'A Birthday', 'All We', and 'In Love For Long'.[6]
'A Birthday' opens with sharply defined images of sensuous delight:

> The tingling smell and touch
> Of dogrose and sweet briar,
> Nettles against the wall,
> All sours and sweets that grow
> Together or apart
> In hedge or marsh or ditch.

And by the end of the first stanza the delight extends to all things, plants and creatures and the elements:

> I gather to my heart
> Beast, insect, flower, earth, water, fire,
> In absolute desire,
> As fifty years ago.

the line, 'As fifty years ago', introduces a new element into the poem. The poet's enjoyment of the world is like the wonder he experienced as a child, and now he finds he is seeing the world with a more than child-like innocence; it is as if the wonder and innocence precede life itself:

> Before I took the road
> Direction ravished my soul.

And it is this prelapsarian innocence and delight that allow him to see the
pattern of the completed pilgrimage in the closing lines of the poem:

> Now that I can discern
> It whole or almost whole,
> Acceptance and gratitude
> Like travellers return
> And stand where they first stood.

In 'All We', the second poem in the trilogy, Muir expresses his profound
satisfaction as an artist in having the whole world as his subject matter. This
brief lyric conveys the solemn ecstasy of the poet's marriage vow with the
world, and of the mysterious power of the poet not only as the maker
of poems but, through the imagination, as the re-maker of the world he
celebrates:

> All we who make
> Things transitory and good
> Cannot but take
> When walking in a wood
> Pleasure in everything
> And the maker's solicitude,
> Knowing the delicacy
> Of bringing shape to birth.
> To fashion the transitory
> We gave and took the ring
> And pledged ourselves to the earth.

In the 1952 radio broadcast already referred to Muir introduced the third of
these lyrics, 'In Love For Long', with this comment on its origins:

> The genesis of . . . 'In Love For Long', I can remember vividly. I was up at
> Swanston in the Pentlands one Saturday morning during the War. It was in late
> summer; a dull, cloudy, windless day, quite warm. I was sitting on the grass,
> looking at the thatched cottages and the hills, when I realised that I was fond of
> them, suddenly and without reason, and for themselves, not because the cottages
> were quaint or the hills romantic. I had an unmistakable warm feeling for the
> ground I was sitting on, as if I were in love with the earth itself, and the clouds,
> and the soft subdued light. I had felt these things before, but that afternoon they
> seemed to crystallise, and the poem came out of them.[7]

But between the starting point of the poem as Muir describes it here and the
poem itself there is an unexplained development; the poem includes none of
the imagery in the prose introduction—the grass, the hills, the cottages, the
quality of light. These details are omitted, and the poem reads as if Muir
knew that the object of his love was more than the configuration of a place,
more even than the spirit of a particular place. Throughout the poem Muir
admits that he cannot name or define the thing he loves and yet at the same
time he knows the indefinable thing is real:

> It is not any thing,
> And yet all being is;
> Being, being, being,
> Its burden and its bliss.

If the thing is to be named at all it can be named only as 'being', with both its burden and its bliss. The love 'Is sieged with crying sorrows', is 'A little paradise/Held in the world's vice' and yet within that grip the thing 'Flourishes sweet and wild'. The poem ends with a complex image in which the indefinable quality

> Is like the happy doe
> That keeps its perfect laws
> Between the tiger's claws
> And vindicates its cause.

The indefinable thing is the quality of original innocence that survives the fall, the moment of eternity surrounded by time.

In this trilogy, and particularly in 'In Love For Long', Muir penetrates the mystery of being by means of joy as he does in other poems by means of suffering or by a form of Christian revelation. What Muir says about Wordsworth in 'Wordsworth: Return To Sources', the second lecture in *The Estate of Poetry*, is relevant here and equally true of Muir himself:

> Wordsworth returned to a source of poetry when he returned to incidents and situations of common life; but his return took him further back; it took him back to the earth itself. He knew with unique clearness that we depend on the earth for our life . . . this is a common fact; but Wordsworth was aware as no other poet has been of the countless less palpable gifts which we owe to the earth, or to nature. His knowledge came to him, as we have seen, in that blessed mood when we see into the life of things.[8]

Like Wordsworth, Muir is aware of our dependence on the earth, and like Wordsworth he too experiences the blessed mood and sees into the life of things.

This insight is expressed in two pairs of matching lyrics in *One Foot In Eden*: 'The Animals' and 'The Days', and 'The Late Wasp' and 'The Late Swallow'. 'The Animals'[9] is a simple tribute to the order of living things that exist in a perpetual present, 'the unchanging Here/Of the fifth great day of God'. The final line of the poem, 'On the sixth day we came', stands alone, and one feels that Muir's purpose is to show man's emergence from—his nearness and yet separation from—the animal world. But here Muir seems to have miscalculated the days of the creation. In the Genesis myth the fifth day was the day of the creation of fish and birds, while the sixth day was the day of the creation of both animals and mankind. Muir's implied point about the kinship of man and animals gains added impact when one notes that the two, man and the animals, are of the same Biblical order of creation.

'The Days', which first appeared as a companion poem to 'The Animals', also has its starting point in the creation myth but its scope is greater than that of 'The Animals'. 'The Days' is a response to all the days of the creation, all the elements and creatures, the colours and movements; at the same time the poem is a celebration of the human senses that make it possible for man to enjoy the world. It is enjoyment, delighted recognition, in the sense in which Traherne knew it.

In the closing chapter of *The Story And The Fable* Muir expresses his admiration for 'the wonderful first two sections of Traherne's *Centuries Of Meditation*', and he quotes the beginning of Section 14 of the First Century:

> When things are ours in their proper places, nothing is needful but prizing to enjoy them. God therefore hath made it infinitely easy to enjoy, by making everything ours, and us able so easily to prize them. Everything is ours that serves us in its place.[10]

The attitude that runs through 'The Days' is that of Traherne's *Centuries*, a reverence and exultation for all things. Muir must also have known Section 29 of the First Century, which is perhaps Traherne's supreme expression of this attitude:

> You never Enjoy the World aright, till the Sea it self floweth in your Veins, till you are Clothed with the Heavens, and Crowned with the Stars: and perceiv your self to be the Sole Heir of the whole World; and more then so, becaus Men are in it who are evry one Sole Heirs, as well as you. Till you can Sing and Rejoyce and Delight in GOD, as Misers do in Gold, and Kings in Scepters, you never Enjoy the World.[11]

In 'The Days' Muir imagines the inchoate universe taking shape, the chaos being differentiated into water and land, light and shadow, heaven and earth:

> The waters stirred
> And from the doors were cast
> Wild lights and shadows on the formless face
> Of the flood of chaos, vast
> Lengthening and dwindling image of earth and heaven.

The first half of the poem speaks of the creation and is itself an image of creation; the second half of the poem is an extended image of the completeness of the fully formed world. In the closing lines Muir suggests that the harmony of the world is part of an even greater harmony and that the 'fragmentary day' will be gathered into an everlasting day:

> The women praying
> For the passing of this fragmentary day
> Into the day where all are gathered together,
> Things and their names, in the storm's and the lightning's nest.
> The seventh great day and the clear eternal weather.

The seventh day, the day God blessed and sanctified,[12] is the completeness of the creation. And when the poet too blesses the seventh day he is celebrating a way of seeing, a wholeness of vision in which the seventh day, 'the clear eternal weather', is an image of eternity.

There is a different sense of completeness in 'The Late Wasp' and 'The Late Swallow'.[13] In these two poems the sense of fulfilment has elegiac undertones as if in the images of the insect and the bird—the *late* wasp and swallow—the poet senses his own approaching death. In a radio broadcast in 1954 Muir offered a brief introduction to the two poems:

> The last two poems are more in the nature of songs, with only a floating residue of meaning, and a faint echo of thought. The first has to do with the eternal return of things; the second with the bourne towards which all things move.[14]

It is clear that the two poems are more than the titles indicate, and clear too that Muir's introduction understates—or perhaps deliberately avoids—part of the meanings of these poems. In these lines from 'The Late Wasp', 'You and the earth have now grown older,/And your blue thoroughfares have felt a change', Muir is surely speaking of his own condition. And in the closing lines of 'The Late Swallow' it is as if he sees his own fate reflected in that of the bird:

> Shake our your pinions long untried
> That now must bear you there where you would be
> Through all the heavens of ice.

The swallow will fly through 'the heavens of ice', through a literal and metaphorical winter, into another climate and another order of existence:

> Till falling down the homing air
> You light and perch upon the radiant tree.

In saying that 'The Late Swallow' is concerned with the bourne towards which all things move, Muir is clearly suggesting more than the destination of the migrating bird. The bourne is also the end of the human journey, and 'the radiant tree' at the end of the journey is the cross unmade and growing eternally as the tree of life. The radiance at the end of the journey is not simply sunlight but also the divine light that is the universal symbol of spiritual enlightenment at the end of the religious way.[15]

This eternal radiance appears again in one of the last poems Muir wrote, the posthumously published 'Sunset'.[16] It seems certain that the starting point of the poem was an actual sunset, but what begins as a nature lyric becomes a beatific vision. As Muir looks he sees not only the setting of the sun but:

> Fold upon fold of light,
> Half-heaven of tender fire,
> Conflagration of peace,
> Wide hearth of the evening world.

The beauty of the light, and the poet's way of seeing, combine to give a double transfiguration: the world is redefined by the evening radiance and by the poet's vision of a harmony that is both natural and mystical:

> Man, beast and tree in fire,
> The bright cloud showering peace.

With its intensity of vision and with its imagery of light, heaven, and peace—horses 'Are bridled and reined by light/As in a heavenly field'—'Sunset' has the apocalyptic effect of the marriage of heaven and earth.

A greater but more sombre statement of the marriage of heaven and earth is the poem, 'One Foot In Eden'.[17] In the opening lines Muir re-affirms his belief that an element of original innocence remains in the fallen human condition:

> One foot in Eden still I stand
> And look across the other land.

And the third line, 'The World's great day is growing late', introduces a sense of urgency that may be prompted by Muir's feeling that little time remains for him personally or prompted by the wider fear of a nuclear holocaust.

When the poet looks at 'the other land', this world, he sees that opposites are inextricably interwoven—love and hate, corn and tares, the weed bound about the stalk—and he concludes:

> Evil and good stand thick around
> In the fields of charity and sin
> Where we shall lead our harvest in.

The stanza is like a version of Christ's parable of the wheat and the tares but the second stanza departs from, and finally rejects, Christ's interpretation of the parable. The divergence between poem and parable is striking. Matthew quotes Christ as saying:

> He answered and said unto them, He that soweth the good seed is the Son of man; the field is the world; the good seed are the children of the kingdom; but the tares are the children of the wicked one; the enemy that sowed them is the devil; the harvest is the end of the world; and the reapers are the angels. As therefore the tares are gathered and burned in the fire; so shall it be in the end of this world. The Son of man shall send forth his angels, and they shall gather out of his kingdom all things that offend, and them which do iniquity; and shall cast them into a furnace of fire: there shall be wailing and gnashing of teeth.[18]

But the first lines of Muir's second stanza interrupt the symbolism of sowing and harvesting to re-introduce the idea of the continuous flow of goodness and innocence from the eternal, prelapsarian source:

> Yet still from Eden springs the root
> As clean as on the starting day.[19]

Muir offers this hopeful note but follows it immediately with another change of direction; the root springs from Eden but the plant grows in the fallen world of time, and time is like the reaper in the parable, casting all things that offend into the furnace:

> Time takes the foliage and the fruit
> And burns the archetypal leaf
> To shapes of terror and of grief
> Scattered along the winter way.

It is as if the conflict of the earlier poems, the old dualism of time and eternity, mutability and immortality, has returned. An earlier poem might have ended with the dualism unresolved or with a forced resolution, while some of the later poems resolve the dilemma through Christian faith. But here Muir does something different: he accepts time and its consequences, the terror and the grief, and in accepting them he rejects the conclusion of the New Testament parable. Muir looks at this fallen world and finds not the wailing and gnashing of teeth that Christ promised but a form of earthly redemption through those qualities that make us truly human:

> But famished field and blackened tree
> Bear flowers in Eden never known.
> Blossoms of grief and charity
> Bloom in these darkened fields alone.

Muir's response here is not that of 'the blessed fall', welcoming the expulsion from Eden as the first move in a divine plan that leads to the incarnation and finally to the resurrection of Christ and the redemption of mankind. There is no reference to Christ in Muir's poem. Instead, and with an undertone of almost defiant celebration, Muir welcomes the fall as the means through which mankind discovers the riches of humanity:

> What had Eden ever to say
> Of hope and faith and pity and love
> Until was buried all its day
> And memory found its treasure trove?

Man fell from the innocence of Eden, from the paradise of unconscious childhood, into this imperfect world of time and mutability. But it is only in this fallen world, and only with his consciousness of good and evil, that man can enjoy the great human qualities that did not exist—could not exist— before the fall. And it is on this note that the poem ends:

> Strange blessings never in Paradise
> Fall from these beclouded skies.

'One Foot In Eden' celebrates the human condition and the triumph of the human spirit, and yet this vision of existence is part of the wider vision. Man has 'One foot in Eden still' and 'still from Eden springs the root/As clean as on the starting day'. This vision of life seen against eternity is in turn part of the even greater vision that emerges from Muir's work. It is a vision that reveals the underworld of the unconscious, acknowledges man's kinship with animals and with gods, imagines the formation of the cosmos and the creation of the earth, penetrates the mysteries of man's origin and end, and even sees the possibility of the destruction of mankind and the world. Muir's vision is in fact the 'supertemporal drama' he describes in the essay, 'Yesterday's Mirror':

> The third glance into the mirror is given only to the greatest poets and mystics at their greatest moments, and is beyond rational description. The world the mystical poet sees is a world in which both good and evil have their place legitimately; in which the king on his throne and the rebel raising his standard in the market place, the tyrant and the slave, the assassin and the victim, each plays a part in a supertemporal drama which at every moment, in its totality, issues in glory and meaning and fulfilment. This vision is too dangerous for us as human beings struggling in the arena; it would be safe only if we felt no touch of evil; and it is given to men only when they are at the very heart of good, and, in a sense very different from Nietzsche's, beyond good and evil. St Augustine saw it and so did Blake; it is the supreme vision of human life, because it reconciles our moral struggle, for in life we are ourselves the opposites and must act as best we can.[20]

Muir does not make this claim for himself, but the third glance in the mirror is a true account of his own achievement. His vision of existence includes the horror, the degradation and the futility, but it is also a vision that includes the mystical, the sublime. At its most joyful Muir's is a beatific vision, and such a vision beatifies the visionary so that he too can be seen as a source of grace.[21]

REFERENCES

THE RISE AND FALL OF THE SUPERMAN pp 8 to 18

1   Edwin Muir, *We Moderns* (Published under the pseudonym Edward Moore) (London, 1918), p 68
2   P H Butter, *Selected Letters of Edwin Muir* (London, 1974), p 21
3   Edwin Muir, *An Autobiography* (London, 1954), p 134
4   *We Moderns*, p 171
5   Ibid. pp 172–3
6   Friedrich Wilhelm Nietzsche, *Thus Spoke Zarathustra* (Harmondsworth, 1969), Introduction, pp 28–9
7   *An Autobiography*, p 151
8   Ibid. pp 157–67
9   Maurice Nicoll, *Dream Psychology* (London, 1920), p 40
10 See *An Autobiography*, pp 158, 163
11 Maurice Nicoll, op.cit. Introduction, ix
12 Ibid. Introduction, ix, x
13 Ibid. p 180
14 Ibid. p 80
15 *An Autobiography*, pp 158–9
16 Ibid. p 158
17 Jung writes: 'Symbols were never devised consciously, but were always produced out of the unconscious by way of revelation or intuition. In view of the close connection between mythological symbols and dream symbols, and of the fact that the dream is "le dieu des sauvages", it is more than probable that most of the historical symbols derive directly from dreams or are at least influenced by them.' *The Structure And Dynamics Of The Psyche* (London, 1960), p 48
18 *An Autobiography*, pp 159–62
19 *Collected Poems*, pp 26–31
20 Kathleen Raine, 'The Journey From Eden', *New Statesman*, 23 April 1960, p 595
21 P H Butter, *Edwin Muir: Man And Poet* (Edinburgh and London, 1966), p 98
22 Elizabeth Huberman, *The Poetry of Edwin Muir: The Field of Good and Ill* (New York, 1971), p 45
23 Nicoll, op.cit. p 24
24 C G Jung, *Modern Man In Search of a Soul* (London, 1961), p 186
25 'A Note On The Scottish Ballads': *Freeman*, VI; January 17, 1923, pp 441–4. Reprinted in Andrew Noble, *Edwin Muir: Uncollected Scottish Criticism* (London, 1982), pp 155–65
26 C G Jung, *The Archetypes and the Collective Unconscious* (London, 1959), p 180
27 C G Jung, *Mysterium Coniunctionis* (London, 1963), p 253. See also J A Hadfield, *Dreams and Nightmares* (Harmondsworth, 1969), p 136. Hadfield writes: 'The

analogy of a deep lake may suggest the idea of the unconscious mind much more comprehensively than the word "unconscious", bringing before our minds, as it does, the picture of vast depths, and of living processes going on in these depths which are not visible on the surface of consciousness and of which we know little, but which every now and then cause trouble on the face of the waters.'

28 C G Jung, *Mysterium Coniunctionis*, p 223. Freud's interpretation of this kind of symbolism is this: 'I added from my own knowledge derived from elsewhere that climbing down, like climbing up in other cases, described sexual intercourse in the vagina.' *The Interpretations of Dreams* (London, 1967), p 365

29 *An Autobiography*, p 158

30 Freud, op. cit. pp 399–400

31 'In Search Of Edwin Muir', BBC Broadcast of 28 April 1964; p 20 of script.

VERSIONS OF EVERYMAN pp 19 to 25

1 *An Autobiography*, pp 48–9

2 Ibid. p 14

3 Ibid. pp 24–5

4 Ibid. p 206

5 Ibid. p 25

6 Ibid. p 246

7 P H Butter, *Selected Letters of Edwin Muir* (London, 1974), p 95

8 P H Butter, *Edwin Muir: Man and Poet*, pp 168–9

9 P H Butter, *Selected Letters of Edwin Muir*, p 115

10 Ibid. pp 154–5

11 C G Jung, *Psychology and Religion: East and West*, translated by R F C Hull (London, 1958), p 157

CHILDHOOD AND PARADISE pp 29 to 38

1 *An Autobiography*, p 274

2 Willa Muir, *Belonging: A Memoir* (London, 1968), p 249

3 *An Autobiography*, p 151

4 Ibid. p 52

5 Edwin Muir, *We Moderns* (Published under the pseudonym Edward Moore) (London, 1918), p 63

6 Ibid. pp 63–4

7 Ibid. p 64

8 Ibid. p 64

9 *An Autobiography*, p 157

10 Sigmund Freud, *Totem and Taboo: Some Points of Agreement Between the Mental Lives of Savages and Neurotics* (London, 1961, first published 1913), pp 68, 141, 146; Freud does not refer directly to the myth of the fall or to the tree in Eden, but his associate, Theodor Reik, argues that the Eden myth is a remnant of tree totemism and that the primal crime—the original sin—was an act of cannibalism in which the father of the tribe, the god-king, was eaten. Reik then goes on to draw parallels between this and the Crucifixion and the Eucharist. See Theodor Reik, *Myth And Guilt: The Crime And Punishment Of Mankind* (London, 1958)

11 James George Frazer, *The Golden Bough: A Study In Magic And Religion* (London, 1963, first published 1922) and *Folk-Lore In The Old Testament: Studies In Comparative Religion, Legend And Law* (London, 1923)

12 The literature is extensive. Works consulted for this study are: Normal Powell Williams, *The Ideas of the Fall and of Original Sin* (London, 1927); C S Lewis, *The Problem of Pain* (especially Chapter V) (London, 1940); J S Whale, *Christian Doctrine* (London, 1957, first published 1941); John James, *Why Evil? A Biblical Approach* (Harmondsworth, 1960); Peter de Rosa, *Christ and Original Sin* (London, 1967)

13 *We Moderns*, p 64

14 Ibid. p 65

15 Ibid. p 69

16 Ibid. p 70

17 *The Golden Bough*, p 223

18 *Totem And Taboo*, p 68

19 Williams, op. cit. p 13

20 Ibid. p 514

21 C G Jung, *The Structure and Dynamics of the Psyche* (London, 1960), p 388

22 *We Moderns*, pp 68, 71

23 *Poor Tom*, p 93

24 Neil M Gunn, from 'In Search Of Edwin Muir'; BBC Radio Broadcast, 28 April 1964; p 29 of script

25 Lewis, op. cit. p 67

26 *Collected Poems*, p 19

27 Ibid. p 144

28 Ibid. p 244

29 'Scottish Life And Letters'; BBC Radio Broadcast, 23 May 1954; p1 of script

30 *Collected Poems*, pp 272–3

31 P H Butter, *Selected Letters of Edwin Muir*, p 191. In a letter to the poet, Kathleen Raine, Muir writes (24 January, 1957): 'I am trying to write one now about a dream I had recently about my two brothers, Willie and Johnny, dead fifty years ago. I watched them playing in a field, racing about in some game, and it was not a game which either of them was trying to win (there was no winning in it), and because of that they were infinitely happy in making each other happy, and all that was left in their hearts and their bodies was grace. It is very difficult to convey this in a poem. I had not thought of them for a long time. And when I did know them (I was little more than a boy then) there was affection, but also little grouses and jealousies, assertions of the will, a cloud of petty disagreements and passions which hid their true shape from me and from themselves. In the dream it seemed to me the cloud was dispelled and I saw them as they were.'

THE BROKEN CITADEL pp 39 to 46

1 *Collected Poems*, pp 128–9

2 James Kinsley (ed), *The Oxford Book of Ballads* (London, 1969), pp 598–602

3 *The Three Brothers*, p 9

4 Ibid. p 13

5 Ibid. p 15

6 *Collected Poems*, pp 71, 72–3

7 Ibid. pp 76–7

8   Ibid. pp 183–6
9   *Chapbook*, 'The Poems of Edwin Muir'; BBC Radio Broadcast of 3 September 1952: p 12 of script
10   Edwin Morgan, 'Edwin Muir' in *The Review*, Number 5, February 1963
11   See *An Autobiography*, pp 251–2
12   Ibid. p 268. See also pp 266–73

THE HOLOCAUST pp 47 to 58

1   *An Autobiography*, p 194
2   Ibid.
3   Ibid.
4   *Collected Poems*, pp 246–7
5   P H Butter, *Selected Letters of Edwin Muir*, p 205
6   *Listener*, 10 May 1951, pp 753–4
7   *Collected Poems*, pp 267–8
8   Ibid. p 298
9   Ibid. p 265
10   Peter Alexander, *Atomic Radiation and Life* (Harmondsworth, 1965, first published in 1957), pp 132–51
11   Ibid. pp 150–1
12   Ibid. p 169
13   *Collected Poems*, pp 282–5
14   P H Butters, *Selected Letters of Edwin Muir*, pp 202–3, 204
15   *The Estate Of Poetry*, p 8
16   *Collected Poems*, pp 300–301
17   Ibid. p 8; Introduction by Willa Muir and J C Hall
18   *The Three Brothers*, pp 333–37
19   Peter Butter, *Edwin Muir: Man and Poet*, pp 290–91
20   Edith Sitwell, *The Canticle of the Rose: Selected Poems 1920–1947* (London, 1949), pp 253–63

THE LOST GARDEN pp 59 to 68

1   ' "Royal Man": Notes on the tragedies of George Chapman', in *Essays on Literature and Society* (London, 1966, first published 1949), p 28
2   *First Poems* (London, 1925)
3   Ibid. p 11
4   Ibid. p 13
5   Ibid. p 19
6   *Chorus of the Newly Dead* (London, 1926)
7   *Variations on a Time Theme* (London, 1934). *Collected Poems*, pp 39–53
8   *Scottish Journey*, p 124; (London, Heinemann in association with Gollancz, 1935)
9   *An Autobiography*, p 92
10   Peter de Rosa, *Christ and Original Sin* (London, 1967), p 27
11   For the concept of alienation and the myth of the fall see D M Baillie, *God Was In Christ* (London, 1961), p 204; E W Kemp (ed), *Man: Fallen and Free* (London, 1969), p 184; C S Lewis, op. cit. p 83; Peter de Rosa, op. cit. p 76

12   *The Narrow Place* II, 'Postscript' (London, 1943)
13   *Collected Poems*, p 132
14   Ibid. p 142
15   Ibid. pp 210–212
16   See Genesis, Chapter 3, verses 17–19

THE KILLING BEAST pp 71 to 78

1   *Collected Poems*, pp 24–6
2   Homer, *The Iliad*, XXII
3   Sir James Frazer, *The Golden Bough* (London, 1963), p 189
4   *The Three Brothers*, pp 47–9
5   *An Autobiography*, p 42
6   *An Autobiography*, pp 32–3
7   *The Three Brothers*, p 316
8   *An Autobiography*, p 213. See also *The Three Brothers*, p 254
9   See Willa Muir, *Belonging*, Chapter 8
10   Muir's tribute to Holms—in effect, an obituary—appears on pages 177 to 181 of the *Autobiography*; the portrait is detailed and analytical but is clearly prompted by affection and gratitude. But the Holms who accompanied the Muirs on their tour of Italy was 'indulgently authoritative', 'eager for agreement', and 'came between us and the Italy we wished to see for ourselves', Muir says on page 211 of the *Autobiography*, just before the account of the murderous dream.
11   *Collected Poems*, pp 94–5
12   Frazer, op. cit. p 191
13   See *Matthew*, 27, 55. See also *Luke*, 23, 55
14   *Collected Poems*, pp 179–180
15   *An Autobiography*, p 65
16   Ibid.
17   *Revelation*, 13, 2
18   *Daniel*, 7, 4–6
19   Butter (ed), *Selected Letters of Edwin Muir*, p 157
20   Peter Butter, *Edwin Muir* (Edinburgh, 1962), p 84

THE THREATENING WORLD pp 79 to 86

1   'The Inheritors', BBC broadcast of 27 March 1955; p 35 of script
2   *Latitudes* (London, 1924), p 218
3   *Poor Tom*, p 111
4   *An Autobiography*, p 35
5   Peter Butter, *Edwin Muir: Man and Poet*, p 12
6   *An Autobigraphy*, p 35
7   Ibid. p 37
8   *The Three Brothers*, p 29
9   *An Autobiography*, pp 90–129
10   *The Marionette*, p 10
11   *An Autobiography*, p 150
12   *The Marionette*, p 37

13   *Poor Tom*, p 142
14   *The Three Brothers*, p 240
15   *Collected Poems*, p 96
16   Willa Muir, *Belonging: A Memoir*, p 36
17   For a detailed study of this psychological division see R D Laing, *The Divided Self* (Harmondsworth, 1970)
18   *Poor Tom*, p 242
19   *The Three Brothers*, p 203. See also *An Autobiography*, p 52 where Muir has a vision of people as animals.
20   *The Three Brothers*, p 269
21   *An Autobiography*, p 121
22   *Collected Poems*, pp 50–52
23   Ibid. p 82
24   Ibid. pp 180–81
25   *An Autobiography*, p 154

AGAINST TIME pp 87 to 95

1   The conflict with time is clearly recognised as a search for faith at a crucial point in the novel, *Poor Tom*, when Mansie Manson 'longs for a faith that shall transfigure life'. The passage in the novel begins with Manson summarising and then rejecting a view of time and the universe that is similar to the theory of J W Dunne in the final chapter of his *An Experiment With Time*. The book was widely reviewed and discussed when it first appeared in 1927, five years before the publication of *Poor Tom*. It seems likely that Muir knew of Dunne's theory, and equally likely that he would feel uneasy at Dunne's claim for the theory: 'Its proof of the unity of all flesh in the Superbody and of all minds in the Master-mind supplies the logical foundation needed by every theory of ethics.'

The passage in *Poor Tom* goes on to express the need for faith as a means of penetrating the mystery of time and existence, and it ends with an admission of the powerful appeal exerted on Manson—and on Muir—by Nietzsche's theory of Eternal Recurrence. The passage reads:

> . . . if one were to comprehend the How from beginning to end, seeing every point in the universal future as luminously as the momentary and local point at which one stands, and seeing oneself with the same clarity as part of the whole, the universe might turn out to be merely a gigantic crystalline machine before which one must stand in blank contemplation, incapable any longer of even looking for a Why in it, so finally, though inexplicably, would that one thing be excluded by the consummated How. A man who has realized this fear, yet who longs for a faith that shall transfigure life, will be betrayed into a final mad affirmation, and in the vision of the Eternal Recurrence will summon from the void a blind and halt eternity to provide a little cheer and society for blind and halt time, and so alleviate its intolerable pathos.

Poor Tom, p 190
2   *The Story and the Fable*, p 263

3 *An Autobiography*, pp 194–5
4 Ibid.
5 *Collected Poems*, p 21
6 See this study, p 88
7 *Collected Poems*, pp 40–2
8 Gwendolen Murphy (ed), *The Modern Poet* (London, 1945, first published 1938), pp 168–70. An extract from Muir's letter to Gwendolen Murphy appears in P H Butter's *Selected Letters of Edwin Muir*, pp 213–4
9 Murphy, op. cit. p 169
10 *An Autobiography*, p 246
11 *Collected Poems*, pp 47–8
12 Ibid. pp 48–50
13 Ibid. pp 99–101
14 *The Story and the Fable*, pp 240–1
15 *Collected Poems*, pp 102–4, 105
16 *An Autobiography*, p 128

CONVERSIONS pp 96 to 101

1 *An Autobiography*, pp 85–7
2 Ibid. p 88
3 Ibid. p 87
4 Ibid. p 88
5 Ibid. p 113
6 Ibid. p 114
7 *Poor Tom*, p 102
8 Ibid. p 103
9 Ibid. p 103
10 *An Autobiography*, p 113
11 *Scottish Journey*, pp 146–7
12 Ibid. p 147
13 'Bolshevism and Calvinism' in *European Quarterly*, I (May 1934), pp 3–11. (Reprinted in *Edwin Muir: Uncollected Scottish Criticism*, edited by Andrew Noble (London, 1982))
14 Ibid. pp 3–4 (Noble, pp 123–4)
15 Ibid. p 7 (Noble, p 128)
16 Ibid. p 10 (Noble, p 129)
17 *Social Credit and the Labour Party* (London, 1935)
18 Ibid. pp 24–5
19 Ibid. pp 6–11
20 Ibid. p 13
21 Ibid. p 20

THE IRON TEXT pp 102 to 111

1 *An Autobiography*, pp 72–3
2 Ibid. pp 27–8
3 Ibid. p 26

4   Ibid. p 97
5   See WIlla Muir, *Belonging: A Memoir*, p 145
6   *John Knox: Portrait of a Calvinist*, pp 102–103
7   Ibid. pp 105–106
8   Ibid. pp 106–108
9   Ibid. pp 224–5
10 Jung writes that when the Protestants abandoned the Mass, the individual burdened himself with immense problems which the church had previously borne and solved for him. The resulting dissatisfaction, Jung argues, 'explains the demand for systems that promise an answer—the visible or at least noticeable favour of another (higher, spiritual, or divine) power.' See *Psychology And Religion: East And West* (London, 1958), p 531

    In *The Structure and Dynamics of the Psyche* Jung makes the interesting observation: '. . . fanaticism is always found in those who have to stifle a secret doubt. That is why converts are always the worst fanatics.' (London, 1960), p 307
11 *The Three Brothers*, p 296
12 *Poor Tom*, p 234
13 *Scott And Scotland*, p 23
14 Ibid. p 23
15 Ibid. pp 60–61
16 John MacQueen, *Ballatis of Luve* (Edinburgh, 1970), p lxviii
17 *Collected Poems*, pp 97–8
18 *John Knox*, p 116
19 *An Autobiography*, p 235
20 *Scottish Journey*, p 38 and *Collected Poems*, pp 229–30
21 *The Story and the Fable*, pp 246–7
22 *An Autobiography*, p 277
23 For a theological comment on 'logotheism' see D M Baillie, *God Was In Christ: An Essay on Incarnation and Atonement* (London, 1961), p 53
24 *Collected Poems*, pp 228–229. 'The Incarnate One' first appeared in the Edinburgh literary magazine, *The Saltire Review*, and one imagines that Muir may have chosen deliberately to make his statement in the city in which Knox had preached his brand of Calvinism.

THE ROAD pp 115 to 125

1   Stephen Spender, *World Within World* (London, 1951), p 290
2   H Harvey Wood, BBC broadcast of 31 August 1969, p 8 of script
3   See Nora Chadwick, *The Celts* (Harmondsworth, 1970), p. 206
4   *Collected Poems*, pp 45–7
5   *The Story and the Fable*, p 258
6   For the elements that make up the trickster figure see C G Jung, *The Archetypes and the Collective Unconscious*, Chapter V, 'On The Psychology Of The Trickster Figure' (London, 1959)
7   See the opening paragraph of the chapter, 'The Threatening World', for another version of the contradictory dialogue between the conscious and the unconscious mind.
8   'A Note on Franz Kafka', BBC broadcast of 23 September 1951 in *Scottish Life And Letters*, p 4 of script

9   *Essays on Literature and Society* (London, 1966), p 121
10 See Edith B Schnapper, *The Inward Odyssey* (London, 1965)
11 Op. cit.
12 *Selected Letters of Edwin Muir*, pp 111–13
13 Ibid. p 137
14 *Collected Poems*, pp 129–30
15 *An Autobiography*, p 251

For other critics on the theme of the journey in Muir's work see: Margaret Bottrall, in *The Critical Quarterly* II, Summer 1960, pp 179–80; J M Cohen, *Poetry of this Age: 1908–1965* (London, 1966), p 81; Fred Grice: 'The Poetry Of Edwin Muir', in *Essays in Criticism* Vol 5, 1955, pp 243–52; J R Watson, 'Edwin Muir And The Problem Of Evil', in *The Critical Quarterly* Vol 6, 1964, pp 231–49.

THE LOST WAY pp 126 to 130

1   *An Autobiography*, pp 34–35
2   Ibid. pp 149–150
3   Lamentations, Chapter 3, verses 6–9
4   *An Autobiography*, p 179
5   Anne Ridler (ed), *Thomas Traherne: Poems, Centuries and Three Thanksgivings* (London, 1966), p 275
6   *Collected Poems*, pp 80–81
7   *Journeys And Places* (London, 1937), p viii
8   *Selected Letters of Edwin Muir*, pp 85–6

THE BRIDGE OF DREAD pp 131 to 139

1   Willa Muir, *Belonging: A Memoir*, pp 43–7
2   Maurice Nicoll, *Dream Psychology* (London, 1920), Introduction pp ix, x
3   *An Autobiography*, p 163; Willa Muir, op. cit. p 46
4   Maurice Nicoll, op. cit. p 180
5   J A Hadfield; *Dreams And Nightmares* (Harmondsworth, 1954), pp 103–109
6   *An Autobiography*, p 246
7   *Collected Poems*, pp 101–102
8   In Jung's *Man and his Symbols*, Jung's associate, Jolande Jacobi, writes: 'A mountain pass is a well-known symbol for a "situation in transition" that leads from an old attitude of mind to a new one.' (Jung et al, *Man and his Symbols* (London, 1964), p 279)
    Freud offers his characteristic interpretation of the same symbol: 'A large number of dreams, often accompanied by anxiety and having as their content such subjects as passing through narrow spaces or being in water, are based upon phantasies of intra-uterine life, of existence in the womb and of the act of birth.' (Freud, *The Interpretation of Dreams* (London, 1967), p 399)
9   Jung, *The Archetypes and the Collective Unconscious* (London, 1959), p 21
10 *Collected Poems*, pp 108–109
11 Frazer, *The Golden Bough* (London, 1963), p 1
12 See Theodor Reik, *Myth and Guilt—The Crime and Punishment of Mankind* (London, 1958), pp 124–9
13 *Collected Poems*, pp 126–8

14   See Edith B Schnapper, *The Inward Odyssey* (London, 1965), pp 24–35; Jung et al, *Man and his Symbols*, p 171
15   *Collected Poems*, pp 175–6
See the traditional balad, 'A Lyke-Wake Dirge', stanzas 5 and 6:

> From whinny-muir when thou may'st pass,
>   — *Every nighte and alle,*
> To Brig o' Dread thou com'st at last;
>   *And Christe receive thy saule.*

> From Brig o' Dread when thou may'st pass,
>   — *Every nighte and alle,*
> To Purgatory fire thou com'st at last;
>   *And Christe receive thy saule.*

(Arthur Quiller-Couch (ed), *The Oxford Book of Ballads* (Oxford, 1924), p 139)
16   Exodus, Chapter 3, verse 2
17   See *An Autobiography*, p 157
18   Freud, op. cit. p 356
19   Gerhard Adler, *The Living Symbol—A Case Study in the Process of Individuation* (London, 1961), p 97
20   *The Story and the Fable*, pp 262–3
21   Juan Mascaro (ed), *The Upanishads* (Harmondsworth, 1970), p 121. See also Mascaro's Introduction, p 7
    Nietzsche too uses the symbol of the bridge. He conveys a similar sense of spiritual ordeal and transformation but it is the transformation from animal to Superman and a denial of humanity:

> 'Man is a rope, fastened between animal and Superman—a rope over an abyss.
> A dangerous going-across, a dangerous wayfaring, a dangerous looking-back, a dangerous shuddering and staying-still. What is great in man is that he is a bridge and not a goal; what can be loved in man is that he is a *going-across* and a *down-going*. . . .
> 'I love the great despisers, for they are the great venerators and arrows of longing for the other bank. . . .
> 'I love him who keeps back no drop of spirit for himself, but wants to be the spirit of his virtue entirely: thus he steps as spirit over the bridge. . . .
> 'I love him whose soul is deep even in its ability to be wounded, and whom even a little thing can destroy: thus he is glad to go over the bridge. . . .
> 'Behold, I am a prophet of the lightning and a heavy drop from the cloud: but this lightning is called *Superman*.'

(*Thus Spoke Zarathustra*, Part 1, 'Zarathustra's Prologue', 4; Trans R J Hollingdale, (Harmondsworth, 1969))

THREE MYSTERIES pp 140 to 151

1   *An Autobiography*, p 56
2   Ibid. p 57

3   See Reinhold Neibuhr, *The Nature and Destiny of Man*, Volume II, *Human Destiny* (London, 1943), p 297
4   *We Moderns*, p 68
5   Ibid.
6   'Yesterday's Mirror—Afterthoughts to an Autobiography', *Scots Magazine*, New Series, XXXIII, 1940, p 404
7   Ibid.
8   *An Autobiography*, p 192
9   Ibid. p 193
10 Ibid.
11 Ibid. p 44
12 Ibid.
13 *Collected Poems*, pp 57–9
14 Ibid. pp 62–3
15 *An Autobiography*, p 119
16 *Collected Poems*, pp 68–70
17 *An Autobiography*, p 56
18 *Collected Poems*, pp 163–5
19 'Chapbook: The Poems of Edwin Muir', BBC Broadcast of 3 September 1952, p 9 of script
20 See Sir James Frazer, *The Golden Bough*, pp 280–81

THE GOLDEN HARVESTER pp 152 to 160

1   *Collected Poems*, pp 168–75
2   See *An Autobiography*, pp 48–9, *Essays On Literature And Society*, p 225, *The Estate of Poetry*, p 88
3   *The Estate of Poetry*, p 89
4   *An Autobiography*, p 158
5   Ibid.
6   Peter Butter: 'Edwin Muir: "The Journey Back",' *English* Vol XVI, Number 96, Autumn 1967, pp 218–22
7   Ibid. p 220
8   Ibid.
9   See Shearer, Groundwater, Mackay, *The New Orkney Book* (London 1967), pp 1–2. See also Eric Linklater, *The Man On My Back*, (London 1947), pp 1–2; George Mackay Brown, *An Orkney Tapestry* (London 1969), pp 25–6

REDEMPTION pp 163 to 171

1   Plato, *Timaeus*, 4. Trans H D P Lee (Harmondsworth 1965)
2   *Collected Poems*, pp 198–200
3   See Matthew 17, 1–8; Mark 9, 2–8; Luke 9, 28–36
4   Selected Letters, p 148
5   *One Foot In Eden*, pp 38, 39–40, 43, 45
6   *Selected Letters*, p 206
7   *T S Elliot: Selected Prose*, John Hayward (ed), (Harmondsworth, 1953), pp 32–44

8   *The Story and the Fable*, pp 254–5
9   *An Autobiography*, p 244
10 Ibid. p 247
11 *The Story and the Fable*, pp 256–7
12 'In Search of Edwin Muir', BBC Broadcast, 28 April 1964, p 34 of script
13 *Selected Letters*, p 154
14 '*Chapbook*: The Poems Of Edwin Muir', BBC Broadcast, 3 September 1952, p 16 of script
15 Matthew 17, 1–5
16 *An Autobiography*, p 55. See also p 115
17 Op. cit.
18 *Selected Letters*, p 148
19 See Edith B Schnapper, *The Inward Odyssey* (London, 1965), pp 193–9. See also Richard Wilhelm and C G Jung, *The Secret of the Golden Flower: A Chinese Book of Life* (London, 1962), pp 30–52
20 *Collected Poems*, pp 223–224
21 *An Autobiography*, p 278

Daniel Hoffman in his book, *Barbarous Knowledge: Myth in the Poetry of Yeats, Graves, and Muir* (New York, 1967), p 255, writes:

> Muir's fable resembles the Christian story—without the Redeemer. Perhaps it is his unexorcised Calvinism (as well as Romantic longing), which makes the Fall, rather than Christ's rising, the moment of greatest psychological power in the pattern. But if Muir is a recusant Calvinist he is so in his own fashion; he cannot believe in a redemption through another's sacrifices—it must be won by his own sufferings, whose meaning he must seek himself.

Hoffman is persuasive in what he says about the balance between the Fall and Christ's rising in the overall pattern of Muir's poetry, but his other statements are clearly wrong. Muir accepts the Christian story *and* the Redeemer; his Calvinism is completely exorcised, as the chapter, 'The Iron Text', shows; and it is the fact that Muir *cannot* find redemption through his own suffering that he is driven to look for a wider faith.

THE EARTHLY SUCCESSION pp 172 to 182

1.   *An Autobiography*, p 170
2   *The Estate of Poetry*, p 89
3   'Yesterday's Mirror: Afterthoughts to an Autobiography', *Scots Magazine* (New Series) XXXIII (1940), p 404
4   *Essays on Literature and Society*, p 94
5   *The Estate of Poetry*, p 91
6   *Essays on Literature and Society*, p 225
7   *Collected Poems*, pp 139–40
8   C G Jung, *Memories, Dreams, Reflections* (London, 1971), p 217
9   'The Inheritors', BBC Broadcast, 27 March 1955, pp 34–44 of script
10 *Collected Poems*, pp 200–201
11 Reprinted in *C G Jung: Psychological Reflections*, selected and edited by Jolande Jacobi (London, 1971), p 323

12 *Collected Poems*, pp 221–2
13 *Selected Letters*, p 172
14 *Collected Poems*, pp 237–8
15 'The Decline of the Imagination', *The Listener*, XLV, 10 May 1951, pp 753–4
16 *Essays on Literature and Society*, p 226
17 *Collected Poems*, pp 249–50
18 The symbol of the rose appears in Section 5 of 'The Journey Back', in 'Song', *Collected Poems* p 248; and in 'The Island', *Collected Poems* pp 248–9

ONE FOOT IN EDEN pp 183 to 192

1 *Latitudes*, p 219
2 '*Chapbook:* The Poems of Edwin Muir', BBC Broadcast, 3 September 1952, page 2 of script
3 *Collected Poems*, pp 154–5
4 *Scott and Scotland*, p 40 (p 21 of the 1982 edition)
5 Ibid. p 62 (p 36 of 1982 edition)
6 *Collected Poems*, pp 157–60
7 Op. cit. p 19 of script
8 *The Estate of Poetry*, pp 35–6
9 *Collected Poems*, pp 207–208
10 *The Story and the Fable*, p 260
11 Thomas Traherne, *Poems, Centuries and Three Thanksgivings*, Anne Ridler (ed) (London, 1966), p 177
12 Genesis, 2, 3
13 *Collected Poems*, p 253
14 *Scottish Life and Letters*, 'Poet's Choice', BBC Broadcast, 23 May 1954, page 5 of script
15 See Edith B Schnapper, *The Inward Odyssey* (London, 1965), p 198
16 *Collected Poems*, p 299
17 Ibid. p 227
18 Matthew 13, 37–42
19 See Milton, *Paradise Lost* Book II, lines 382–4: '. . . to confound the race/Of mankind in one root, and earth with hell/To mingle and involve'; Book III, lines 287–9: 'As in him perish all men, so in thee,/As from a second root, shall be restored,/As many as are restored'.
20 'Yesterday's Mirror', p 406
21 Muir's autobiography ends with the words:

> As I look back on the part of the mystery which is my own life, my own fable, what I am most aware of is that we receive more than we can ever give; we receive it from the past, on which we draw with every breath, but also—and this is a point of faith—from the Source of the mystery itself, by the means which religious people call Grace.

BIBLIOGRAPHY

WORKS BY EDWIN MUIR

We Moderns: Enigmas and Guesses (under the pseudonym, Edward Moore) (London, Allen & Unwin, 1918)
Latitudes (London, Melrose, 1924)
First Poems (London, Hogarth Press, 1925)
Chorus of the Newly Dead (London, Hogarth Press, 1926)
Transition: Essays on Contemporary Literature (London, Hogarth Press, 1926)
The Marionette (London, Hogarth Press, 1927)
The Structure of The Novel (London, Hogarth Press, 1928)
John Knox: Portrait of a Calvinist (London, Cape, 1929)
The Three Brothers (London, Heinemann, 1931)
Six Poems (Warlingham, Samson Press, 1932)
Poor Tom (London, Dent, 1932)
Variations on a Time Theme (London, Dent, 1934)
Scottish Journey (London, Heinemann with Gollancz, 1935)
Social Credit and the Labour Party (London, Nott, 1935)
Scott and Scotland: The Predicament of the Scottish Writer (London, Routledge, 1936)
Journeys and Places (London, Dent, 1937)
The Present Age from 1914 (London, Cresset Press, 1939)
The Story and the Fable: An Autobiography (London, Harrap, 1940)
The Narrow Place (London, Faber, 1943)
The Scots and their Country (London, Longmans, 1946)
The Voyage (London, Faber, 1946)
Essays on Literature and Society (London, Hogarth Press, 1966, first published 1949)
The Labyrinth (London, Faber, 1949)
Collected Poems 1921–1951 (London, Faber, 1952)
Prometheus (London, Faber, 1954)
An Autobiography (London, Hogarth Press, 1954)
One Foot In Eden (London, Faber, 1956)
Collected Poems 1921–1958 (London, Faber, 1960)
The Estate of Poetry (London, Hogarth Press, 1962)
Collected Poems (London, Faber, 1963)

OTHER WORKS BY EDWIN MUIR

'Bolshevism and Calvinism', in *European Quarterly*, 1, 1934, pp 3-11
'The Scottish Character' in *The Listener*, XIX, 23 June 1938, pp 1323–5
'Time and the Modern Novel', in *Atlantic Monthly*, CLXV, April 1940, pp 535–7

Yesterday's Mirror: Afterthoughts to an Autobiography', in *Scots Magazine* (New Series), XXXIII, 1940, pp 404–410

'The Book of Scotland—1', BBC Broadcast, 21 October 1941 (unpublished script)

'The Book of Scotland—6', BBC Broadcast, 17 March 1942 (unpublished script)

'Salute to Czechoslovakia', BBC Broadcast, 1 November 1942 (unpublished script)

'The Decline of the Imagination', in *The Listener*, XLV, 10 May 1951, pp 753–4

'A Note on Franz Kafka', BBC Broadcast, 23 September 1951

'The Fabric of Scottish Literature', BBC Broadcast, 16 December 1951 (unpublished script)

'The Fabric of Scottish Literature', BBC Broadcast, 13 January 1952 (unpublished script)

'The Poems of Edwin Muir', BBC Broadcast, 3 September 1952 (unpublished script)

'Poet's Choice', BBC Broadcast, 23 May 1954 (unpublished script)

'Some Conclusions' from the series, 'Is the Novel Dead?' in *Observer*, No 8521, 26 September 1954, p 8

'The Inheritors', BBC Broadcast, 27 March 1955 (unpublished script)

'Problems of Prosperity', in *Observer*, No 8588, 5 February 1956, p 10

'Toys and Abstractions', in *Saltire Review*, IV, 1957, pp 36–7

Selected Letters of Edwin Muir, edited by P H Butter (London, Hogarth Press, 1974)

Edwin Muir: Uncollected Scottish Criticism, edited and introduced by Andrew Noble (London, Vision Press, 1982)

WORKS REFERRING TO EDWIN MUIR

Aitchison, James, 'The Limits of Experience: Edwin Muir's "Ballad of the Soul",' in *English* Volume XXIV, Number 118, Spring 1975

—— 'Edwin Muir', in *The Scottish Review*, Number 10, 1978

Blackmuir, R P, 'Edwin Muir: Between the Tiger's Paws', in *Four Poets on Poetry*, Don Cameron Allen (ed) (Baltimore, Johns Hopkins Press, 1959)

Bottrall, Margaret, Review of *Collected Poems* in *The Critical Quarterly*, II, Summer 1960, pp 179–80.

Brown, George Mackay, *An Orkney tapestry* (London, Gollancz, 1969)

Bruce, George, 'Edwin Muir: Poet' in *Saltire Review*, Volume 6, Number 18, Spring 1959, pp 12–16

—— and Lindsay, Maurice, 'Edwin Muir', BBC Broadcast, 11 March 1959 (unpublished script)

—— (with George Mackay Brown, Stanley Cursiter, Neil M Gunn, Eric Linklater, and Willa Muir), 'In Search of Edwin Muir', BBC Broadcast, 28 April 1964 (unpublished script)

—— (ed), *The Scottish Literary Revival* (London, Collier-Macmillan, 1968)

Butter, P H, *Edwin Muir* (Edinburgh, Oliver & Boyd, 1962)

—— *Edwin Muir: Man and Poet* (Edinburgh, Oliver & Boyd, 1966)

—— 'Edwin Muir: "The Journey Back",' in *English*, Volume XVI, Number 96, Autumn 1967, pp 218–22.

—— *Selected Letters of Edwin Muir* (London, Hogarth Press, 1974)

Cohen, J M, *Poetry Of This Age—1908–1965* (London, Hutchinson, 1966)

Cox, C B, 'Edwin Muir's "The Horses",' in *Critical Survey*, I, 1962, pp 19–21

Fraser, G S, *The Modern Writer and his World* (Harmondsworth, Penguin Books, 1972)

Fulton, Robin, 'The Reputation of Edwin Muir', in *Glasgow Review*, II, 1965, pp 17–19

Gardner, Helen, *Edwin Muir* (The W D Thomas Memorial Lecture, December, 1960) (Cardiff, University of Wales Press, 1961)

Grice, Fred, 'The Poetry of Edwin Muir', in *Essays In Criticism*, Volume 5, 1955, pp 243–52.

Grubb, Frederick, *A Vision of Reality* (London, Chatto & Windus, 1965)

Hall, J C , *Edwin Muir* (London, Longmans, Green, 1956)

Hamburger, Michael, 'Edwin Muir', in *Encounter*, December 1960, pp 46–53

—— *The Truth of Poetry* (Harmondsworth, Penguin Books, 1972)

Hart, F R and Pick, J B, *Neil M Gunn: A Highland Life* (London, John Murray, 1981)

Hoffman, Daniel, *Barbarous Knowledge: Myth in the Poetry of Yeats, Graves, and Muir* (New York, Oxford University Press, 1967)

Hollander, Robert B, Jr '*A Textual and Bibliographical Study of the Poems of Edwin Muir*', Unpublished PhD thesis, Columbia University, 1962 (manuscript in National Library of Scotland)

Holloway, John, 'The Poetry of Edwin Muir', in *Hudson Review*, Volume XIII, Number 4, Winter 1960–61, pp 308–313

Huberman, Elizabeth, *The Poetry of Edwin Muir: The Field of Good and Ill* (New York, Oxford University Press, 1971)

Jennings, Elizabeth, 'Edwin Muir as Poet and Allegorist', in *London Magazine*, VII, 1960, pp 43–56.

Kemp, Robert, 'Edwin Muir', BBC Broadcast, 23 August 1955 (unpublished script)

Knight, Roger, *Edwin Muir: An Introduction to his Work* (London, Longman, 1980)

Lindsay, Maurice, *Modern Scottish Poetry* (London, Faber, 1946)

—— (ed), *A Book of Scottish Verse* (London, Oxford University Press, 1967)

—— (ed), *A Book of Scottish Verse* (London, Hale, 1983)

MacCaig, Norman, 'Edwin Muir: A Great Literary Figure', in *Radio Times*, 18 January 1957

MacDiarmid, Hugh, *The Company I've Kept: Essays in Autobiography* (London, Hutchinson, 1966)

—— 'Edwin Muir' (first published 1925), 'On Making Beasts of Ourselves' (first published 1949), in *The Uncanny Scot*, Kenneth Buthlay (ed) (London, MacGibbon & Kee, 1968)

Maycock, F H, 'Edwin Muir and the Predicament of Man', in *Man: Fallen And Free*, E W Kemp (ed) (London, Hodder & Stoughton, 1969)

Mellown, Elgin W, *A Bibliography of the Writings of Edwin Muir* (London, Kaye & Ward, 1970)

Moore, Geoffrey, *Poetry Today* (London, Longmans, Green, 1958)

Morgan, Edwin, 'Edwin Muir', in *The Review*, Number 5, February 1963, pp 3–10

Morgan, Kathleen E, *Christian Themes in Contemporary Poets* (London, SCM Press, 1965)

Muir, Willa, *Belonging: A Memoir* (London, Hogarth Press, 1968)

Murphy, Gwendolen, *The Modern Poet* (London, Sidgwick & Jackson, 1954)

Noble, Andrew (ed), *Edwin Muir: Uncollected Scottish Criticism* (London, Vision Press, 1982)

O'Connor, Philip, *The Lower View* (London, Faber, 1960)

Pick, J B, 'The Poetry of Edwin Muir', in *Scottish Periodical* Volume I, Number 2, Summer 1948 pp 89–93

Raine, Kathleen, 'The Journey From Eden', in *New Statesman*, 23 April 1960, pp 595–6.

—— *Defending Ancient Springs* (London, Oxford University Press, 1967)

Reid, Alexander, 'Eden and the Boneyard', in *Scotland's Magazine*, Volume 58, Number 6, June 1962, pp 47–8

Rosenthal, M L, *The Modern Poets: A Critical Introduction* (New York, Oxford University Press, 1960)
—— *The New Poets: American and British Poetry Since World War II* (New York, Oxford University Press, 1967)
—— *Poetry and the Common Life* (New York, Oxford University Press, 1974)
Scott, Alexander, 'Scots in English' in *Glasgow Review*, II, 1965, pp 12–16
Selden, Lee B, '*The Use of Myth, Legend and Dream Imagery in the Poetry of Edwin Muir*', Unpublished PhD thesis, Tulane University, 1963 (microfilm in University of Strathclyde Library)
Spender, Stephen, *World Within World* (London, Hamish Hamilton, 1951)
Stanford, Derek, 'Absolute Values in Criticism: A Study of the Work of Edwin Muir', in *The Month*, 1951, New Series, Volume 5, Number 1, pp 237–44
—— 'Sancta Simplicitas', review of *Collected Poems* in *Time and Tide*, 14 May 1960
Thwaite, Anthony, *Contemporary English Poetry* (London, Heinemann, 1959)
Tschumi, Raymond, *Thought in Twentieth Century English Poetry* (London, Routledge & Kegan Paul, 1951)
Watson, J R, 'Edwin Muir and the Problem of Evil', in *The Critical Quarterly*, Volume 6, 1964, pp 231–49
Wiseman, C S, '*Symbol and Structure in the Late Poetry of Edwin Muir*', Unpublished PhD thesis, University of Strathclyde, 1970
Wiseman, Christopher, *Beyond the Labyrinth: A Study of Edwin Muir's Poetry* (Victoria, British Columbia, Sono Nis Press, 1978)
Wittig, Kurt, *The Scottish Tradition in Literature* (Edinburgh, Oliver & Boyd, 1958)
Wood, Harvey, 'Edwin Muir', BBC Broadcast, 31 August 1969 (unpublished script)

INDEX

The Works Of Edwin Muir

SUBJECT INDEX